Designing Instruction for the Adult Learner

for the

Adult Learner

Systemic Training Theory and Practice

Rita Richey

KOGAN
PAGE

For Charlie
with memories of our times
talking about research, scholarship, and teaching
and for Allison and Andy,
with hopes that learning continues to play an
important role throughout their lives.

First published in 1992

Kogan Page Limited
120 Pentonville Road
London N1 9JN

British Library Cataloguing in Publication Data
A CIP record for this book is available from the British Library.
ISBN 0 7494 0477 9

Typeset by BookEns Ltd, Baldock, Herts.
Printed and bound in Great Britain by Biddles Ltd, Guildford

Contents

Appendices

List of Figures

List of Tables

Acknowledgements

This project, like so many others, was completed because of the assistance and support of many. First, I must express my great appreciation to those people at Ford Motor Company and the United Auto Workers who gave me the opportunity to examine their training. Their interest in employee training and evaluation of those programmes contributes greatly to the professional development of the workforce as well as to corporate productivity. In addition, they have made it possible for an abstract idea of mine to become rooted in the real world.

I am especially indebted to Anthony Ruggiero and Joe Peters UAW-Ford co-chairmen of the National Joint Committee on Health and Safety and to William Stevenson, currently executive director of the UAW-Ford National Education and Development Training Center who was previously co-chair of the Joint Committee. The UAW-Ford research was also consistently aided and supported by Mickey Long, a member of the UAW-Ford National Joint Committee on Health and Safety and Doris Morgan, corporate safety engineer at Ford Motor Company. Each of these persons did far more than give organizational approvals; they devoted time and energy to discussing the projects, working on data collection instruments, and helping collect data from the various plants.

Special credit must be given to Hank Lick, manager of the Industrial Hygiene Department at Ford Motor Company. He played a very important role in this research. He initially introduced me to UAW-Ford health and safety training and specifically to power lock-out and the issues related to this procedure. Hank officially served as a liaison between the Joint Committee and the first study, but more importantly he became involved in the world of instructional design and design research. Hank continues to be dedicated to instructional design excellence in industrial training.

While not directly connected to these projects, I would also like to note the work of Jerry Steele, supervisor of the Ford Instructional Method Research Section of the Employee Development and External Planning Department. His dedication to instructional systems design and efforts to incorporate it throughout the corporation are noteworthy. He is responsible for the ISD dissemination work at Ford which is cited in the first chapter.

There were many others who participated in conducting the UAW-Ford training research. I am grateful to them all for their work, and hope that the experiences were also useful to them. In addition to Hank Lick, these persons include Dan Chasteen, Sandy Murphey, Andrea Taweel, Alan Rockwell, and Hamid Siddique. Hamid especially is to be thanked for his data analysis skills and his extraordinary patience with me since I always wanted to explore 'just one more thing'. The clerical and administrative support of Clora Patterson and Joyce Martin was also important to keep these projects on track.

Finally, I am grateful to those who helped shape this manuscript: Alan Rockwell for his skill in graphics design, and George Weber's editing expertise. Alan was especially helpful and always supportive throughout his work in these projects.

While they also provided editing suggestions, the contributions of Barbara Seels of the University of Pittsburgh and James Moseley of Wayne State University were far more substantive. Each provided insights and challenges for me. They were very helpful and I thank them both.

1 The Rationale for a New Approach to Designing Instruction for Adults

Instructional design as a discipline is currently experiencing rapid expansion on a variety of fronts – theoretical, technological, philosophical and in the spheres of practice. This book is about changing design theory and practice to meet the challenges of this growth. The pressures on this expanding profession have caused many design practitioners to seek more specific guidelines. At the same time, the propriety of the field's theoretical foundation is also being questioned.

The tenets of instructional design are being applied in many settings, but one of the most active is that of adult learning, especially employee training. Lifelong learning has become not only a common value of society, but also an economic necessity as business and industry turn to education and training as a means of increasing productivity and profit. This training is not only necessary to keep abreast of change, but work-related training encompasses a wide range of needs, including qualifying training, upgrading – and now in many settings – basic literacy instruction. While universities and adult and continuing education centres share in this task, the bulk of instructional designer involvement is through the design and development of formal employee education and training programmes.

In 1990 this was a $45.5 billion endeavour in the United States alone, up from the 1985 estimate of $30 billion reported by the American Society of Training and Development. The growth in the training industry has been steady. At times this growth was explosive, such as the 12 per cent growth registered in 1989; at other times, it has been more modest, as with the 2½ per cent 1990 growth ('Industry Report,' 1990). The prospects of continuing this expansion are good.

Moreover, the United States is not unique. The overall costs of training in Britain in 1986/7 were £33 billion, of which £18 billion was borne by employers (Institute of Training and Development, 1991). This level of activity is destined to expand rapidly when trade barriers are lifted for members of the European Community in 1992.

This new competition will be especially important for the United Kingdom which has 62 per cent of its workforce consisting of unskilled labour (Barrett *et al.*, 1991).

Both the magnitude and the rate of growth of employee training highlights the significance of the principles of both instructional design and adult learning. To a great extent, the market place has been the primary factor which has intertwined these two separate areas of research and practice. While learning theory has always formed a critical foundation for instructional design as a discipline, the more general principles formed on the basis of pre-adult research have been typically used. Now, practitioners and theorists alike are looking to principles of adult learning for direction. Therefore, a combined examination of these two areas of study provides another avenue of development for the changing field of instructional design.

A RATIONALE FOR THE THEORETICAL GROWTH OF INSTRUCTIONAL DESIGN

Current reliance upon instructional systems design models

Instructional design, to most practitioners, is a procedural activity that is governed by both generic prescriptions and creative applications. Instructional systems design (ISD) techniques are a series of recommended steps which have been substantiated by experience in many settings, including the military, business, industry, health care and education. The general procedures are so accepted among those trained in the field that ISD paradigms now seem to be the closest description that instructional technologists, as a body, has as a standard for professional practice. These design models, and their variants, can be defined, taught, and prescribed for use in a variety of instructional contexts.

The more comprehensive ISD models typically include six core elements. The generic version of this model begins with a determination of learner needs. Using this information, instructional goals and objectives and assessment procedures are constructed. The major task is to design or select the delivery plan. After careful try-out and revision of the instruction, the designer specifies plans for the installation and maintenance of the system. One of the most popular descriptions of instructional systems design is the Dick and Carey (1990, pp2–3) model. This is a macro-design model useful in structuring the overall design task. It is shown in Figure 1.1.

Typically, designers use models such as that of Dick and Carey regardless of contextual variations – variations which may relate to organizations, instructional goals, or types of learners and instructors. Instruction is adapted to specific situations through the use of

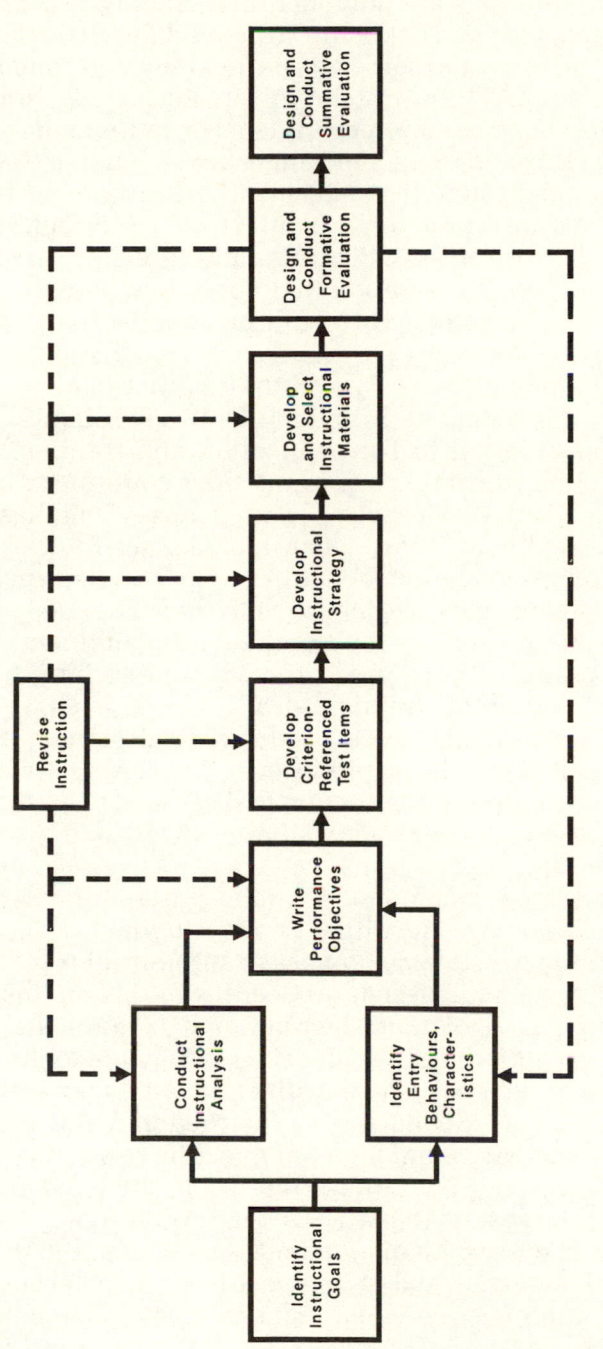

Figure 1.1 *The Dick and Carey systems approach model for designing instruction*

psychologically oriented micro-design models which guide lesson development.

Many corporations are now institutionalizing ISD principles and models similar to the Dick and Carey model. Often the procedures have been adapted to their own particular environment. IBM, for example, uses SATE, a Systems Approach to Education, which is rooted in the business and performance requirements of the organization. SATE has 'become the banner for rallying executive support and for communicating the concepts and strategies of the corporate education organization throughout IBM' (Bowsher, 1989, p113); moreover, all major areas of the corporation are now using the systems approach with the expectation that not only will high quality levels be attained, but also that costs will be contained.

Similarly, Ford Motor Company has designed a plan which articulates a recommended version of the instructional systems design procedures. The intent of this plan is to provide standards for worldwide implementation in Ford education and training, focusing on the corporation's business needs and their continuous improvement policy. The Ford ISD proposal puts a heavy emphasis on needs assessment and evaluation which includes all four levels of Kirkpatrick's (1976) evaluation model. As such, the plan speaks to measuring participant reactions, changes in their knowledge, behaviour, and ultimate impact on the company. In addition, this version includes a product survey phase, providing procedures for evaluating existing off-the-shelf training products; this phase establishes standards for selecting such products or designing Ford-specific training. In all cases, the emphasis is on the Ford mission and quality improvement training. Instructional systems design techniques are used to ensure knowledge acquisition, as well as transfer to on-the-job application.

These are two examples of major international corporations which are seriously committed to instructional design excellence and are willing to establish policies to support their ideologies. General use of systematic design procedures in this manner has been a long-standing goal of most instructional technologists. However, even with the growth of ISD advocacy, others are looking ahead and are becoming concerned with the effects of what they see as a blinding adherence *only* to ISD models as the predominant, and often sole, guide for designers. Bonner (1988) questions 'whether and in what way designers may be limiting the design of good instruction by adhering to the systematic process' (p5). And Davies (1984) sees that the emphasis on systematic methods has resulted in a 'tendency to freeze methodologies and techniques in a fixed form . . . the "one best way" approach has often reduced creative ideas to cookbook-like recipes, and promising heuristics to algorithms' (p9). Finally, Winn (1989a) argues for reasoning 'from basic principles of learning and instruction rather than simply following design models' (p36). These criticisms typically are not based upon a desire to eliminate use of ISD models; rather, they are attempts to build upon the strengths of ISD, expanding the theoretical and practical scope of instructional design activities.

Challenges to the philosophical base of instructional design

The prevailing orientation to instructional design is embedded within a scientific context. Quantitative research is valued, and the goal is for instruction and instructional outcomes which can be replicated. There are also advocates of a more qualitative approach, not only to the field's research base, but also to its espoused procedures. However, this position still tends to be a minority view. Within this context though, there is a growing call for a critical examination of the underlying philosophical stance of the field (Hlynka and Belland, 1991).

One response to this criticism is the post-modernist orientation. Hlynka (1991) has defined this term in the following manner:

> Post-modernism is a way of thinking which celebrates the multiple, the temporal, and the complex over the modern search for the universal, the stable, and the simple. Other synonyms for postmodern include breakup, irony, and violent juxtaposition (p28).

The implications of this philosophy on instructional design focus upon the recognition of multiple views and approaches, especially those which emphasize design as art, rather than science. In addition, there is an amplification of the complexities of a teaching-learning situation (Hlynka, 1991).

Advocates of post-modernist positions typically find traditional approaches to systematic instructional design too confining and too simplistic. They seek alternative procedures which permit increased flexibility and creativity.

Challenges to the psychological base of instructional design

Instructional design both as a discipline and a profession is intimately coupled with learning. While the earliest links were primarily with behavioural learning theory, the predominant theoretical orientation today is cognitive. There are two diametrically opposing challenges in this arena: 1. the standard systematic design procedures do not conform to cognitive theory as much as they should and 2. the cognitive orientation does not sufficiently account for human learning.

Demands for more pervasive cognitive design
The first criticism is especially important to those who take the position that the use of cognitive principles 'can lead to teaching for *understanding* rather than simply memorization and skill application' (Winn, 1989b, p15). They are concerned that the typical practitioner is far more aware of principles of the systems approach than those generated by cognitive considerations.

However, there are popular cognitively oriented procedures in use. The most frequently used models of this type tend to be micro-design models which prescribe procedures for presenting a specific lesson. Most notable among these models are the Events of Instruction described by Gagne *et al.* (1988) and Component Display Theory presented by Merrill (1983). There is a similarity between these approaches to design. Both provide a sequence of instructional moves which facilitate human information processing, and are usually used in conjunction with a comprehensive ISD model. Both assume one designs instruction differently dependent upon the type of learning task; they also provide methodology for attention-getting, integrating instruction into prerequisite knowledge, presenting stimuli and activities to promote the demonstration of new behaviours or knowledge.

But there is a demand from many quarters for an even more pervasive incorporation of cognitive theory into design practice. Bonner (1988) identifies ways in which each of the stages of the ISD process can be modified by assuming a cognitive orientation. She describes cognitive-based techniques for completing a task analysis, specifying goals and objectives, assessing skills, classifying skills, addressing learner characteristics, and selecting learning strategies. For example, the cognitive approach would conduct task analyses of various levels of expertise; it would focus more on describing the content to be learned; it would consider the learner's mental models and schemata as important input.

In a similar vein, Hannafin and Rieber (1989a; 1989b) have shown detailed applications of learning and cognition research to instructional design, specifically to computer-based instruction. They describe ROPES+, a plan for incorporating cognitive procedures into an ISD framework. ROPES+ addresses techniques for retrieving information, orienting, presenting, encoding, and sequencing instruction within a given context.

Other representative attempts to highlight cognitive theory in design have been made by DiVesta and Rieber (1987) who developed a model for cognitively-engineered instructional design, by Schmid and Gerlack (1986) who present an algorithm-based design approach, and by Tennyson and Rasch (1988) who propose an instructional design model which links cognitive learning theory with instructional prescriptions.

While promoting far more wide-spread use of cognitive-based design techniques, Winn (1989b) questions whether even this approach will meet all of the demands put upon instructional design. He challenges the underlying belief in the predictability of human behaviour (especially when we are promoting understanding rather than specific performances), and he anticipates that this inconsistency will negate many of our plans. If this premise is substantiated, then neither cognitive theory alone, nor cognitive principles coupled with instructional systems design techniques, will meet all of the demands placed upon the field of instructional design.

Constructivism and the role of context

There is support emerging in some quarters for constructivism, a psychological position which is seen as an alternative to the cognitive learning paradigm. Seels (1989) indicates that the 'constructivist paradigm states that learning occurs because personal knowledge is constructed by an active and self-regulated learner who resolves conflicts between ideas and reflects on theoretical explanations' (p13). Constructivism further holds that meaning is based upon experience and the context in which that experience takes place (Duffy and Jonassen, 1991).

Merrill (1991) most likely represents the view of many designers and design theorists when he asserts that only extreme constructivism presents a true alternative to the traditional cognitive/ISD approach. Many of the more moderate tenets are consistent with the standard position. In either case, the context of instruction is an especially interesting variable cluster for designers, since practitioners function in very diverse settings – formal educational institutions, health care training, business and industrial training, military and other governmental agencies, as well as more informal community-based educational environments.

The assumption has always been that the general design procedures are valid regardless of setting. The more powerful influence on learning is the pre-designed instructional plan. However, the role of context in the learning process is being examined in more detail by theorists such as Brown *et al.* (1989) and Suchman (1987). Suchman (as described by Streibel, 1991) concludes that,

> human learning is phenomenologically and contextually bound. Whereas a cognitive model of the processes of human learning is mechanical, the actual processes of human learning are experiential. And finally, whereas plans determine the meaning of actions in the cognitive model of human learning, the *in situ* interpretations of lived experiences by the participants determine the meaning of actions in the 'life-world' of situated actions (p548).

Brown *et al.* (1989) have built upon the work of Suchman and present an epistemology of cognition emphasizing its situational nature. They speak to the importance of activity and enculturation in the learning process. 'All knowledge is, we believe, like language. Its constituent parts index the world and so are inextricably a product of the activity and situations in which they are produced'. (p33).

Streibel (1991) has already begun to examine the implications of the principles of situated cognition for instructional design and, in the process, questions the compatibility of situated learning with the cognitive paradigm. However, generic instructional design strategies which reflect a sensitivity to learners' perceptions of their environments have not yet been proposed.

Context-specificity is also of interest with respect to content selection. Perkins and Salomon (1989) review critical research on the effects of general cognitive skills and context-specific knowledge on learning and transfer. They present an approach which 'calls for the intimate intermingling of generality and context-specificity in instruction' (p24). This is a debate between the utility of general heuristics as opposed to specific knowledge.

Constructivism has many other implications for instructional design in addition to the use of context and personal experience. Some advocates encourage more concentration on instructional exercises which involve the active learner and problem-solving tasks. Others call for a change in the traditional testing procedures (Duffy and Jonassen, 1991). The debate will undoubtedly continue, as this newer theoretical emphasis impacts the design field.

Other challenges to instructional design

The struggle to deal with new philosophical and new psychological viewpoints are not the only examples of efforts to expand the theoretical base of instructional design. Martin and Briggs (1986) developed a theoretical 'framework for an instructional theory that will help us synthesize what we know about the development of attitudes, values, and feelings with what we know about the development of intellectual abilities' (p9). This emphasis reflects the stress placed on student attitudes in much of the teaching effectiveness research conducted primarily with school-age children. Another specific attempt to expand design theory with respect to learner attitudes has been made by Keller (1983; 1987b). He has constructed a descriptive theory to govern the manner in which designs incorporate motivation strategies into instruction. Keller's ARCS model also extends the theoretical foundation into concrete procedures for practitioners.

The nature of the delivery process is also being re-examined in terms of its effect on design and learning outcomes. While delivery systems are a very traditional component of design activities, their role is being reconsidered in light of the new technologies. Many new media provide for an ongoing process of adaptive teaching. Adaptive teaching has been defined by McFarland and Parker (1990) as 'optimal instructional adaptations that effectively meet the individual needs of the students while they are actively working in controllable learning environments' (p179), and 'microadaptations involve moment-to-moment decisions required to attend to the step-by-step processes of systematic instruction' (p182). The adaptations are typically computer-based. The possibilities presented by such technology for addressing individual differences are great. However, they also interject additional elements in the learning process which should be addressed in design theory.

Addressing the issues underlying these challenges is a difficult task, and often the critics, in their fervour for identifying what should be changed, neglect to provide specific direction on how to change. One general orientation – the systemic approach – may present some general guidance in this task.

The systemic approach to instructional design

A definition of systemic design
The rumblings of dissatisfaction with excessive reliance on ISD procedures are complemented by others who argue for using a *systemic*, rather than a systematic view of instructional design (Beckwith, 1988). Beckwith defines a systemic approach as 'the creation of unified and dynamic wholes (from previously separated components) to effect the transformation of learning' (p4). What does this mean and how does it actually differ from a systematic approach? Does this vantage point offer a response to the philosophical and psychological criticism?

The use of the word 'systematic' implies using specified procedures to design instruction, while 'systemic' infers concurrent consideration of the many aspects of a situation which can affect the learning process. Systemic design has more to do with creative problem-solving (Romiszowski, 1981) than it does with using the scientific method to address the teaching-learning process. While few would say that systematic design negates the possibility of creativity, its typical use has been associated with 'the applied science concept of a system which is well regulated by rules and routines, which is methodical and requires uniformity of behavior' (Hlynka and Nelson, 1991, p115). This may be an extreme viewpoint; clearly, those working in the area of systems interactivity would protest that they are using the new technologies precisely for the reason of avoiding uniform behaviour among learners.

In addition to the notion of creativity, there is also an implication of increased interactivity and vibrancy in a systemic orientation.

Hlynka and Nelson (1991) compare the systemic approach to a chess game in which 'there is no one best strategy, no one best opening move, no one best procedure. Rather, a good game requires a holistic or systemic view' (p114). There is more of an emphasis on flexibility and adaptability in the systemic approach than is typically associated with systematic design.

The implications of a systemic approach

How do designers create a 'dynamic whole'? Using a systemic approach implies:

- avoiding the use of inflexible lock-step design procedures;
- increased attention to the dynamics of a given instructional context; and
- more consideration of the nature of the individual learner.

Adherence to these general principles requires two fundamental changes in the typical design process: 1. the steps must be more interative, and 2. the instruction must address a wider spectrum of variables than only those which concern learner prerequisites and the nature of the content.

By incorporating these principles into instructional design practice, there is also some recognition of the difficulties focused on by critics in the field. The relevant complexities of the larger instructional system are being addressed. Flexibility and creativity are less alien. The wider scope of design-relevant variables can encompass critical aspects of the learning environment, as well as broader experiential, attitudinal and cognitive bases of learning.

While some may see the systemic approach as a major break with design tradition, others can easily claim that this represents an extension of current practice. On a macro level one still designs and manages instructional systems, even though the boundaries may be stretched. Procedures need not be ignored, but rather they should be used in a more flexible fashion. On a micro level systemic design can be seen as an extension of Gagne's (1985) view of internal and external conditions of learning. Internal conditions can be expanded beyond those normally associated with information processing. Likewise, one can also expand the usual range of pertinent external conditions which prompt such processing to include more contextual elements.

The systemic approach highlights instructional design's fundamental emphasis on learning rather than instructional products. Moreover, since its use does not demand alignment with any particular philosophical or psychological school, a systemic, rather than systematic, approach to design seems to provide one direction for the continued development of design as a discipline of study and an area of practice. However, using this approach does not guarantee that designers will give an increased emphasis to the learning process as has also been suggested.

A RATIONALE FOR BASING INSTRUCTIONAL DESIGNS ON ADULT LEARNING PRINCIPLES

If one heeds the calls for new emphases on learning, those designers who work in training and other adult educational environments would naturally look to theories of adult learning for direction. A question which plagues many is whether distinct theories for the adult learners are really necessary, or whether learning theory is generic. The outcomes of this debate influence the extent to which adult learning theory should impact the design process. This issue has two major components: 1. the overriding power of individual learner variables in relation to the instructional design process, and 2. the extent to which adult learning is different from that of pre-adults.

Defining the adult learner and adult learning theory

The discussion of these issues is based upon certain assumptions surrounding the adult learner and adult learning theory. First, the adult learner is viewed here as an age-bound entity. The term does not denote one's level of maturity or development as a learner. Thus, typical descriptions of the adult learner as 'self-directed' and 'problem-oriented' should be viewed as personality characteristics rather than attributes of the definition.

This stance is not consistent with all of the literature. Brookfield (1986) is representative of the alternative point-of-view when he states that,

> the exercise of autonomous self-direction in learning is proposed as the distinguishing characteristic of adult learning . . . . There are many individuals who are chronologically adult but who show a marked disinclination to behave in anything approaching a self-directed manner . . . . Self-directedness is rather being advanced as a prescriptively defining characteristic of adulthood (pp25-6).

In contrast, an adult learner is simply defined here as *anyone over 18 years of age in an instructional situation, formal or informal*. Within this framework, there are extreme variations, as well as many frequently occurring characteristics. This position is being taken not only because of its objectivity, but because the variations produced by the definition are desirable from a research viewpoint, creating the potential for identification of learning principles from a life-span development orientation.

Theories of learning with respect to adults encompass a range of topics, many of which are unlike those addressed in the more generic learning theory. Hartree (as cited by Merriam, 1987) has indicated that an adult learning theory should speak to three concerns: how adults learn, what they learn when it is distinctive, and why they learn. Such learning theory has implications for areas of study such as factors which influence participation in learning activities, adult motivation and persistence, on-the-job transfer, attitude formation and stabilization, and cognitive development.

A theory is fundamentally different from a philosophy; it is also different from a hypothesis, in this context. Theory is a position supported by research. This approach reflects Hartree and McKenzie's critique of andragogy as a theory (cited in Brookfield, 1986). They see andragogy not as a theory, but rather 'as an essentially philosophical construct that has come to prescribe elements of "good" practice' (p95). Since there is a concentrated attempt here to be data oriented, 'theories' of this nature will not be addressed.

The role of individual learner variables in instructional design

When considering the need for design theory directed towards adult learning situations, one is really evaluating the predominance of individual learner variables in instructional design. Since ISD design procedures are typically seen as generic, the same procedures are not only recommended for any type of setting, but also for learners of all ages, interests, and capabilities. The instructional design process itself is considered to be self-regulating since (among other reasons) it relies on an initial needs assessment; thus, the resulting instruction can be adapted to any learner group, as well as to any situation.

However, practical realities often pose time constraints on designers when it comes to assessing learner characteristics; thus, Bonner's (1988) point is well taken. In spite of 'some interest in attribute [sic] treatment interaction (ATI) research, instructional design has not placed a great deal of emphasis on learner characteristics' (p9). This not only contradicts the desires of many leaders in the field for increased recognition of the principles of learning, but violates an assumption of the larger field of instructional technology which puts great value on the individualization of instruction.

The practical reluctance to attend to such detail has also been duplicated by theorists. However, in responding to the theorists' complaints, Snow, a leading proponent of aptitude-treatment-interaction research, has said that 'ATI does not make theory impossible; it makes general theory impossible' because 'individual difference variables operating in ATI show the essential importance of detailed description of both specific instructional situations and specific groups of people' (Snow, 1977, p12).

There are two questions subsumed in the issue relating to the degree of attention given to individual differences in the design process. The time necessary to deal with detail is a practical obstacle, but trivial theoretically. The more crucial question relates to the relative influence of learner characteristics, as opposed to instructional characteristics, in explaining the variance in instructional outcomes.

This issue is at the heart of mastery learning and is fundamental to Bloom's (1976) model of school learning which was constructed 'to predict, to explain, and to modify individual differences in school learning' (p12). His conclusions were that 'Where conditions for learning in the home and school approach some ideal, we believe that individual differences in learning should approach a vanishing point' (p16). Thus, at least for children, Bloom would optimistically emphasize instructional characteristics as a means of ameliorating the effects of learner characteristics. Such a position would support the general neglect designers give to learner characteristics.

But Bloom's (1976) research does show the powerful effects of learner entry characteristics on instructional outcomes. Cognitive entry behaviour (both content-specific prerequisites and general learning skills) accounts for up to 50 per cent of the variance in cognitive achievement; moreover, the specific cognitive entry behaviours seem to be highly alterable for children in early elementary school. (There is less evidence to support this conclusion for older children or young adults). Affective entry characteristics (encompassing subject-related and school-related affect, and academic self-concept) are highly related to motivation. Bloom concludes that these variables account for up to 25 per cent of the variance in achievement. Therefore, his conclusions show that three-quarters of the variance is attributable to learner entry characteristics! The job of the schools is to alter these effects with the instructional programmes.

Other arguments in the individual differences-instructional characteristics debate include Carroll's (1989) conclusions after a review of both his work on his model of school learning and that of others over a 25 year period. He asserts if there is appropriate quality of instruction and an opportunity to learn, student motivation difficulties will be resolved. Snow, as might be expected from his ATI research, still highlights the interactive effects of ability. He concludes that highly structured learning environments seem to benefit low ability students, while the environments with low structure benefit high ability students (Snow, 1989). Similarly, Snow has found a strong relationship between the effects of learner control and ability, with the higher ability students having the most to gain from self-managed instruction (as cited in Williams, 1990).

Feuer and Geber (1988) have noted that 'the adult education camp has often faulted the instructional design contingent for being so concerned with the methodology and outcomes of instruction as to lose sight of the learner in the process' (p32). The research literature with a school-age population clearly supports the important role of learner characteristics. While there is also evidence that high quality instruction does modify these effects, the extent to which this happens and how it happens are not always clear.

There has been no comprehensive research of this nature with adults, although there are studies which have identified effects of various adult learner characteristics. The stability of the cognitive and affective adult learner entry characteristics has not been fully determined.

The uniqueness of adult learning

The question of the propriety of design theory and design procedures directed toward only the adult learner parallels the question of to what extent adults learn differently from people of other ages. The literature is mixed in this regard. While the popular approach is to emphasize the differences, some see the learning processes of adults and pre-adults as essentially the same. For example, Jarvis (1987) asserts that the facts do 'not suggest that there is an intrinsic difference in the learning processes, only that there is a difference in the external processes that accompany the teaching and learning process. In short, there is a social difference rather than a pscyhological one' (p11). Houle also took the position that child and adult learning are fundamentally the same (Merriam, 1987). Even Knowles is saying that 'what he once envisioned as unique characteristics of adult learners, he now sees as innate tendencies of all human beings, tendencies that emerge as people mature' (Feuer and Geber, 1988, p33).

Demographic effects

Nevertheless, it seems appropriate to scan the research literature to determine if it is possible to distinguish adults, or particular groups of adults, from other learners. Shipp and McKenzie's (1981) study is representative of a body of literature which identifies income, education, age and occupational status as the variables which are most discriminating between active adult learners and non-learners. The active learners are younger, more affluent, better educated, and hold higher-status occupations. The obvious question is whether these findings represent independent relationships, or whether they may be understood as simply a matter of intelligence and other capacity variables.

Capacity effects

Do people continue to learn throughout the various stages of their lives? In general, it is believed that they do, but there are caveats to this conclusion. Information processing abilities may vary, depending upon the learner's age and upon the content being learned. Information control processes (short and long-term memory, storage and retrieval) may be altered with age. The literature shows mixed results on this issue, although some measured declines have been attributed to testing instrumentation and procedures, the importance of the items being remembered, and general health conditions (Ford and Roth, 1980).

Rybash *et al.* (1986) contend that adults do become less adept at general learning as they age, but that there is continuing development of expert knowledge and processing skills which are domain-specific. Reduced capacity in novel situations is compensated for by growth in specializations, selected areas of interest and practice. This conclusion is consistent with Cattell's (1963) concepts of fluid and crystallized intelligence. Fluid intelligence, more reflective of neurophysiological structure, can decline with age, while crystallized intelligence, which is dependent upon experience and culture, continues to grow.

Competence effects

While learning is limited by natural capacities, demonstrated competence (or achievement) also plays an important role in all human learning. Competence can be divided into two major areas – prerequisite skills and experiential background. Acquisition and demonstration of prerequisite skills encompass both content-specific knowledge and general cognitive skills. As previously noted, Bloom (1976) has voiced concerns about the ease of modifying cognitive entry characteristics of older learners if the prerequisites have not been initially mastered. Others may further conclude that adult learners may differ from younger learners with respect to their abilities to acquire some prerequisite skills. This latter position could be substantiated by notions that fluid intelligence declines with age.

It is more certain that life experiences not only clearly distinguish adults from pre-adults, but that they probably play an important role in understanding the adult as a learner. They serve a primary role as a stimulus to educational participation. For example, Aslanian and Brickell (cited in Cookson, 1986) found that 83 per cent of all adults seek learning situations in response to experiences such as job changes, marriage, arrival of children, and retirement. Participation, in turn, is closely tied to motivation and other attitudes.

Attitude effects

The adult education participation literature highlights self-confidence, course relevance, personal priorities (Darkenwald and Valentine,

1985), and various attitudes towards one's job (Cookson, 1986) as critical. These elements are important as aspects of motivation. However, attitudes have also been recognized for their influence on behaviour changes following a learning experience (Murphy, 1989). Positive attitudes must either be present or be developed to facilitate use of new knowledge.

While such a phenomenon is undoubtedly not unique to adult learning situations, there are questions concerning the stabilization of attitudes during one's life span which do pertain primarily to adult learners. Commonly, attitude stabilization is thought of as being 'set in your ways', a characteristic of many as they age.

Jennings and Markus (1984) studied this phenomenon in another arena, that of political attitudes. They identified socio-political attitude consolidation and persistence which seemed to occur between the mid-20s and the mid-30s. Moreover, they found similar patterns of attitude crystallization occurring in non-political domains. If those attitudes which play pertinent roles in the learning process develop and operate in a similar fashion to that in the Jennings and Markus research, attitudes critical to learning and application may also be fairly firm by the mid-30s. If so, the role of attitudes may distinguish adult from pre-adult learning.

Overall effects

In summary, while there are surely many similarities between the learning patterns of adults and pre-adults, there also appear to be characteristics unique to adults. While one may still argue that many of these characteristics reflect either social or experiential situations (ie, job-related motivation, self-confidence), there are many attributes of human learning which seem to be a reflection of life-span development. These include changes in cognitive processing represented by levels of fluid and crystallized intelligence, effects of life experiences at the various stages of development, attitude stabilization, and ease of altering general and specific prerequisite skills.

Therefore, learning for those over 18 does seem different in many (but probably not all) respects from learning situations of those who are younger. Correspondingly, younger adult learners should probably be distinguished from older adults. But the position is only valid from an instructional design point of view if there is first a commitment to an emphasis on individual differences in general.

A RATIONALE FOR ORIENTING DESIGN THEORY TOWARD THE TRAINING ENVIRONMENT

Arguments have been made to support further development of design theory and practices and simultaneously others are calling for design procedures specifically directed toward adult learning situations. The philosophical and psychological arguments focus to a great extent upon an assertion that the current theoretical framework is too narrow. It is confined not only by too great a reliance on ISD models and behaviourism but also by inadequate emphases on human learning. More emphasis should be placed upon a greater range of factors in the teaching-learning process. The second argument is that instructional designers should increase their concerns for individual differences among learners; since adult learners are to some extent unique, special consideration should be given to the circumstances surrounding their learning.

However, designers are also faced with market pressures posed by the rapidly expanding training enterprise. While these forces easily influence the expansion of design practice, they also should have implications for design theory. In the process of exploring these implications, three points will be discussed: 1. What is the nature of a training setting? 2. What is the influence of a training environment on the design process? and 3. To what extent must design theory be empirically supported by data from varying contexts?

Employee training environments

It has been noted that, given the current and predicted labour trends, most new occupational needs will have to be filled by retraining the existing workforce (Lynton, as cited in Morse, 1984). This prediction is supported by the growth in money spent yearly on employee education and training. Such activity constitutes a large portion of current adult learning endeavours with 39.5 million Americans participating in employee training programmes in 1990 (Industry Report, 1990), approximately 30 per cent of the civilian workforce. This can be compared to the 13.1 million people who are in the American higher education system (US Department of Commerce, Bureau of Census, 1990). Furthermore, as early as 1986/7 in Great Britain over 8.6 million people, nearly *half* of the workforce, participated in employee training programmes (Institute of Training and Development, 1991).

Corporate-based learning is growing and in many organizations it encompasses all three categories of human resource development as viewed by Nadler and Nadler (1989) – employee training, employee education, and employee development. Training is specifically job-related with a view to immediate application; education is generally job-related with future use anticipated; development is not job-related. While a number of corporations are moving into non-traditional learning programmes such as remedial and basic literacy instruction and corporate colleges, the major focus for most organizations, and consequently for most adult learners, is employee training.

Organizational characteristics

An analysis of *Training* magazine's 1990 industry-wide survey results shows that training in the United States spans the array of corporate enterprise, occurring primarily in eight general industrial groups: manufacturing, finance/insurance/banking, public administration, wholesale/retail trade, business services, transport/communications/utilities, education services, and health services. The largest survey response, and presumably the largest amount of training, occurred in the manufacturing industry, but the highest average training expenditure per employee was in the transport/communications/utilities group.

Not unexpectedly, a disproportionate amount of training occurs in the larger organizations. For example, only 1.1 per cent of the businesses surveyed by Dun & Bradstreet have 10,000 or more employees; however, 19.6 per cent of the survey sample was from these large corporations ('Industry Report,' 1990). On average, it has been shown that business organizations have training budgets which are 3.3 per cent of the amount allocated to total personnel costs (Lee, cited in Watkins, 1989).

In the 1986/7 report on employers' activities in 'Training in Britain' it was shown that the greatest amount spent on British training also occurs in the area of manufacturing with other major expenditures in the finance/business services area, followed by education services, personal services, health, and retail fields (Institute Training and Development, 1991).

Trainee characteristics

The 1990 *Training* report ('Industry Report', 1990) also presents findings relative to the types of persons typically participating in employee training programmes. According to their data, the professional employee is the most likely trainee, with the office/administrative employee least likely to be participating. However, production workers spend close to the same amount of time in training as do the professionals – 30.7 hours per year as compared to 35.5 hours per year in 1990. This compares with the Lee study (cited in Carnevale, 1988) which stated that the 2.5 million top managers in the United States received 36.3 hours of formal training per year. However, the technical professional workers (almost 4.8 million in the American workforce) get the most education and training in preparing for their jobs, and the most upgrading once they are in their jobs with 23 per cent receiving formal employer-provided training (Carnevale and Schulz, 1988).

This pattern is similar to that of Great Britain where management/professional groups are the most likely to be involved in training, and those in personal services and other manual occupations the least likely to be trained (Institute of Training and Development, 1991).

As training programmes become generally available to all levels of employees, participants will more closely reflect the profile of the total workforce. Therefore, the sociological changes in the workplace will be mirrored in the typical group of trainees. It is anticipated that by 1995 59 per cent of American women over 16 years of age will be in the workforce. This general principle also applies to Great Britain; although many of these women are likely to be employed in those jobs which currently receive less training (Barrett *et al.*, 1991). However, in voluntary education and training situations, women have already surpassed men in terms of numbers. In 1980 American women assumed the majority role among higher education freshmen, and in 1981 they surpassed men in job-related adult education courses taken in the United States (Rachal, 1989).

Other pertinent demographic changes in the United States relate to the effects of eliminating mandatory retirement policies in the private sector and the Age Discrimination in Employment Act of 1967. These two statutes can stimulate continued employment and new employment after formal retirement. Of additional concern is the growing number of Americans who do not have English as their primary language.

In Great Britain, the problems will tend to center on a large unskilled population in which 'sixty percent of the young people in the UK leave school at the age of sixteen, with about forty percent of them attaining minimal academic qualifications' (Barrett *et al.*, 1991, pp62–3). Creative training approaches will be required to develop and maintain a competitive workforce.

Training content characteristics
Training programmes in the early 1990s, according to 'Industry Report (1990)' will be responding most to technological changes (16.2 per cent of the organizations); customer service, and quality improvement topics are also prevalent (in 14.9 and 14.4 per cent of the organizations respectively). Whether one analyses the data by industry or by size of organization, the training patterns remain the same with respect to general offerings. Organizations most commonly offer training in management skills/development, technical skills/knowledge, and then supervisory skills. The least frequent type of training was remedial basic education, then customer education, and sales skills, although with respect to these last three types there was a trend for these topics to be more likely offered as the size of the organization increased.

The most prevalent specific type of training was new employee orientation, followed by performance appraisals and leadership; the

least commonly offered specific training related to foreign lan-
guages, reading skills, and purchasing. It appears that employee
training is, thus, more common than employee education.

Content of training programmes is increasingly being determined
by technological changes. In the 1980s such change prompted a
large amount of computer-related training, including personal computer applications, and word processing. In fact, over half of the
organizations still offer such training (Industry Report, 1990). Technical changes in our society are not only increasing the technical
skill requirements of many jobs, but also the basic skill requirements,
sometimes to the point of creating new occupations (Carnevale and
Schulz, 1988). These changes point to the need for much training to
take the form of employee upgrading or retraining. The need for this
type of training in Great Britain has been previously emphasized.

The relationship between training environments and instructional design

What are the implications of data from the training industry and
knowledge of typical training environments for instructional design
practice? Can one find direction for new procedures from these statis-
tics? Are there different patterns of adult learning emanating from
specific job-related training that are not present when analysing
adult behaviour in community education, in formal continuing education classes, or in higher education? These questions again highlight
the need to determine the effects of context on learning, and consequently on instructional design.

Organizational implications
In most organizations time allocated to training is usually at a pre-
mium; consequently those topics selected for training programmes
are considered essential to the productivity of the company. As a
result of this stance, two patterns emerge: 1. training is typically
mandatory for most employees, and 2. learning efficiency is critical.

This situation has direct influence on delivery of instruction.
Ideal delivery systems need to:

* reduce effective learning time to a minimum;
* attend to participant motivation;
* provide for replicability; and
* incorporate flexible pacing to accommodate the trainee's pressing
  job demands.

Of course, all of these traits must be blended into a cost-effective
instructional plan; and cost-effectiveness can be determined best by
relating the effects of training to the goals of the organization.

Trainee profile implications

Typically, employee training programmes are directed towards persons with the same or similar job titles. This frequently results in a less varied trainee group, ie, predominantly one gender, similar educational backgrounds, similar socio-economic status. In addition, the attitudes of these trainees may reflect the nature of the organizational climate, and their basic competence may be greatly influenced by common occupational experiences. However, while similar work environments may compress learner diversity, ranges of age and personal experience tend to accentuate the differences among those in employee training programmes.

Of primary importance are the interactive effects of age and experience. (Ordinarily, work experience is the most critical type of experience, although other personal experiences may also be pertinent to a given training topic). If the training involves 'unlearning' old habits, being older and having more experience can be detrimental; however, in most situations work experience facilitates learning new topics in one's area of interest and expertise.

These characteristics also speak to the design process. The amount of diversity in a group affects the necessity to individualize instruction in terms of pacing, degree of developmental support or enrichment, adjustment to varying cognitive styles, and even modification of content. The age/experience blend of the group has implications for the way in which instruction builds upon prerequisites and content is tied to past learning. If it is necessary for trainees to modify previously learned information, skills or habits, then increased practice is typically required. This practice may not only be of the new skill, but also of the information retrieval process itself.

Training content implications

Employee training programmes are usually confined to limited and specific goals. In this sense, training objectives are easier to achieve than broader educational goals; however, the ultimate expectations relate to on-the-job behaviours, rather than simply knowledge acquisition. Therefore, the issue becomes one of both long-term retention and transfer, a more ambitious target. This target may be made even more difficult when one considers the role of attitudes, perhaps very long-standing, stable attitudes.

Transfer goals alter design tactics. The following are examples of some of these transfer-oriented procedures. First, the initial task analysis is often expanded to include analysis of the larger work situation in which the task will be used. New performances need to be practised and critiqued during training under either actual or simulated conditions. If possible, efforts are made to insure continued application on the job. Perhaps simple job aids are constructed which foster review of key points after training, or even periodic refresher seminars are offered.

The design task in its ideal form is not isolated from the setting in which the instruction will occur. Designers often need to base their decisions in part on the nature of the organization, the nature of the learners, and the type of content. It is not unusual for these three elements to interact and in combination affect design practice, but these factors also have theoretical implications as well.

The utility of environment-specific data for theory development

Frequently when good designers adapt their products to the situation and the learners it is done intuitively, rather than as an exact science. The preceding discussions can be viewed as a brief example of such an activity. After an attempt at a somewhat systematic analysis of data, logical extensions have been made to recommended design tactics. The extent to which this is done typically depends upon practical constraints such as time, money, cooperation and finally, expertise. The question here is how research conducted within specific training environments contributes to the development of this expertise.

This question has both technical and practical elements. Technically, it relates to the extent to which one can generalize and apply the findings of design and learning research conducted in one context to another education or training setting. Does theory based upon research with a college population apply to employee training populations? Practically, the question has to do with the credibility of academic research and theory in the marketplace. However, the issue is more complex than one of communication or researchers simply selecting appropriate samples.

The use of situational data in research

Research efforts have been divided into two fundamental orientations, theoretical and practical (Schubert, 1980). Theoretical approaches are used to identify generalizable conclusions. Within the context of traditional research categories, both basic and applied research have a theoretical orientation. Basic scientific research attempts to generate knowledge and theory; the researcher is not primarily concerned with practical consequences. While applied research seeks to explain and understand the complexities of practice, its findings can also 'suggest boundaries of generalizations' (Shaver, 1979; p5).

On the other hand, practical research concerns itself entirely with the resolution of specific problems. Not only are its roots in the context of the problem situation, but its goals are 'situationally specific decisions and action' (Schubert, 1980, p18).

Instructional design practitioners may be interested in both kinds of research if they think it is appropriate for their own situation, but practical research is usually easier to immediately apply providing there is sufficient similarity between one's own situation and that of the research. Design theorists typically are interested in all types of research – basic, applied or practical – if it is possible to generalize the findings to other settings. However, most design theory relies upon applied research.

The validity of situational data initially appears to be dependent upon whether one is interested in theory development or practitioner direction. However, this position may oversimplify the question. Theorists may find situation-specific data useful, especially when identifying generalized principles. In this case, it is important to know if certain findings have been replicated in a number of situations, or if they vary between settings.

Applied instructional design research has not been systematically replicated across settings to any great extent, nor has it encompassed a broad base of settings. Most of the applied design research is conducted with children or young adults in a higher education setting. Moreover, research stemming from typical adult learning situations is even rarer. The literature is not only limited in terms of subject age and setting, but the majority of studies do not even have contextual ramifications.

Though little design research is replicated, the field does use meta-analyses or other techniques for summing results across studies. In addition, some design researchers are calling for increased use of qualitative techniques which rely more on contextual elements, but these studies are seldom replicated either. Consequently, there is a self-fulfilling prophecy. Elements of the learning context are undervalued because they are not emphasized in the original research designs or in follow-up research. However, context is still very important to practitioners.

If one looks to other educational research for guidelines relating to the importance of contextual differences in learning behaviour, one finds a 'mixed bag'. Gage (1979) analysed research on teaching studies to answer this question. His findings support both sides of the question. In some studies, results were consistent across context variables; in others, there were differences. He concluded that 'when more adequate evidence becomes available, the resulting picture will not be either completely general or completely specific' (p278), and he recommends the inclusion of both types of variables in subsequent research. The ultimate goal would be a hierarchy of dimensions related to teaching effectiveness which would show the range of predictive variables from situation-specific to generic.

The use of contextually-different research in theory development
Instructional designers do not always expect to find answers to their

problems from research or colleagues in exactly the same situations. Areas of design application are extremely diverse. They usually interpret and draw conclusions based upon the experiences of others and studies of other instructional situations. However, even though one is willing to take advice based upon different work contexts, the lessons must first be deemed relevant.

The relevance of research is dependent not only upon contextual similarities, but also upon the perceived credibility of the topic and the results. It is possible for research to have general findings which are credible and relevant in a variety of situations, although determining relevancy is a complex task laden with personal values. The question is always, relevant to whom?

> Situations do not become problems unless we approach them with values which specify what properties these situations ought to have . . . our ideologies turn events into problems, and . . . tell us what human needs are . . . (Strike, 1979, p10).

Therefore, without a similar situational foundation or common values, research and theory can be irrelevant to the user. With a common base of professional values, contextually generic research can be seen as quite useful.

To be credible, theory and its foundational research must also be basically consistent with current professional thinking and values and 'common sense'. Instructional design procedures are likely to be implemented if they have support from respected colleagues or consultants, even if they have no empirical support whatsoever. Even carefully designed research is often seen as irrelevant if it conflicts with conventional wisdom. For example, there are many devout followers of the andragological approach to teaching adults. The literature includes many positive reports of this methodology which are experience-based; there is little research support for these principles. Moreover, data which contradict andragogy tenets most likely would have little impact on the committed follower.

These conclusions can be applied to theory directed toward instructional design for employee training. The ideal situation would be to expand design theory and practice using a base of research conducted in actual training programmes with typical adult learners. While other research bases can be useful, they are relevant in a practical sense only to the extent that the research conforms with the thinking and values of designers in the training industry. Even theory developed out of relevant situations may suffer credibility problems if the propositions deviate greatly from current practice.

SUMMARY

Instructional design, having progressed through two decades of technological growth and expansion, is now being challenged in a very fundamental fashion. These challenges appear to signal developmental growth of both a philosophical and psychological nature which will likely alter some established design procedures. At the same time design practitioners are now working to a great extent within training environments, rather than traditional educational settings. This setting is currently the most prevalent context for formal adult learning in both the United States and Great Britain. It encompasses all major industries, and includes persons in most of the major job categories. Furthermore, continued growth is almost guaranteed by new organizational missions and technological change.

The combined pressures from theorists and the marketplace alike may result in more flexible design practices and practices which incorporate a wider range of elements in the instructional environment. Given the preponderance of designers working in the training arena, at least some of these new procedures should address the unique needs of adult learners and corporate learning environments. Given the weight of the theoretical arguments, it seems justified to approach the intellectual base of these new design procedures from a systemic orientation, expanding upon the traditional systematic viewpoint.

While instructional designers have always been influenced to some extent by the nature of the learner and by the learning environment, some may doubt the necessity or the practicality of design theory which specifically addresses employee training. Nevertheless, a research base has been established which supports a theory of training design. This theory:

- responds to the calls for more emphasis on learning and less emphasis on lock-step procedural models of design;
- expands the range of variables typically addressed in design theory, including an emphasis on the role of the learning context; and
- gives increased emphasis to individual learner differences, especially to adults.

The next chapter provides an overview of the theory of Systemic Training Design and its conceptual base. In addition it introduces the procedural model which forms the basis of its practical applications in employee training.

2 Systemic Training Design: An Overview of the Models and the Theory

Systemic Training Design (STD) is the result of an investigation to determine which factors impinge upon training interventions, and as such influence adult learning. The investigation was prompted by a desire to test a conceptual model of design factors which was more comprehensive than those typically considered. It was prompted by concerns that those principles of adult learning which should guide training design were typically based upon convictions rather than empirical evidence. Finally, it was prompted by a belief that the outcomes of research should be purposefully directed toward theory development as well as practice.

This overview of STD has three major components:

- a conceptual model of factors which affect adult learning in the training environment;
- a procedural model to guide design practice; and
- a theory consisting of propositions which both describe the learning process and prescribe the design process.

This theory and its accompanying models are products of replicated research involving large-scale employee training programmes. STD is primarily outcomes-oriented rather than process-oriented. In other words, it emphasizes learning, adult learning in particular. It is tied to learning outcomes which reach beyond immediate knowledge acquisition, a somewhat limited perspective of learner achievement within the training context. Instead the theory encompasses knowledge retention, attitude change, and transfer of training content to on-the-job behaviour.

This orientation assumes the learning process varies depending upon the nature of the outcomes, an approach consistent with the Gagne tradition of altering the conditions of learning for varying learner outcomes. It is especially compatible with Component Display Theory (Merrill, 1983) which suggests different design rules depending upon interactions between the type of content and the type of performance expected after learning.

Finally, it is a theory which has a cognitive orientation to the extent that the major components of the model reflect a belief in learning as a product of complex interactions between external conditions and internal reactions. However, there are elements of a constructivist stance in terms of the emphasis given to individual reactions to their environment and to their past experiences.

THE RESEARCH FRAMEWORK

The research model

The general model for the research upon which STD is based is shown in Figure 2.1. The model, basically an input-process-output model, shows multiple training outcomes and input from the learners, the environment and the design and delivery characteristics. In addition, it is a model which suggests causal relationships.

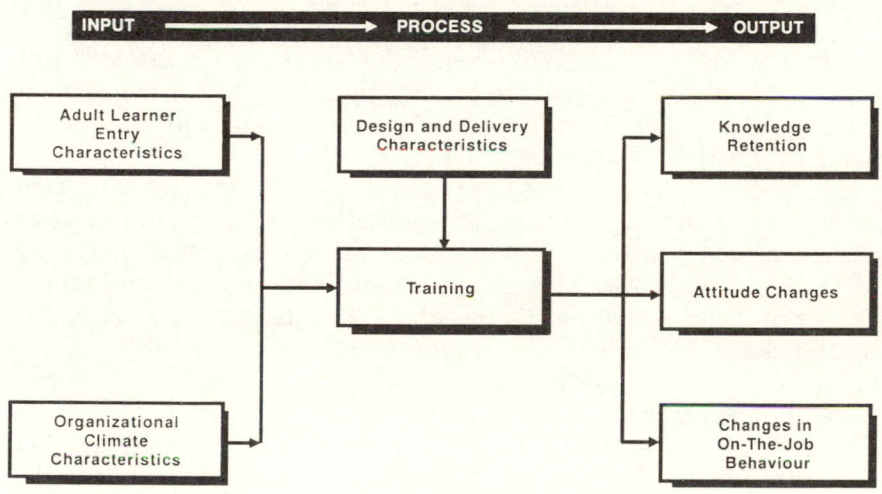

Figure 2.1 *Model of industrial training research*

This model is reminiscent of other instructional effectiveness models. However, it is not a process-product model like those which have been used to guide a substantial portion of the teaching effectiveness research. Rather than attributing learner outcomes to teacher performance as do many process-product paradigms, this model provides for the possibility of various types of outcome predictors.

This research framework also incorporates the major components of a previously constructed conceptual model of variables critical to instructional design (Richey, 1986). This model consists of four clusters of factors which influence design outcomes, but are distinct from those factors (such as sequencing or text layout) which are inherent to the instructional product or programme itself. These variable groups relate to:

- the learner;
- the content;
- the environment; and
- the delivery of instruction.

These clusters are very general groupings constructed after an analysis of the knowledge bases upon which the discipline of instructional design is built. The specific elements within each cluster have implications for many instructional design decisions. There is considerable research evidence to warrant a belief that these factors affect learning outcomes either directly or indirectly by interacting with other elements of the model. As such, they provide a direction for instructional design theory development (Richey, 1986).

The research model used here is most appropriate for a systemic, rather than a wholly systematic orientation to instructional design. First, the model provides for simultaneous consideration of a variety of factors which may influence learning and, correspondingly, the design process. Learning can be affected by design, by environment, by the characteristics of the students or by a combination of these elements.

While the research framework on the surface appears to have a linear pattern, it actually implies an interaction between all of the variables within the training programme. Such interactivity is also characteristic of a systemic orientation.

The nature of the variable clusters in the model is the most systemic feature. Rather than relying primarily upon design and delivery factors, the distinctive properties of the learner and the environment are emphasized as well. The instructional system is conceived from a broader perspective than is typically the case. This is especially true with respect to environmental factors. The environment is not interpreted as the immediate instructional environment, but as the context in which trainees work. Content is also viewed broadly, as evidenced by the range of learning outcomes addressed. Therefore, STD originated in a base that was not only empirical, but was also systemic in design.

The foundational studies[1]

The target training programmes
The research framework was used to study real training programmes. These programmes were conducted with all the complexities of a natural work situation. The training programmes were considered by most to be well designed but, as with any realistic situation, they were not perfect. They incorporated both the richness and the constraints of real life.

The target training programmes were major corporate-wide efforts to improve plant safety, and were jointly sponsored by the United Automobile Workers and the Ford Motor Company's National Joint Committee on Health and Safety. Three programmes were studied. The first related to energy control and power lock-out in the plants (Locking-out involves shutting down the assembly line while completing diagnosis and/or repair tasks. It is expensive since production stops, but failure to lock-out can be life-threatening.) The second programme related to safe techniques for driving and controlling vehicles in the plants, and the third covered safety procedures for plant pedestrians. Almost 200,000 employees participated in these training programmes, including both hourly and salaried personnel.

A summary of the research process
The research on these three training programmes spanned approximately four years, and during this time a study using the research model shown in Figure 2.1 was conducted and replicated twice. Thus, both the STD theory and the design practice recommendations are made with some degree of assurance.

The studies included both quantitative and qualitative components, using a pre-test/post-test survey design with structured follow-up interviews of both trainees and trainers to refine and verify the survey data. A major product of each study was a statistically constructed diagram of those variables which predicted the trainees' knowledge gains, their changes in attitude, and the extent to which they used the information acquired in the training programmes back on the job. These diagrams form the basis for the STD conceptual model. However, interpretation of this model and its sub-models is facilitated and supported by the structured interviews.

THE STD CONCEPTUAL MODEL: PREDICTORS OF ADULT LEARNING IN EMPLOYEE TRAINING

The general model

The function of a conceptual model
Instructional designers and researchers alike commonly use models of various sorts to guide their work. The research model just discussed is one example of this practice. Conceptual models are particularly useful in theory development. As with other types of models, the conceptual model 'implies a representation of reality presented with a degree of structure and order' (Richey, 1986, p16).

The STD conceptual model has three key functions:

- it identifies the relevant aspects of the adult learning process in training settings;
- it shows the relationships among these various components; and
- it provides the foundation for STD theory and STD practice.

While conceptual models can take a number of different forms, this one is presented visually and verbally in chart form. This model, as with most conceptual models, is shown in a generalized format, even though it is based upon research in a specific context. It summarizes fairly complex findings and facilitates their use by design practitioners, but it also serves as the basis for constructing theoretical propositions.

The direction established by the STD conceptual model is characterized by the comprehensive scope of those factors included in the model. This is the essence of the systemic approach.

The systemic nature of the STD model
The idealized goal of instructional design is to facilitate consistent learning which is not only effective and interesting, but is also efficient and error-free. Traditionally, designers have approached this task in a systematic fashion, basing design moves on knowledge of the structure of the content, the nature of human information processing, and the capabilities of the learner and the instructional media. Gagne's (1985) position has provided fundamental guidance to today's instructional designers: 'the external situation needs to be arranged to activate, support, and maintain the internal processing that constitutes each learning event' (p20).

The external situation, as typically interpreted by design practitioners, primarily encompasses learning activities, including materials, delivery techniques, and learner undertakings. These are the factors most likely to be within the control of the instructional designer. They are the essence of instructional programmes.

Instructional materials, however, are not developed in isolation from implementation issues. The best training programmes are predicated upon a thorough needs assessment, the first phase of the ISD process. Rossett (1987) defines this phase, in the training context, as an analysis of performance discrepancies in the workplace. Feelings, causes and solutions are directed toward the performance problem. Cause analysis encompasses skills or knowledge, incentives, environmental support or motivation. Training is suggested as a solution, only if the performance discrepancy is precipitated by knowledge or skill deficiencies.

The more systemic approach to design as presented here demands that the development of employee training programmes also be initiated by a comprehensive needs assessment using procedures such as those suggested by Rossett (1987). However, in some situations it may be appropriate to address incentives, environmental support, or motivation in the workplace in the training itself so that target skills and knowledge can be enhanced.

While quality instruction has been produced without attending to the dimensions suggested here, it does not, by itself, always produce the desired outcomes in the workplace. This model suggests that by attending to issues such as the non-instructional environment and a broader array of learner attributes and attitudes, achievement will be more consistent, in addition to being more efficient and error-free.

The conceptual model upon which the STD theory is based is displayed in Figure 2.2. It is applicable to a range of training situations, but has not been tested with other adult learning environments. The more detailed sub-models[2] show adaptations of this general set of variables to specific training outcomes: knowledge gains, attitude changes, improvement of on-the-job behaviours specifically related to the training, and improvement of more generally related behaviours.

This model portrays training outcomes as a function of the trainee, the environment, and the instructional design and delivery. While the trainee and environmental characteristics are fixed, the design and delivery patterns obviously can be altered. These modifications control the extent to which instruction affects learning outcomes as opposed to the effects of other elements in the environment. This is the traditional dilemma of educators – how to help people learn in spite of all the instructional barriers such as little motivation, or little family and peer support. This model implies that regardless of the quality of the instructional design, other factors in the instructional system will always partially predict human learning.

The STD conceptual model portrays learning as a product of a network of interrelated factors. All major clusters of variables have

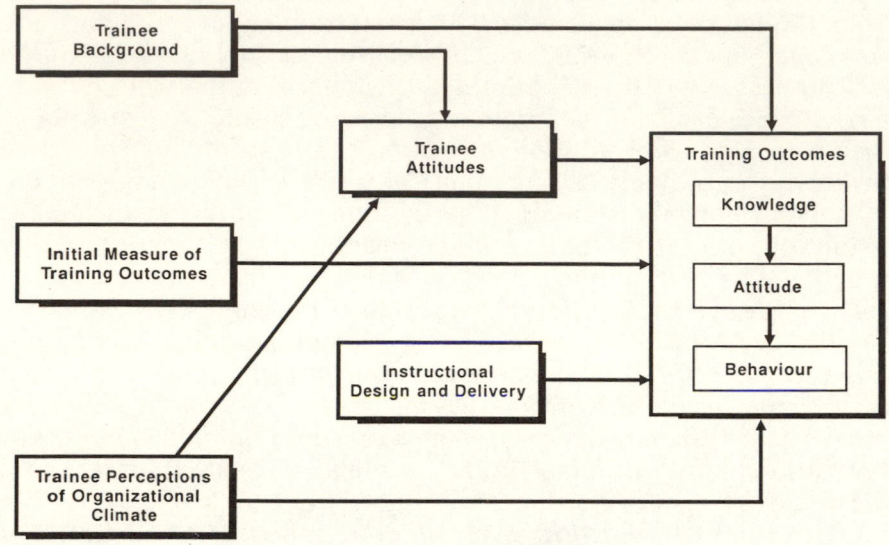

Figure 2.2 *A systemic model of factors
predicting employee training outcomes*

direct influence on learning outcomes; however, some also exert indirect, and at times hidden control of the training process. It is easy to ignore or minimize these effects.

In general, the most distinctive features of the STD conceptual model are:

- the relationships among learning outcomes;
- the major influence of factors external to the instruction itself; and
- the dominance of the adult trainee's pre-training knowledge, attitudes, and work habits.

Each of these aspects of the general model will be explored.

Relationships among the primary outcomes of training
As one might expect, the different types of training outcomes are not independent of one another; however, they are not totally dependent on one another either. It is logical to assume knowledge precedes both attitude and behaviour. Furthermore, popular wisdom usually assumes 'good' attitudes predict 'good' behaviour, and 'poor' attitudes anticipate 'poor' behaviour.

The STD model only partially supports such assumptions. Based upon the research data, there is a direct causal link only between knowledge and attitude, with a subsequent connection between attitude and behaviour. Knowledge does not directly influence behaviour.

However, even these relationships are tenuous. They do not occur in every training situation. The implications of this research are that such patterns are present only in the most effective training. In other programmes, one can not be assured of any relationship at all between knowledge outcomes, attitude change, and on-the-job behaviour! However, training programmes, even those which are not of top quality, can produce isolated changes in participants; there is simply not a coordinated pattern of change.

This phenomenon speaks primarily to the complexity of transfer of training in the workplace. While the hierarchical relationship between knowledge and application of knowledge seems initially obvious, those situations which foster the use of knowledge are not self-evident. For adults it seems a possibility that the abilities to demonstrate knowledge acquisition (ie, take a test) and to utilize knowledge in a work setting can be independent processes.

While this model and its underlying research show a causal relationship between attitude and behaviour in only some situations, the literature related to such phenomena is also mixed. For example, there is research indicating behaviour may precede attitude. Representing this alternative line of thinking, Guskey (1986) proposes a model based upon his analysis of the literature which shows that both behaviour and perceived results of such behaviours are first necessary to effect a change in beliefs and attitudes of another group of adult learners. In this case he was addressing the behaviour of teachers who had participated in formal in-service training.

The role of systemic factors
The STD approach suggests that the conditions of learning reach beyond learning activities to encompass the work environment and a broad range of learner characteristics, including a variety of attitudes and experiential background. There are multiple categories of stimuli outside the realm of planned instructional activities which affect one's internal processing of information, as well as the practical application of information in work situations. These are referred to here as the 'systemic design factors'. They are distinguished from those factors which are elements of the delivery process, such as type of media, grouping strategies, or reinforcement patterns.

It is not surprising that adult attitudes and background experience have emerged as general categories of systemic factors which affect learning. These factors have been especially helpful for some time in answering the question of who participates in adult education (Merriam and Caffarella, 1991). Nor are the effects of organizational climate on workplace behaviour unanticipated. Pfeffer (1985) shows the integral role of the organization in explaining employee behaviour within that context. However, the interactive and causal relationships among the three categories of variables which are suggested by this model have not been well documented, especially as predictors of adult learning in training programmes.

The systemic aspects of the STD model are those which exert both direct and indirect influence on training outcomes. Trainee background variables can partially shape attitudes as well as directly determine some outcomes. Likewise, one's perception of the work environment also plays an important part in forming work-related attitudes in addition to influencing the outcomes of training. Perhaps the indirect nature of much of the influence of systemic factors has served to suppress their major role in the learning process.

The role of entry-level knowledge, attitude, and behaviour

Another critical input to the training process is the trainee's entering knowledge level, initial attitudes, and pre-training work habits. Unlike the systemic factors, these learner characteristics have only direct and very profound effects on the training outcomes. For each type of outcome the trainee's pre-training demonstration of that performance predicts the major portion of the ultimate learner achievement not attributable to design factors. This supports the standard research conclusion that the best predictor of future performance is past performance.

Such an axiom is especially true for adult learners in employee training settings. Low entry pre-training performance does not serve as a barrier to improvement, but actually facilitates gain. This pattern of relationship is consistent whether one considers knowledge improvement, changing employee attitudes, or even changing daily work habits.

Implications of the STD conceptual model

Training designers, as do most educators, typically believe quality instruction has a primary influence upon learning. This seems almost true by definition. These convictions are reflected in numerous educational innovations. For example, mastery learning procedures are built upon the belief that quality design, competent delivery and careful management of instruction can compensate for individual learner differences.

Research has supported this conclusion in some respects. One example important to those in employee training relates to the relationship between quality instruction and the effects of ageing. Adults, on the whole, apparently do become less adept at *general learning* as they age (Rybash *et al.*, 1986). While reduced capacity in novel situations is often compensated for by growth in areas of specialization, quality instructional interventions can also counteract the effects of ageing in many learning situations. These include lessons pertaining to both novel content and topics in one's field of interest. Thus, the combined effects of job experience and carefully designed and managed instruction often results in successful training programmes for older workers.

What does the STD approach add to this view? As previously noted, the model implies that systemic design factors always influence learning, even learning which originates from instruction with superior design. However, a detailed examination of the data[3] suggests another hypothesis. There is a tendency (especially in instruction oriented toward knowledge gains and changes in on-the-job behaviour) for *the influence of systemic design factors to expand* to assume an even more central role in the learning process *as the design quality decreases*. Environmental factors fill the void created by instruction with inadequate design.

Therefore, design quality does account for learning – but not totally – and when the instruction is not wholly sufficient to produce the best results, other aspects of the environment begin to assume greater control of the learning process. This conclusion, even though tentatively made, does speak to the delicate balance in the learning process between systemic factors, on the one hand, and design and delivery factors on the other.

Moreover, the data upon which the STD conceptual model is based imply that with higher quality instructional design, there is also a more coordinated progression of resulting skills, ie, knowledge and attitude outcomes contribute to the application of training principles in the workplace. This provides some additional support for the faith placed in sound design technique as an avenue to efficient and effective instruction.

This balancing act between design strategies and systemic factors (specifically environment and learner characteristics) may not be a conflict which can conclude in the complete dominance of one set of variables over the others. The theory proposed here suggests that both sets of factors have a profound effect on learning in every situation, at least in every training programme confined by the realities of corporate life. Even the finest training programme may not totally compensate for the effects of the other systemic elements. Therefore, training designers should address components of the STD model in their instructional plans, rather than simply following traditional design practices. That is the central implication of STD. However, the task is more difficult than may first appear in the general STD conceptual model. The specific models of critical factors vary depending upon the training outcomes which are targeted by a given programme.

Building conceptual sub-models

The general STD conceptual model permits one to grasp the overall relationships among those factors which impact learning in employee training. While this version of the model may be useful for general understanding, it has so little detail that actual design guidance is all but impossible. Therefore, more specific conceptual models are required, and the specificity comes in relation to each of the four training outcomes.

Building the STD sub-models is a process of analysing and interpreting the data from three different pieces of research. The sub-models will be developed throughout this full discussion of STD in the following stages:

- present and discuss the full hypothesized sub-model for each training outcome. These initial sub-models will be based upon all those specific relationships among factors shown in the foundational research (see the discussion following in this chapter);
- present and analyse in depth the impact of each cluster of systemic design factors (see the discussions in Chapters 3 – 5); and
- synthesize the replicated research findings, present the final versions of the STD conceptual sub-models, and discuss their implications for design practice (see the discussion in Chapter 6).

The hypothesized STD sub-model for knowledge retention outcomes

A closer examination of the research data permits one to adapt the general STD conceptual model specifically toward knowledge retention as the desired training outcome. Within each component of the general model there are patterns of variables which predict knowledge retention outcomes after training.[4] The initial hypothesized sub-model relating to knowledge outcomes is shown in Figure 2.3. It shows all relationships which have been empirically identified, but not replicated in the foundational research.

In summary, this sub-model shows that knowledge retention is dependent to a great extent upon a complex interaction of:

- learner background characteristics, including profile descriptors, education and training history and job experience factors;
- learner attitudes, including attitudes toward training, job, the content of the training and the delivery system; and,
- learner perceptions of the organizational climate, including general environmental characteristics, factors generally and factors specifically related to the training.

The knowledge sub-model includes all cluster components addressed in the research.

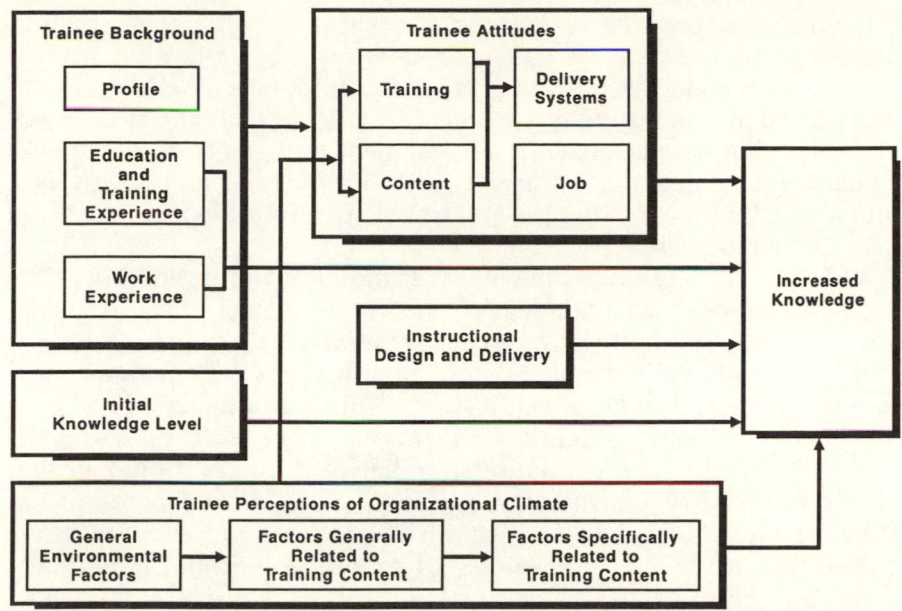

Figure 2.3 *A model of possible factors related to increased knowledge after training*

Overall dimensions of the knowledge retention sub-model
Knowledge acquisition and retention is, in some respects, the easiest training goal to achieve. It is not uncommon for a group to demonstrate knowledge gains, but show little evidence of higher level performances, such as applying their knowledge on the job, or changing attitudes. Even so, knowledge retention can be elusive as well. Coping with this problem can be vexing for trainers.

In the process of addressing knowledge retention issues, certain assumptions were made when interpreting the data. It is possible to account for a certain portion of variance among trainees in knowledge retained by the combined impact of the systemic design factors and the employee's pre-training knowledge level. What then is responsible for the remaining variance? Is it all simply a matter of measurement error? Or can some portion of this remaining variance be attributed to the effects of the instructional design and delivery? The latter position is a fundamental assumption of STD.

Given this assumption, it is possible to analyse the knowledge data (see Figures C.1 and C.2 in Appendix C) and conclude that the trainee and organizational climate entry characteristics, as a whole, can account for *up to 80 per cent* of the knowledge retained after training, leaving instruction and instructional materials responsible for only a maximum of 20 per cent of the variance. Such a conclusion can be unsettling, at best, for instructional designers.

On the more positive side, it appears that the quality of instruction can have more effect on subsequent knowledge retention than it does with respect to the other training outcomes. With excellent design, the instruction may account for up to 60 per cent of the variance, leaving a maximum of 40 per cent control to the systemic design factors and the trainee's initial knowledge level. This is a much greater portion than was shown in relation to attitude and behaviour changes.

This pre-training knowledge level is an important predictor of the training outcomes as a whole. As one would expect, those with the lower pre-training knowledge levels are more likely to gain the most. While this pattern is displayed consistently, excellent design seems to weaken the strength of the trainee's initial knowledge level as a predictor of ultimate retention.

This exemplifies the relationship between instructional design effects and entry characteristic effects on knowledge retention. When the training is less intense or the quality is not as high as one would like, the primary predictor of retention is initial knowledge level. Superior design can compensate for a great deal, but clearly not all, of the effects of pre-training knowledge level.

The hypothesized effects of systemic design factors on knowledge retention

The systemic design variables with the greatest effects on knowledge retention are primarily concerned with trainee's education and training experiences, their attitudes, and to those aspects of the organizational climate related in some way to the training content. Even though a variety of systemic factors are pertinent to knowledge retention, their influence is less, on the whole, than that of an effective design or the trainees' initial knowledge level.

In spite of the diminished influence of systemic variables in quality programmes, they still play an important role. As expected, experiences in formal learning situations do impact one's current performance in employee training programmes, especially with respect to the outcomes most similar to those of traditional schooling – knowledge acquisition and retention. More education and training experience contributes both to knowledge retention in a direct fashion, as well as to the development of other attitudes which influence knowledge acquisition.

Another aspect of a trainee's experiential background is the level and amount of work experience he or she has. This plays a lesser role in knowledge acquisition than does education and training experience, but it does seem to help mould the employee's attitudes toward training in general.

Attitudes toward the training subject matter and toward one's job also play some role in affecting knowledge retention after training.

However, the more important attitudes, with respect to this outcome, relate to past training and to preferences for particular ways in which training is delivered.

Learners' perceptions of organizational climate in the knowledge sub-model serve two roles. First, they act as a force in the formation of attitudes, indirectly serving as an element which influences the development of training motivation. Second, the trainees' impressions of their work environment directly influences how much of the information will be retained.

Those climate factors which exert direct influence on knowledge outcomes tend to be related in some manner to the training content. For example, with respect to safety training a pertinent factor might be the extent to which the plant manager is aware of safety issues.

However, organizational climate factors which contribute to trainee attitudes, especially those related to training motivation, need not have this direct connection to the training programme. For example, general climate elements, such as satisfaction with one's physical working conditions, also affect positive attitudes toward training and one's job. In turn, the attitudes toward training and jobs are the factors which directly influence knowledge retention. This exemplifies the indirect, sometimes hidden, manner in which systemic design factors can influence adult learning.

The hypothesized STD attitude change sub-model

Overview
Attitude change is usually an important, but often unarticulated training goal. While attitude change is sometimes important in its own right, attitudes are often considered important outcomes of a training programme because of the common assumption that attitude change is a precursor of behaviour change. Even though cognitive instruction may lay the groundwork for attitude change, this process typically involves the interaction of other forces as well, such as social and cultural norms or environmental support.

The attitude change sub-model[5] is similar to that of knowledge retention with the following exceptions:

- fewer factors impact the final outcomes, making the process appear to be less complex; and
- attitude changes are almost exclusively determined by other attitudes and opinions of the trainees.

General profile characteristics of trainees are not typically relevant learner characteristics when explaining attitude change, although the trainees' experiential background is important. Attitude change can also be influenced by one's knowledge, but knowledge does not

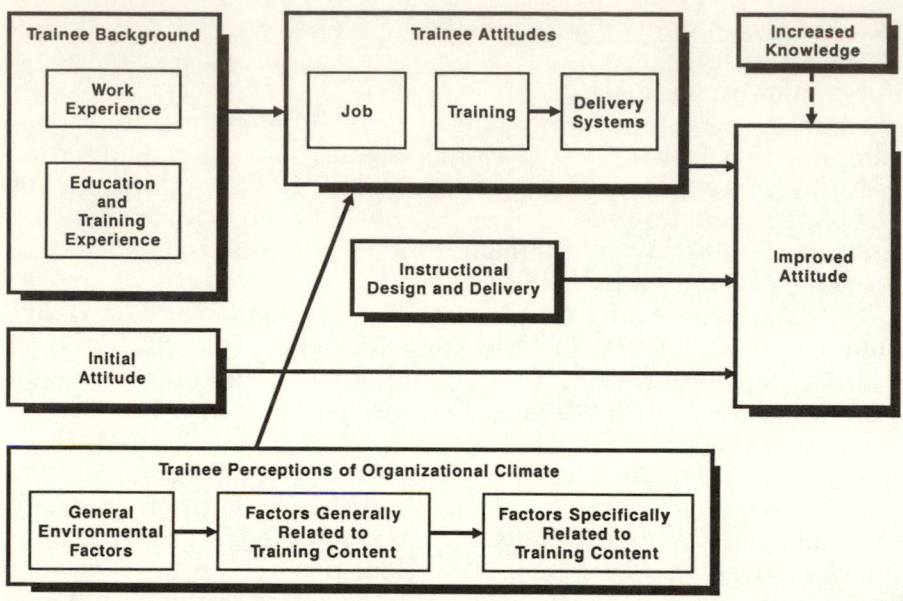

Figure 2.4 *A model of possible factors related to attitude improvement after training*

appear essential. In fact, as previously noted, this only seems to occur in those situations with more intense training or higher quality instructional design. The attitude sub-model appears in Figure 2.4.

The dimensions of the STD attitude change sub-model
Using the same assumptions to guide data interpretation as introduced in terms of the knowledge sub-model, one can infer the effects of instructional design and delivery upon attitude outcomes of training. Outcomes appear to fluctuate less as a result of the quality of the design than do knowledge outcomes. It appears that no more than 35 – 40 per cent of the variance in attitude change can be explained by instructional design tactics.

The influence of one's pre-training attitudes is not only substantial, but appears to be fairly constant from one training situation to another. This is true even in those situations in which knowledge gains influence attitude change. Again, as with knowledge retention, those with the most to gain are the most likely to respond to training directed toward work-related attitude change. For many, this may be a surprising conclusion in light of the common assumption that negative attitudes among many employees are very difficult to alter. Furthermore, this seemingly false conventional wisdom is usually emphasized even more so for older workers.

The effects of systemic design factors
The systemic design factors are especially interesting in relation to the development of attitudes because they account for the majority of the change. While experience and background of the adult learner is critical with respect to other outcomes, it appears to play a lesser role in attitude formation. Instead, other attitudes and beliefs are central.

The dominant influence of organizational climate perceptions in this sub-model is through their role in establishing a variety of attitudes. They contribute to attitudes toward previous training, toward one's work, and toward the training content. In turn, these factors contribute to attitude change in the workplace.

A secondary function of the organizational environment is achieved through social influence and pressure of co-workers and supervisory staff. If prevailing habits and sentiments correspond favourably with the principles introduced in the training, then trainee attitudes are likely to conform to those being promoted.

Even though the age of the trainee seems to have no discernable effect on attitude change, experience does. In the foundational research, the more experienced workers were more likely to exhibit the desirable safety attitudes, but were *less likely* to change their opinions if they did not conform to the training advice. This lends some support to the notion of attitude crystallization during the adult life span.

Finally, attitude changes appear to be facilitated by the more individualized training methodologies. These are exemplified by computer-based instruction, interactive videodisc, and self-instructional modules. Perhaps such delivery techniques permit one to be more introspective during training than does group-oriented delivery. In addition, these methodologies can insulate the learner from the opinions and influence of co-workers during training. In any case, trainees in these studies who prefer self-instruction seem more likely to show attitude growth.

The hypothesized STD behaviour change sub-models

General and specific behaviour
The ultimate purpose of training in most organizations is for employees to actually transfer the newly acquired knowledge and attitudes to the workplace by altering their behaviour patterns. Training is the means; behaviour change is the ends. However, desired performances may be taught, but often are not practised in many corporate training programmes. This distinguishes much group-oriented training from one-to-one instruction in the workplace. Typically in group instruction, performance rules are taught, or model behaviour is simulated through media. At times demonstration is

possible, but even here practice is typically limited. Even so, the aim of most training is still to modify work habits.

Behaviour outcomes of a training programme can be viewed in two ways:

- specific replication on the job of those skills which were addressed in the training programme; and
- adherence on the job to the general principles taught by applying them in a variety of situations.

An example of this distinction follows from the training upon which these models are based. There were three safety training programmes. On-the-job behaviour changes could be achieved in two ways. There could be behaviour changes specifically related to the training; they could make changes in the way they operated industrial trucks in the plants, for example. Or there could be behaviour changes generally related to training, ie, trainees could become more conscious of safety issues in the workplace after training and regularly heed most safety precautions.

Different conditions led to these diverse types of transfer of training, even though the training programmes were identical. Consequently, there are two sub-models of behaviour change. Each sub-model varies in certain respects from those previously discussed, even though the same general cluster of factors is included.

Both general and specific on-the-job behaviour changes can be influenced directly by attitude improvements following participation in a training programme, and indirectly by knowledge also acquired via training. As with knowledge affects on attitude, these patterns seem to exist only in the more intense and the higher quality programmes. Contrary to the expectations of most trainers, knowledge gains do not always directly influence workplace performance according to the data upon which this model is based.

On-the-job behaviour change, whether general or specific, is more comparable to the attitude change process as well as the knowledge retention process in at least one other respect: the role of one's level of entering behaviour as a predictor of ultimate change. Once again, those trainees who are least likely to demonstrate the desired behaviour on their jobs register the largest amounts of behaviour change after training. This finding was consistently replicated.

The hypothesized STD sub-model of specific on-the-job behaviour change
The first of the two sub-models[6] relating to on-the-job behaviour change is shown in Figure 2.5. This initial sub-model pertains to those factors which predict the extent to which employees will use those principles taught during the training programme on a daily

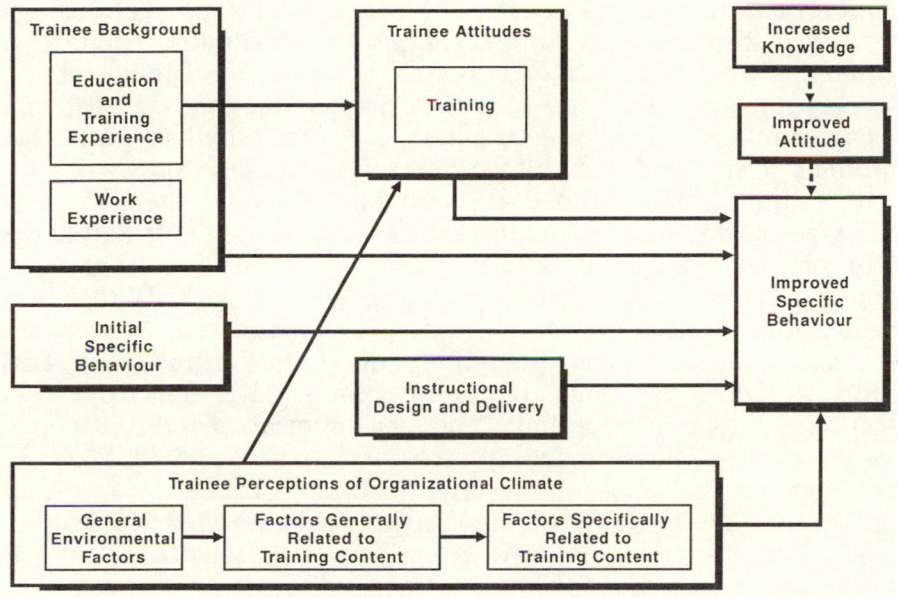

Figure 2.5 *A model of possible factors related to transfer of training to specific on-the-job behaviour*

basis. It is a more complex learning task than knowledge acquisition and retention, involving a complete understanding of the topic in addition to the motivation to consistently apply specified skills or rules of behaviour.

One of the first conclusions that can be drawn from the data related to this topic is that the quality and intensity of the training programme greatly affect the task, even more than some other types of training outcomes. In this respect the process of transferring specific behaviours from the training room to the workplace is more similar to knowledge retention than to changing general on-the-job behaviour or attitudes. More intensive training is able to exert greater influence on specific behaviour transfer. The data from these training studies show that design effects can fluctuate to account for a maximum of only 20 per cent of the variance in post-training behaviour on the job (see Figure C.8) to a maximum of 45 per cent of the variance (see Figure C.6).

These data suggest that some design and delivery patterns may have over twice the effects of others. Moreover, in the situation with more profound design effects, there is some moderation of the dominating effects of pre-training work habits on one's post-training behaviour.

The initial sub-models, as that presented in Figure 2.5 for modification of training-specific behaviour, incorporate all relationships evident in the three foundational studies. In this situation, Figure 2.5 combines what appear to be two separate models – one describing the learning process controlled to a great extent by the systemic design factors (see Figures C.7 and C.8), and another controlled more by design and delivery variables (see Figure C.6).

With less design and delivery variable influence, there are two key types of dominant systemic factors: 1. those elements within the workplace climate relating to modelling of the desired behaviour, and 2. those relating to physical working conditions. With better design and/or more intensive training, organizational climate factors such as these play no direct role. Rather, their influence is of an indirect nature, and their affects are minimized in that respect as well. They are still important, however, in terms of their influence on knowledge retention and attitude formation.

When the influence of the organizational climate recedes and design quality takes a more predominant role, learner background characteristics tend to have greater influence on specific on-the-job behaviour, especially one's education and work experience. The employee's general attitude toward training is also important in this learning environment.

In summary, specific transfer of training seems to be most dependent either upon 1. quality instruction and the trainees' past experiences as learners, or 2. a work environment which has supportive colleagues and a physical setting conducive to the target behaviour.

The hypothesized STD sub-model of general on-the-job behaviour change
The second of the two behaviour-oriented sub-models[7] is portrayed in Figure 2.6. Even though this sub-model pertains to on-the-job behaviour as did the last, it differs in some respects from specific transfer of training.

With close inspection of the supporting data the parallels between general behaviour transfer of training and attitude change are apparent. Even the best instruction seems to account for no more than 40 per cent of the outcome variance. Correspondingly, the systemic factors seem to predict approximately 60 per cent of the change regardless of the quality of the instructional design.

Even though the systemic factors appear to have a consistent degree of influence, it is possible to see different *patterns* of these systemic factors operating on general on-the-job behaviour when design and delivery quality and intensity vary. In this respect, there

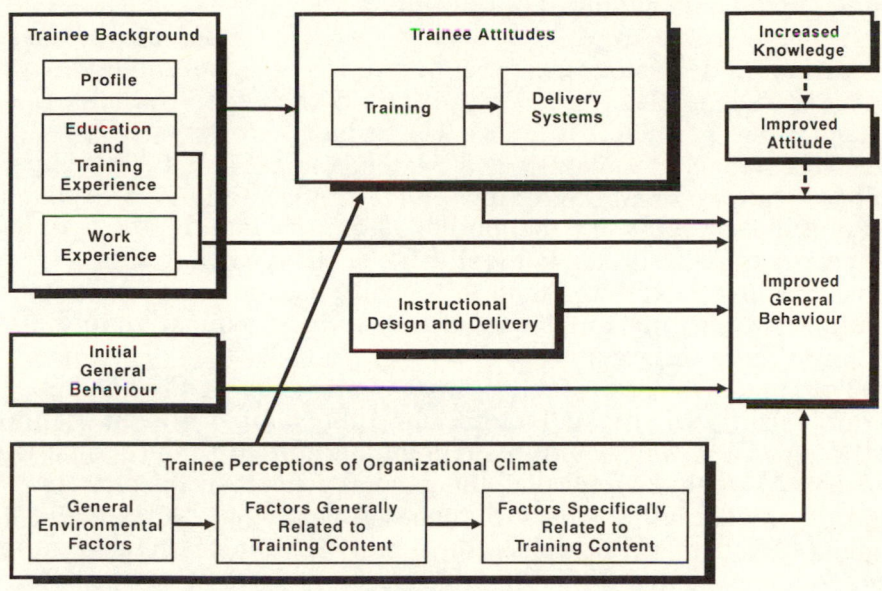

Figure 2.6   *A model of possible factors related to transfer of training to general on-the-job behaviour*

are similarities between the two types of training effects on work behaviour.

The first pattern is obvious when design quality is high or the training was simply less intense (see Figure C.9). There are relatively few systemic variables impacting outcomes here. Instead their influence is substituted by the influence of the employee's relevant knowledge and attitudes. The organizational climate perceptions have no direct influence. The systemic factors which do continue to play a role in determining behaviour outcomes in this situation pertain to the employee's educational and work background, and these effects are minimal.

On the other hand, when the design quality is less or the training is less intensive, the systemic variables are very important (see Figures C.10 and C.11). They serve two general functions in this situation: 1. as a direct influence on behaviour change, and 2. as a contributor to general training attitudes.

For the most part, one can relate those systemic factors with direct influence on general behaviour to one's level of motivation for the training. There is evidence of this motivation in the employees' attitudes toward training and how training is delivered. There is further evidence in terms of their impressions of the extent to which their supervisors support the training.

In these instances of lesser design quality, trainee attitudes are important in determining general on-the-job behaviour, but the systemic variables also exhibit more hidden influence by helping to shape these significant attitudes. The trainee's work experience and age both impact attitudes. In general, the younger and the less experienced trainees exhibit more positive attitudes and are more likely to alter their general on-the-job behaviour. Education and training experience have similar indirect affects; those with a more extensive training background tend to be more anxious to participate in another programme, and those with less formal education look forward to these programmes.

The major systemic effects, however, are generated by the impact of organizational climate factors. They play a major role in shaping training attitudes in lieu of a commanding role of the programme's design. As might be expected, the general aspects of the climate are more critical with respect to general behaviour outcomes. For example, general safety behaviour is more influenced in the training programmes studied by more diffuse impressions of safety factors in the organization than by specific instances of following a particular safety rule.

Regardless of the impact of the instructional design, changes in any type of work behaviour (be it specific or general) are heavily influenced by the pre-training work habits of that employee. It is easier to change poor work habits than it is to facilitate further improvement among those with more desirable pre-training habits.

One could summarize the lessons of this first look at training's impact on work behaviour *generally* related to the training programme in this way: general behaviour changes are most likely with *either*: 1. quality instruction and a more educated employee with greater work experience and positive work habits, *or* 2. a supportive work environment and a younger employee with positive attitudes about training and positive work habits.

A summary of predictors of training outcomes

One general model and four sub-models have been briefly described which show the initial explanations of four types of adult achievement in employee training. The general model speaks to the effects of a broad network of variable clusters upon training outcomes. This network is determined to a great extent by three factors:

- the employees' pre-training knowledge, attitudes, and work habits;
- the quality of the training programme's instructional design and delivery; and

- an array of systemic factors which describe the typical trainees' background and attitudes, and the nature of the organizational climate.

At least half of the variance in most outcomes is predicted by factors outside of those usually considered by most designers. Therefore, even a preliminary examination of these research results appears to warrant the construction of a new model of design procedures specifically directed toward the training arena, as well as a newly hypothesized theory of designing instruction for adult learners in employee training.

THE STD PROCEDURAL MODEL

The feasibility of STD procedures

Designing instruction in a systematic manner is detailed work. It emphasizes phases which already seem superfluous to some, such as front-end analysis or formative evaluation of instructional products. Yet, the STD approach involves consideration of even more factors than is typically attended to in systematic design. This section will introduce the STD model of design procedures based upon the conceptual model just discussed. Will such procedures be feasible and practical or will they be so complex that their implementation will be contingent on using computer-based design tools?

Such aids will be commonly used in the future, and in some settings they are already standard. The development of the Macintosh-based IDioM system for use by both expert and novice course developers is one example in current use. Gustafson and Reeves (1990) describe this system as a computer-based design workstation; while it is not an expert system, IDioM can be further developed into this more advanced format. On the other hand, Merrill *et al.* (1990b) have been working on the construction of an expert system which is being developed to address the shortcomings they see in current ISD procedures. This system will provide for the development of more interactive computer-based delivery of instruction, as well as designs which accommodate a greater number of variables which impinge upon learning outcomes. The completed system will guide knowledge analysis, adaptation of individual differences, and course management.

Clearly, such systems will expedite instructional design projects which address a broad range of learner variables. However, STD procedures are intended to serve today's typical designer of employee training programmes. This is a professional who has expertise, some tools, and often works as part of a team, but one who may lack state-of-the-art technology. This is a designer who must function in an organization with tolerance for a somewhat detailed design and development process, if it is possible to prove the cost-effectiveness of the required time expenditures.

While the research and development work is progressing, any new design model or theory must be adapted to ordinary circumstances. Without some ease of manual use, it is unlikely that these new design models will substantially impact training practice in the near future. Of course, computer-based design offers greater opportunity for more finite adaptation to the employee as a learner, to the peculiar needs of the organization and to the demands of the training content.

Complexity of task is but one perspective of feasibility. A second aspect relates to cost. The expansion of the traditional ISD model, whether the design and delivery processes are computerized or not, involves more detailed data collection and analysis. This means time and money.

While some of the systemic design factors which have been discussed may be addressed in current design procedures, their inclusion is usually based upon logic. Common sense leads to the conclusion that educational level, for example, affects learning in a training context. To commit funds to collecting data such as these is meaningful for a research institution, but not for an organization intended to generate profit, unless there is a more substantial rationale.

This rationale is embedded in the STD conceptual model and its foundational research conducted in real-life training situations. Only those elements of the total system which have proven influence on training outcomes are represented in this conceptual model and, correspondingly, in the STD procedural model and ultimately in STD theory.

Merging systemic and systematic design orientations

Enhancing current ISD models
STD is intended to supplement rather than supplant existing models of instructional systems design procedures. Systematic procedures have significantly improved instruction in many settings by establishing an organized method for planning instructional events based upon the nature of the content and the characteristics of human information processing.

'Micro-design' procedures used to sequence teaching/learning activities have typically been combined with 'macro-design' procedures, steps to follow when producing instructional programmes or materials. This latter framework has become known as the 'systems approach'. This orientation to instructional planning can be viewed, in some respects, as an application of the traditional scientific method. The use of the term 'instructional design' reflects a commitment to procedures such as these which constitute a determined application of scientific knowledge and research to education and training.

Recent instructional systems design applications, using both micro and macro orientations, have major roots in two publications. In the 1965 publication, *The Conditions of Learning*, Robert Gagne provided the theoretical thrust for the development of instructional design as an area of study and practice. Then Bela Banathy's 1968 book, *Instructional Systems*, provided one of the first widely used systematic macro-procedural models.

Now there is an impetus to move beyond this initial conceptualization of instructional design. Merrill's efforts to construct an expert system tool is one attempt to expand the traditional ISD approach. He is calling his work a movement to second generation instructional design. His large-scale project is designed to address the limitations of current design practice. These limitations have been delineated in the following manner:

> content analysis focuses on components, not integrated wholes; there are limited or no prescriptions for knowledge acquisition; prescriptions for course organization strategies are superficial; the theories are closed systems, asserting principles based on a subset of available knowledge, but not easily able to accommodate new knowledge as it becomes available; each phase of instructional development is performed essentially independently of other phases, as the theories provide no means for integration or for sharing data; the resulting instruction teaches components but not integrated knowledge and skills; the resulting instruction is often passive rather than interactive; and finally, all of these theories are very inefficient to use because an instructional designer must build every presentation from fundamental components (Merrill *et al.*, 1990a, pp7–8).

This critique of current instructional design procedures does not come from a new philosophical or psychological stance. The work of Merrill *et al.* is still within the ISD school; it is still framed by a cognitive view of the world. The impetus for their 'second generation instructional design' is not only their impressions of current practice, but also the design possibilities offered by new technologies. The solution to the dilemmas proposed by Merrill and his associates will be initially tool-oriented, with the expectation that theory will evolve from the tool.

The tactic proposed here is to devise related instructional design theory and models which are based upon replicated research. This solution for new design direction consists of three parts, including a systemic procedural model. This provides for STD's impact on design practice.

Using procedural models to guide design practice

Procedural models differ from conceptual models even though they may appear similar when both are presented in a chart format. Their function is clear: they suggest how to perform a task. There are many procedural models in the instructional design literature; the Dick and Carey model shown in Figure 1.1 is a prime example.

Procedural models are prescriptive, contrasting with the descriptive character of conceptual models. For many, they are almost design project management blueprints. They provide designers with a summary of 'how to' information.

The underpinnings of procedural design models vary. Some summarize effective practice. Others have a more theoretical base. While few have grown from a research base, it is possible for evaluation data resulting from their use to confirm or shape existing theory. The following section introduces this STD procedural model.

The systemic model of employee training design procedures

Many ISD models have been produced, each designed to meet unique situational needs or constraints. Previously six core elements of ISD models have been identified (Richey, 1986). These were derived from the analysis of 60 such models by Andrews and Goodson (1991). The elements are:

- determine learner needs;
- determine goals and objectives;
- construct assessment procedures;
- design/select delivery system approaches;
- try out instructional system; and
- install and maintain system.

When merging the systemic and systematic design models for employee training, these core elements serve as the foundation of the expanded model. Therefore, the new systemic model of design procedures strongly reflects the traditional ISD approach. In addition, it addresses employee training concerns, giving a pivotal position in the model to the trainee and the organization. This new procedural model is shown in Figure 2.7.

The design process is initiated by a training needs assessment. This is the process described by Rossett (1987). A fundamental objective of this phase is to determine whether training is the appropriate solution to the organizational problem. If so, the methodology continues with standard systematic design procedures. However, the analysis of employee and organizational climate characteristics is central to the entire task. This analysis activity influences every other phase in the design process.

One may still ask what makes this model systemic? It looks tradi-

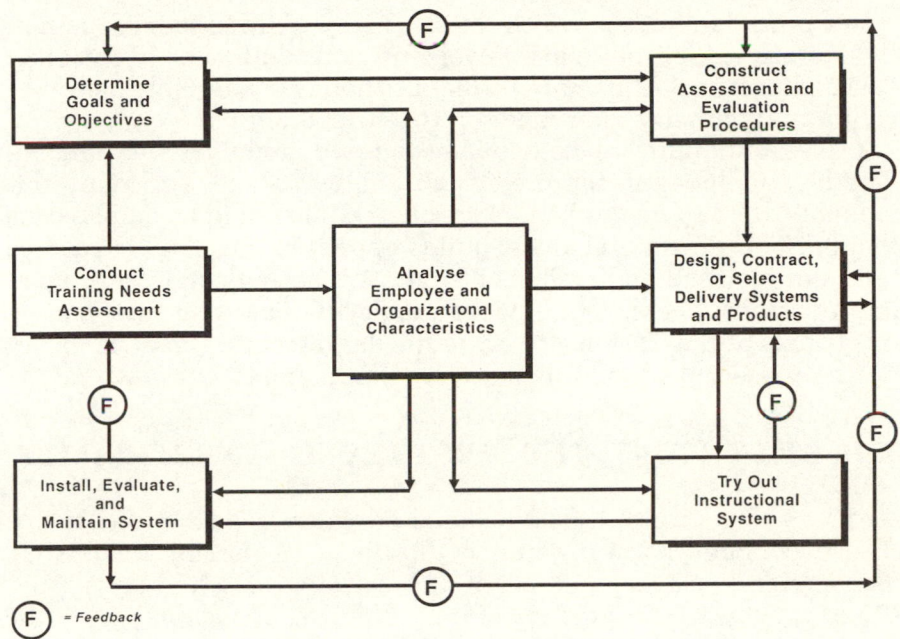

Figure 2.7 *A systemic model of employee training design procedures*

tional, not unlike many standard models in the literature. This is true; however, there are three clearly systemic features embedded in the model. They are:

- an expanded range of factors included in the front-end analysis;
- a process more responsive to the instructional context; and
- an iterative process.

The front-end analysis is more extensive than is usually the case. Not only is there a full training needs assessment, but also further analysis of employee and organizational characteristics. This makes the design process more responsive to the environment and to the background and experiences of the learners.

The model is not linear as are many ISD models; it is based upon the designer reflecting upon interactions between the training and the social and organizational environment. As such, it is not a closed system. Instruction can change with the characteristics of the organization and the learner, as well as adjust to the reactions of individuals to the instructional materials and delivery as in an ISD model.

Many of these same issues have been incorporated into other ISD procedural models. Most recently Jonassen *et al.* (1991) have presented a new procedural model which reflects many of these same concerns. It is iterative; the front-end analysis interacts with each of the other design stages, exerting more influence than is usual. However, they continue to classify their model in the ISD mould.

The essential difference between the two models is the range of variables included in the pre-design analysis stage. For many this would be the key distinction. Nevertheless, it should be emphasized that the STD procedural model builds upon the proven and accepted tenets of instructional systems design. It is seen as an evolutionary improvement. The model, however, is dependent upon the substantive details of the STD theory for particular direction since the theory has both descriptive and prescriptive components.

THE STD THEORY: THE FIRST LEVEL OF GENERALITY

As previously suggested, instructional designers need comprehensive theory, comprehensive in terms of the range of variables addressed and comprehensive in terms of the settings to which it applies (Richey, 1986). STD responds to only one part of the challenge: the need for theory which is comprehensive in terms of its component design factors. It has not been tested with learners of all ages, nor with learners in settings other than employee training.

STD theory still reflects ongoing theorizing and reflection. Even though the findings discussed have supporting data with some replication, the conclusions are far from being confirmed. This is a theory at the proposition stage, at best. Nevertheless, this proposed theory offers some explanation of the relationships between instructional design and adult learning, and their roles in employee training.

The first level STD propositions

The object of research is theory, and theory in its most general and most verified form is cast into statements of law. Propositions stem from conclusions derived from research. Typically several propositions which have been further tested and supported are synthesized into laws. Therefore, propositions have some degree of certainty but are intermediate steps in the theory development process.

The STD theory is presented in proposition form at two levels of generality. The first level of generality speaks to those relationships which pertain to overall training design without reference to the details of a given cluster of predictive variables. The second level of generality speaks to the effects of these causal factors. The propositions at this second level will be introduced in subsequent chapters.

The following list of first-level propositions has been derived from the STD conceptual model and sub-models of factors which predict outcomes in employee training. They serve as a basis for further research and testing of this explanation of adult learning and the effects of instructional design in training contexts. The propositions speak both to the training process and to instructional design methodology.

Propositions which describe training outcomes and learning processes

The first section of the STD theory is a description of those factors which predict overall training outcomes, and describe adult learning in employee training programmes. The descriptive STD propositions at the most general level are:

- Training outcomes can be predicted by a combination of:
  a. the quality of the instructional design and delivery;
  b. the employees' pre-training knowledge, attitudes, and work habits;
  c. the attitudes of the trainees;
  d. the employees' perceptions of the organizational climate; and
  e. the experiential background of the employees.
- The trainee's entering level of knowledge, attitude, or behaviour is the primary determinant of training outcomes. Those with lower knowledge levels tend to show the most gains after training; those with more positive pre-training attitudes and/or work habits tend to show the most improvement.
- Quality instructional design more easily influences knowledge retention and on-the-job application of the specific behaviours taught in the training programme.
- Transferring general behaviours to the workplace and affecting attitude changes are both facilitated by high quality instructional design, but these outcomes are primarily determined by other environmental factors and learner characteristics.
- As instructional design quality increases, the array of non-instructional factors which have primary impact on transfer of training varies. With higher quality design, the learners' experiential background is most influential; otherwise, organizational climate and pre-training attitudes are critical.
- Given higher quality programmes, there is a coordinated and hierarchical relationship between knowledge gains, attitude improvement, and changes in work habits after training; otherwise these are independent outcomes.

Propositions which prescribe instructional design procedures
The second part of the theory is prescriptive, suggesting particular design techniques based upon this explanation of adult learning in the training setting. These statements, combined with the STD procedural model, provide step-by-step guidance for training designers. When combined with the more detailed prescriptive propositions which are forthcoming, they provide the necessary direction to fully expand traditional ISD procedures to also reflect the systemic approach. The prescriptive STD propositions at the first level of generality are:

- Instructional designs should specifically address systemic factors, as well as adhere to systematic processes, especially if the training goals focus on attitude changes or general transfer of training.
- Front-end analyses for training programme design should be very comprehensive, encompassing not only analysis of performance discrepancies on the job, but also analysis of the organizational setting and a wide range of trainee characteristics and attitudes.
- Training programmes should be designed to accommodate learners with a range of entry levels. Pre-test results should be used to modify the training interventions to accommodate the employees' pre-training knowledge levels, attitudes and work habits.
- When selecting media and delivery systems, equal emphasis should be given to learner characteristics as is given to content demands, media attributes and other practical considerations.
- When incorporating motivation design into instructional programmes, emphasis should be given to the typical trainee's personal motives and opinions, as well as the environmental characteristics and reinforcement provided within the work setting.

The character of STD

These 11 propositions begin the delineation of STD theory. The theory will be developed in terms of the effects of learners' background characteristics and attitudes, and the organizational climate. As a whole, the theory presents an orientation to design which is even more analytical than ISD, and simultaneously more complex and more flexible.

SUMMARY AND NEXT STEPS

STD is a research-based approach to instructional design theory and practice. The STD conceptual model forms the basis of both the proposed model of design procedures and the proposed theory of designing instruction for adults in employee training programmes. The theory and recommendations for design practice will be further developed within a detailed explanation of the components of the STD conceptual model. This explanation will be integrated with the current literature as well as with the foundational data base.

Chapter 3 examines the affects of learner background characteristics on training outcomes with specific discussion of age, education and training experience, and work history. Chapter 4 addresses the role of learner attitudes as predictors of effective training, especially in terms of their roles as motivators. Atittudes toward previous training are considered separately and in relation to trainees' delivery system preferences to which they are so closely related. In addition, this chapter analyses the implications of the employee's attitudes toward the training content and the new delivery technologies being used in many training programmes.

Chapter 5 describes the role of the work environment in training, with an emphasis on organizational climate. The particular effects of behaviour modelling by management and co-workers are discussed, in addition to the impact of the physical working conditions and aspects of employee empowerment. The link between trainee's perceptions of the work environment and other employee attitudes is also examined. Finally, Chapter 6 synthesizes the theoretical and practical positions developed by summarizing the recommendations for designing instruction to promote knowledge gains, attitude changes, and near and far transfer of training. The final conceptual sub-models are presented and discussed here. Special consideration is given to creative design and ways of simplifying and streamlining the systemic design process.

Throughout the remaining chapters of the book the issue of the extent of STD's applicability is addressed. Is it appropriate for other types of adult learning? Does it apply to pre-adult learning as well? These discussions speak to the total comprehensiveness of STD.

NOTES

[1] See Appendix A for a more complete description of the training programmes, as well as their design and delivery characteristics. In Appendix B there is a fuller description of the research techniques used in studying these programmes, and the specific way each variable was measured.

[2] The path diagrams and their supporting data which serve as the basis for both the general model and for the sub-models related to specific types of training outcomes are found in Appendix C. The variables in these diagrams have been measured according to the specifications listed in Appendix B.

[3] The conclusions in this discussion are based upon a comparison of the path diagrams in Appendix C interpreted in light of knowledge of the comparative effectiveness of the three target training programmes. Especially note the comparisons of Figures C.1 and C.2, and Figures C.6, C.7 and C.8.

[4] The initial knowledge outcome sub-model is supported by two path diagrams in Appendix C. See Figures C.1 and C.2. The corresponding data follow each chart.

[5] This initial attitude change sub-model is supported by three path diagrams found in Appendix C. See Figures C.3, C.4 and C.5 and their matching tables of data.

[6] The initial sub-model describing transfer of specific behaviours on the job is supported by the path diagrams in Figures C.6, C.7 and C.8 found in Appendix C. The corresponding data follow each chart.

[7] The initial sub-model describing transfer to general on-the-job behaviour is supported by three path diagrams found in Appendix C with the others. The general behaviour diagrams are in Figures C.9, C.10 and C.11. The data upon which these path diagrams were constructed follow each figure.

3 Age and Experiential Background

This chapter explores the nuances of 'trainee background' as a predictor of employee training outcomes, and describes the role of these characteristics in the design process. These attributes are the first major cluster of variables identified in the STD conceptual model as highlighted in Figure 3.1.

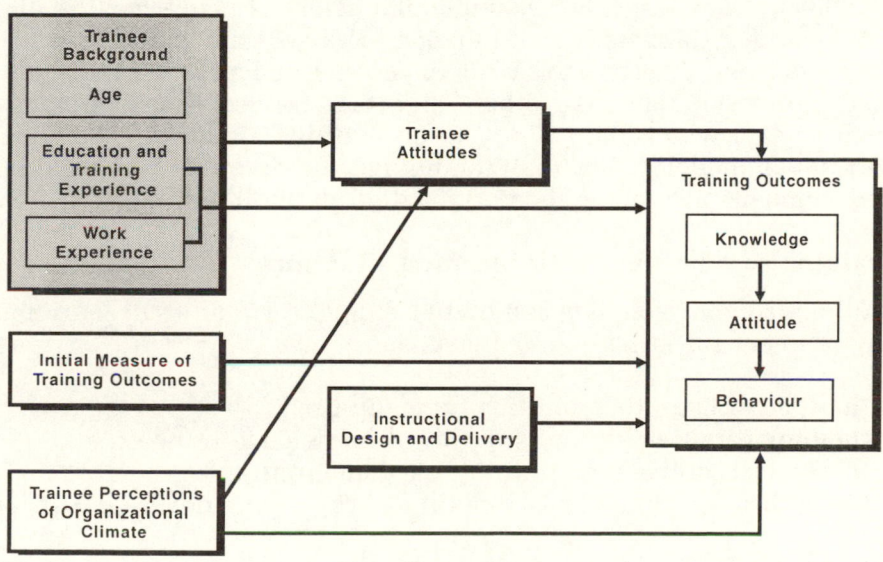

Figure 3.1 *A systemic model of factors predicting employee training outcomes: trainee background emphasis*

While little is totally predictable with respect to human learning, one can be sure of at least two attributes which distinguish adult from pre-adult learners. Adults are older than pre-adults, and with this age usually comes experience in many aspects of life. Even though these statements are self-evident, the nature and extent of their influence on learning is debatable. The model of training outcomes presented here identifies three categories of background characteristics which appear to partially determine employee training effectiveness: age, education and training experience, and work experience.

The issue here is the influence these variables have in determining the more specific outcomes of a training programme. Do these factors play similar roles with respect to knowledge retention, attitude formation, and behaviour change?

ADULT BACKGROUND CHARACTERISTICS AND EMPLOYEE TRAINING

Any learning situation is characterized to some extent by the nature of the learners. Employee training is no exception. Here, the distinctive nature of adults as learners influences the course of learning. However, training differs from other adult learning environments in a number of key ways. For example, the nature of employee training emphasizes certain aspects of the learner's background and psychological makeup, such as one's work experience and his or her reactions to it. However, there are other important trainee characteristics, such as age, which impact any adult learning situation. The STD conceptual model builds upon the unique characteristics of training environments as well as those typical of all adult learning.

Training as a unique adult learning situation

Training can be seen as a somewhat unique form of adult learning environment for at least four reasons:

- the type of cognitive abilities typically used;
- the opportunities for and support of knowledge transfer;
- the typical motives for training participation; and
- the nature of trainee involvement in programme development.

First, most adults participating in employee training programmes have prerequisite knowledge and skills gathered from practical on-the-job experiences as well as formal schooling. This implies the use of multiple types of intelligence and abilities.

Resnick (1987) has highlighted the differences between formal learning in school and practical learning outside school. The more practical learning tends to rely on shared activity, the use of physical and cognitive tools to acquire and demonstrate one's knowledge, and a close relationship with real events and objects. People who excel in practical learning situations often differ from those who excel in individual, symbol-based learning which emphasizes 'pure thought'. The expertise and competence of the practical learners tends to be situation-specific. On the other hand, expertise and competence from formal schooling is thought to promote more general transfer.

The kinds of intelligence developed from both formal schooling and practical learning create some of the diversity among adult trainees. These distinctions are compounded by the multiple types of basic intelligences relating to linguistic, numerical, pictorial, and social systems (Gardner, 1983) which have been developed in varying degrees in all adults.

Second, for most types of employee training, there is an immediate opportunity for application of the knowledge and skills addressed in the programme. This presents the possibilities of increased learner motivation due to relevance of the subject matter, as well as occasions for reinforcement of those principles which have been taught. On the other hand, these natural job situations also can create scenarios which quickly demonstrate a general lack of support for the target knowledge and skills.

The opportunity for transfer of training content is coupled with the emphasis business and industry places on transfer as the most important outcome of employee training. While other adult education settings also value knowledge acquisition as an end in itself, knowledge without use in the world of work is simply not cost effective.

A third key characteristic of employee training, as opposed to other adult learning situations, relates to participation. Typically, employees participate in training because it is required or because progress in the organization is dependent upon compliance. In other adult learning contexts, such as basic literacy programmes or continuing education, participation is usually voluntary.

This characteristic has major implications for trainee motivation and persistence levels. In addition, required training tends to diminish the effects of life changes and transitions. These have been found to influence participation in other types of educational activities. For example, Levinson (1978) called changes such as 'marriage, divorce, illness, advancement or failure at work, retirement, war, flourishing times or "rock bottom" times' (p54) marker events. The effects of these life-points on motivation and participation have been well-documented in the general adult education literature (Brookfield, 1986). They serve as essential motivators. However, their role is usually negligible in employee training.

Required participation naturally expands the trainee population as compared to those adult populations participating in volunteer education and training programmes. This expansion, in turn, exacerbates the range of differences within a group of adult learners.

Finally, not only is training typically mandated, but there is seldom trainee involvement in initial planning and goal-setting. While such cooperation is recommended and often adhered to in general adult education settings, the design of training programmes is usually based upon an analysis of a problem in the workplace, external mandates, or a management decision based upon personal observations or opinion. Thus, a trainee's commitment to the learning endeavour can not be facilitated through this early involvement in establishing programme direction. However, the orientation toward organizational problems, rather than learner participation, can increase the training's relevance since the basic intent is to improve the company and its productivity.

Training as a typical adult learning situation

However, in some respects employee training is similar to other adult learning settings. For example, adult learners as a group are diverse, more so than typical groups of younger learners. This diversity is also a characteristic of most employee trainees. Even though work demands, organizational history and similar job titles often create commonalities among learners, there is still much diversity.

Trainees typically vary in terms of age, educational and cultural background and interests. Moreover, the accentuation of multiple types of intelligence in employee training, as previously discussed, simply adds to this diversity with respect to intellectual functioning. In this respect, there is far more differentiation and complexity among individual adults than there is among pre-adults (Dixon *et al.*, 1985).

An important principle of adult educators is the belief that adults maintain their ability to learn throughout the life-span. This conviction also serves as a foundation for employee training, but it does more than present an optimistic, humanitarian orientation for those involved. It recognizes the importance of content-specific experience and expertise as a facilitator of new learning, even for the oldest trainees.

Training programmes are able to capitalize on the notion of crystallized intelligence. This type of intelligence is dependent on life experiences, knowledge acquired through formal schooling and other societal influences. It tends to increase with age, unlike fluid intelligence, its counterpart, which is a genetically determined characteristic which tends to decrease with age (Cattell, 1963). The concepts of fluid and crystallized intelligence are commonly used to explain the ability of adults to continue to learn in programmes such as employee training, in spite of research which seems to confirm the diminished abilities of ageing adults to excel in learning *general*, typically novel, content.

Implications for designing adult instruction

Viewing employee training within the context of the adult learning literature lays a foundation for analysing the role of learner background as a predictor of training outcomes. This orientation can emphasize the impact of learner profiles on training outcomes as well as stress the role of individual differences, rather than instructional design quality, as the basis of training success. However, it does not negate the role of training interventions in compensating for differences in learner background.

The instructional design literature, and much of the research, typically addresses individual differences in terms of ability level. However, other factors seem of equal or even more importance for adult learners in employee training, but these factors often vary depending upon the particular type of training goal being considered. The pertinent background factors will be discussed in relation to the major training outcomes.

THE EFFECTS OF TRAINEE AGE AND DEVELOPMENT

The phases of adult development

A generally supported notion of adults is that they 'pass through a number of developmental phases in the physical, psychological, and social spheres' (Smith, cited in Brookfield, 1986, p30). This approach suggests that adults change as they age, and there is evidence that these life changes have implications for adult learning in terms of learning style, motivation to learn and capacity to learn.

Troll (1982) has identified five basic assumptions of adult development which permeate the stage theories of life-span explanation:

- universality (a common path through life experiences);
- sequentiality (a common order of stages);
- teleology (a predetermined endpoint in each sequence);
- adaptation (indications of preferred approaches to life sequences); and
- class bias (a preference for middle-class values and approaches).

One of the most influential stage theories in adult education has been Havighurst's (1972) developmental tasks. These tasks are presented as representative of early and middle adulthood and old age. Some adult developmental theorists avoid a chronological framework citing the importance of factors other than age *per se*. For example, Erickson (1963) describes eight life-cycle periods beginning with 'basic trust vs basic mistrust' and progressing to 'ego integrity vs despair'. However, even this scheme is related in a general fashion to chronological phases of adulthood.

According to Havighurst's research, early adulthood concerns include: selecting a mate, learning to live with a marriage partner, starting a family, rearing children, managing a home, beginning a career, assuming civic responsibility and locating a congenial social group. Middle adulthood focuses on: achieving civic and social responsibility, establishing and maintaining a standard of living, guiding teenage children, developing leisure activities, relating to one's spouse and adjusting to ageing parents. Finally, the developmental tasks of old age encompass: adjustment to decreasing strength and health, adapting to retirement, reduced income and the death of a spouse, affiliating with one's own age group, meeting social and civic obligations and establishing satisfactory physical living arrangements.

Havighurst's developmental tasks have been widely recognized as one basis for planning relevant learning experiences for adults. The rationale is that activities tied to developmental interests should make the instruction more interesting and relevant for the learner. However, the research of Merriam and Mullins (1981) casts some doubt on the validity of developmental stages as a tool for designing instruction for broad populations. Their findings indicated educational experiences focusing on these tasks would be responsive only to the needs of females, middle-income adults and older people. Nevertheless, many still advocate relating education and training activities to those tasks identified with one's current stage in life in order to facilitate motivation.

However, developmental considerations are seldom stressed in employee training, perhaps because of the disparity among groups of trainees with great age ranges. Perhaps it is because developmentally-related topics do not seem pertinent to the business world. Or perhaps it is because of the frequent lack of attention given to learner differences in general. Even so, it is logical to assume developmental differences among learners affect training outcomes in some manner. The difficulties occur because the developmental changes in adulthood are complex and seldom neatly standardized, involving multiple, interrelated factors including those related to age, to social history and to non-normative life events (Schaie and Willis, 1982).

Age as a predictor of training effectiveness

Overview of the effects of trainee age

According to the STD model, the age of the participant does not *directly* predict the effectiveness of a training programme; instead the effects are all of an indirect nature. This explanation prevails, regardless of the type of training outcome. This is true when considering not only knowledge acquisition and retention, but also the broader outcomes of attitude change and transfer of knowledge to the workplace.

The question that may logically come to mind is 'why discuss a variable that has no direct influence on training outcomes?' Many optimistically believe that ageing does not hinder one's ability to learn and change, and there are many persons who clearly exemplify the principles of lifelong learning. However, common sense and other experience in the world of work produce some scepticism in this regard. Researchers also have explored the issue, and have found the same conflicting results in a variety of settings.

The STD model is consistent with these seemingly uncertain results. Age influences training outcomes, but not directly nor in as powerful a manner as some other factors.

The more detailed explanations of the age effects implied by the STD conceptual model follow. They are based upon the data presented in Appendix C. These explanations expand upon the very general conclusions relating to trainee background characteristics suggested by Figure 3.1.

The direct effects of trainee age on knowledge retention

Cattell's theory of fluid and crystallized intelligence has been interpreted by Knox (1977) as the substitution of 'wisdom for brilliance' (p421) by older adults dealing with intellectual tasks. This compensates for the loss of certain mental facilities, seeming to result in no change, at least until one's 60s and beyond, on average. This interpretation clearly accounts for the negligible direct influence of age upon knowledge retention in training contexts where the subject matter is work-related. The older and presumably more experienced employee shows knowledge gains comparable to the younger trainee who is probably more educated on average.

Knowledge acquisition and retention, if tested at all in training programmes, usually is measured by traditional paper and pencil tests similar to those used in formal education and schooling. Older workers typically have less recent experience with such tests. Moreover, they are likely to exhibit one of two opposing attitudes in these testing situations – anxiety or indifference – and either is detrimental to knowledge demonstration. Younger workers, with more recent formal educational experience, are more likely to perform well on objective knowledge tests. The 'wisdom' derived from job experience becomes the factor which equalizes older and younger workers' performance in training programmes with respect to traditional learning and knowledge acquisition.

There may be another explanation for the older employee's comparatively competent performance as a trainee with respect to knowledge acquisition and retention. In training programmes with traditional knowledge objectives, trainees have the opportunity to practice those cognitive learning skills which may have been unused for some time. They are listening to lectures, analysing explanations and using their reasoning abilities. Perhaps they form arguments opposing a particular position. This explains the position of some that simply participating in training programmes can tap the reserved capacity of fluid intelligence in older adults (Baltes *et al.*, 1988).

Others have explained the differences in the intellectual performances of adults of various ages in terms of declines in reaction time rather than a decline in actual mental functioning. This explanation has most support in those situations in which there is a memory task which is very complex or speed-related (Bee, Schulz and Ewen as cited in Merriam and Caffarella, 1991). For much training subject matter it is possible to define the task so that speed and reaction time are not issues, and consequently age differences are minimized and competence again does not appear to be age-related.

In any case, it seems possible for instructional designers to reduce their concerns regarding the depressing effects of ageing on abilities of those who participate in employee training programmes. The ability to excel in a training programme is not directly determined by age even in relation to knowledge retention, the area in which conventional wisdom might predict a strong relationship (see Figures C.1 and C.2 in the Appendix).

The direct effects of trainee age on attitude

Attitude change has been characterized as a frequently hidden goal of training programmes. The STD model suggests that, like knowledge retention, the extent to which this goal is achieved is not a function of the trainee's age. Instead, an employee's work-related attitudes are shaped more directly by other factors. The question is not whether adult attitudes in a work setting can change; they can and do. The question is whether adults of various ages tend to be more or less rigid in their beliefs, and if they are more rigid, what is the recourse?

Knox (1977) concluded that adult rigidity with respect to attitudes was distributed throughout the life-span. Rigidity was more of a personality characteristic than an age characteristic. This contradicts popular stereotypes of both the young and the old.

However, there are conflicting points of view, both with supporting research, relating to the stability of personality traits across the life-span. Some say there is considerable change; others indicate it is negligible. But there seems to be some additional weight given to the view that personality variables are more stable in the latter half of one's life than in the younger years (Kogan, 1990).

Even so, within the training environments upon which STD is based, age played no direct role in attitude change (see Figures C.3,

C.4, and C.5). It neither inhibited nor facilitated attitude change. In these situations the older employees were as likely to change their work-related attitudes after training as were the younger.

This conclusion may say less about general attitude stabilization than it does about the unique characteristics of work environments. In these settings job experience naturally is highly correlated to employee age. It may be that the adult's experiential background impacts attitude change in much the same way as it can impact knowledge acquisition and retention. Then again, it may also attest to the positive influence of successful employee training on work attitudes.

The direct effects of trainee age on behaviour
Transfer of training is typically a more complex task than knowledge acquisition, perhaps on a par with attitude change. Typically, transfer is viewed from the theory of common elements. In other words, the likelihood of transfer is dependent upon the extent to which the training situation and the application situation are similar. Transfer of training then is viewed as changing one's performance in the new environment as a result of something learned in the prior environment (Butterfield and Nelson, 1989).

In most taxonomies of instructional content transferring knowledge by using it in another situation is a higher order intellectual task. With respect to workplace behaviour, however, more than 'academic' intelligence is used in the transfer process. Wagner and Sternberg (1986) have found that only about 4 per cent of the variance in occupational performance is accounted for by traditional IQ tests. Others point to the existence of a 'practical intelligence' as a way of explaining some types of human behaviour. What is practical intelligence and is it influenced by one's age as is the type of intelligence relied upon for general learning?

Practical intelligence has been defined as the application of intellectual skills to everyday activities (Schaie, 1990). It is logical to conclude that practical intelligence is more sensitive to crystallized intelligence, which responds to interests and experience, rather than fluid intelligence, the more genetically determined capability. Surprisingly, psychological research tends to relate practical intelligence to fluid, instead of crystallized intellect. Consistent with this conclusion, other research found age differences in the performance of everyday tasks, such as interpreting medicine bottle labels, road maps, and warranties. People tended to have more difficulty with these types of tasks as they aged. These age differences were comparable to those usually associated with fluid intelligence (Schaie, 1990).

Such results would lead one to expect that age might also negatively influence on-the-job behaviour outcomes of training, but such a finding is not apparent in the STD conceptual model. The foundational research showed that age did not influence trainees' on-the-job behaviour, positively or negatively (see Figures C.6 – C.11). The benefits of experience did not give older workers an edge; nor did the intellectual advantages of youth produce superior on-the-job performance. If practical intelligence is not closely allied with crystallized intelligence, how can this be explained?

Age effects are apparently overpowered by other factors. Experience, attitude, and organizational climate are more influential. These will be discussed later. Of interest here are those aspects of intellectual functioning which seem to stabilize (rather than decline) throughout adulthood. By emphasizing the common types of mental activity in everyday life, Dixon and Baltes (1986) have identified two principles which are pertinent to this examination of trainees' propensity to transfer their learning to the workplace. Mental functioning stabilizes in practised, skilled and pragmatic areas, and in performances in which there is interest, effort, training, or social support.

These features are characteristic of a good work environment. Thus, while intellect (perhaps even the same types of intellect needed to succeed in formal learning environments) is required to transfer training principles to on-the-job behaviour, other aspects of occupational behaviour compensate for age-related declines. The result is that trainees of all ages, given the proper conditions, can be expected to modify their job performance after participation in training. Perhaps a good training programme actually decreases trainee differences with respect to both practical and basic intellectual functioning. This conclusion is supported by the fact that the employee's age does not directly influence any of the four major types of training outcomes.

The indirect influence of trainee age

Trainee age, however, does influence learning in an indirect fashion primarily through its role in shaping selected pre-training attitudes. Attitudes are presented in the systemic approach as a dominant force in the training process. Not only are they instrumental in promoting on-the-job behaviour changes, but a range of pre-training attitudes directly influences the other major types of training outcomes as well.

There is some evidence of indirect age effects in determining all training outcomes with the exception of transferring specific skills to the workplace. Knowledge retention, attitude change and a more generalized transfer are all influenced to some extent by age effects. Knowledge outcomes appear to be most consistently affected by age's impact on pre-training attitudes (see Figures C.1, C.2, C.3 and C.11). Those attitudes most commonly affected by the employee's age pertain to methods of training delivery, and the pre-training disposition toward the content of the training programme.

The in-depth analysis of these findings follows in Chapter 4. However, it is crucial to a general interpretation of the STD model that one notes the effects of the complex network of systemic design factors on training outcomes. Adult learning is not always fully explained by obvious relationships between outcomes and design and delivery tactics. Rather there is an underlying base of factors, such as age-related attitudes, which play just as important a role in determining outcomes.

Summarizing age effects
On the surface, the STD model proposed here seems to suggest the following principles in relation to the influence of the employee's age on training outcomes:

- it is possible for all persons to learn at any phase in their lives when the instruction is directed toward their work;
- normal intellectual ageing is promoted by a variety of factors other than time; therefore, age alone is not the most salient background characteristic to use when explaining learning proficiency, especially in a training setting; and
- quality instructional design can compensate for the age effects which do pose a barrier to learning.

THE EFFECTS OF EXPERIENTIAL BACKGROUND

An overview of the role of experience

Experience and adult learning
In the current adult education literature, life experiences have been included as an important aspect in the learning process in terms of their role as:

- factors which provide a major distinction between adults and pre-adults (Kidd, 1973);
- fundamental determinants of motivation for adult participation in educational activities (Aslanian and Brickell, 1980);
- a basis for trainers and adult educators to use when constructing meaningful learning situations (Darkenwald and Merriam, 1982); and
- a major resource used by trainees to help themselves in learning situations (Brookfield, 1986).

Such conclusions point to the value of past experience as a vehicle for understanding and interpreting new concepts, a position which reflects a cognitive orientation to learning. The storage of new information in long-term memory is aided by organizing the content in familiar formats. Retrieval of this information is facilitated not only by its organization, but also by its integration with past experience.

However, experience does more than provide the trainee with a context for learning; it also has the effect of shaping abilities. For pre-adult learners, references to individual differences typically imply only variation in cognitive ability. For adults, as previously discussed, the more useful definition of intelligence encompasses multiple abilities and competencies. Many of these capabilities are shaped by one's experiences rather than only by basic intelligence.

With respect to employee training, some of the experiences that matter are easily anticipated. They include one's education and training background and one's work experience. It has been demonstrated with older adults that the education and training experience itself can not only reactivate one's existing cognitive skills, but also provide opportunities for further practice of these skills (Baltes *et al.*, 1988). It is logical to assume that this same phenomenon could occur for young and middle-age adults as well. Work experience also permits similar practise of situation-specific skills, again aiding the adult who is participating in training on similar topics.

Experiences in STD

The STD model presented here suggests that experiential background has multiple effects. It can either motivate or inhibit training performance. It affects training outcomes directly and indirectly as well by serving as an important factor in shaping trainee attitudes.

While the data show that the influence of one's background experiences varies depending upon the type of training outcome, the substance and extent of one's experiences are also critical aspects of each type of learning situation. It is speculated that the influence directly exerted by experiential characteristics is determined in part by the frequency of opportunities provided in the training design for practice, reinforcement, and testing of the content. In other words, when more practice of the expected performance is incorporated into the instruction, the less the trainee needs to resort to using past experiences to interpret and assimilate the content.

Indirectly, the learner's experiences in work, education, and training play a role in all training outcomes, regardless of the design or intensity of instruction. This occurs because of the critical role experiential background plays in shaping pre-training attitudes. Background experiences seem instrumental to success, even though the training may not directly or consciously build upon the learners' history.

The direct effects of experiential background on training outcomes

The direct effects of trainee experiences on knowledge retention
The direct effects of one's experiences on the learning process can be explained by analysing the type of experience and also the type of training outcome. For example, the process of transferring training principles to the workplace differs from traditional knowledge acquisition and retention with respect to trainee experiential background. Moreover, if the goal is changing attitudes after training, there is a third pattern of experience variables which partially predicts the outcome, although experience variables have minimal control of the ultimate consequences of a training programme in these circumstances.

Experience in formal education directly influences knowledge retention, as might be expected (see Figure C.1). This can be easily explained in a number of ways. Schooling, even if it occurred some time ago, provides expertise in learning-to-learn skills which are utilized in training programmes. Such skills are particularly important in those training programmes which use intermittent test-type activities for the trainee's knowledge demonstration and recall practice. Conversely, one can conclude that a trainee's educational experiences would be less important when the programme design emphasizes knowledge presentation by the trainer (or a type of mediated instruction). In these programmes there is less learner interaction and involvement. However, one would assume that educational background is still critical to knowledge acquisition and retention even in programmes such as these, although it may not be obvious because of the lack of testing and overt learner response.

Work experience does not directly facilitate trainee demonstration of new knowledge (see Figures C.1 and C.2). This practical experience may well aid the trainee in assimilating the new information, but 'workplace wisdom' apparently does little to help the adult learner perform formal school-related tasks, such as reading, listening and taking tests.

The direct effects of experiential background on attitude change
Attitude change, as the target outcome of a training programme, is controlled far more by other attitudes than by the dimensions of the trainee's background experiences. The experiential effects are different with respect to attitude change from those operating on knowledge retention and behaviour change. Attitude changes are influenced more by the *lack* of work experience than by the accumulation of such experience (see Figure C.3).

Given the extensive support for the facilitating effects of one's experiences, how can experience now appear to serve as a barrier to successful training? This occurrence can be explained by recalling the tendency for attitudes to crystallize as adults age. A mind-set becomes established as the person ages, and correspondingly as more job experience is acquired. Therefore, those trainees most likely to demonstrate significant attitude changes are younger with less work experience.

The role of past education and training experiences in relation to attitude change is also very different from how knowledge retention or behaviour changes are achieved after training. Similar to the role of work experience, these experiences have no direct positive effects on attitude change either (see Figures C.3, C.4 and C.5). Here there is no connection whatsoever between past learning experiences and changing current workplace attitudes, even though current learning can affect attitudes.

The direct effects of experiential background on workplace behaviour

Is the adult learning literature not as relevant for training situations as for other adult education contexts with respect to the use of one's past experience? Thus far, the effects seem limited. However, the trainee's past experiences do play a more predominant role in certain types of transfer of training. The STD conceptual model highlights the effects of both past learning experience and work experience, but the patterns differ depending on whether one considers general or specific transfer. Completion of a greater amount of formal education facilitates the transfer of specific behaviours to the workplace (see Figure C.6) but, surprisingly, inhibits general transfer (see Figure C.9). This seems unusual, given that one espoused purpose of schooling and general education is to teach basic skills and knowledge to facilitate competent behaviour in a broad range of situations (Resnick, 1987). Typically this goal distinguishes education from training situations.

One explanation for the dichotomous situation suggested by this model is based upon Bruner's (1982) distinction between general and specific transfer. He relates general transfer to non-specific principles and attitudes. General transfer can encompass behaviour in a wide spectrum of situations. The appropriate response in these settings can be determined by following generic principles rather than situation-specific rules such as those typically presented in employee training programmes.

For example, in the automotive training programmes studied here, the trainee exhibiting general transfer skills behaved safely in all plant situations, in addition to consistently following the specific safety rules which were targeted in the training programmes. The new general behaviour could be attributed to a belief that safety is important, as well as an action plan which operationalizes this belief. The plan may have even required the employee to consciously (or unconsciously) generate a new operating rule. General transfer from this viewpoint is dependent upon attitudes and problem-solving capabilities.

However, higher levels of formal education inhibited these general transfer behaviours. Perhaps much schooling does *not* foster generalized behaviour in the workplace. Perhaps many schooling experiences promote only recall and use of those skills which have been directly taught, practised and tested. This conclusion is unsettling since it is diametrically opposed to the presumed value of education as distinguished from training.

Changes in specific and general behaviours on the job also differ in terms of their relationship to the employee's work experience. While job history plays a role in predicting both types of transfer, there are again opposite explanations of its particular role. The use of specific skills on the job is promoted by larger amounts of work experience (see Figure C.6). Here is the place where the 'workplace wisdom' and (perhaps one's practical intelligence) helps performance.

General transfer, on the other hand, is more likely to occur if the employee has had *fewer* years with the company (see Figure C.9). This phenomenon can be explained by re-examining the connection between attitudes and general transfer which was suggested by Bruner. The relationship between younger adults and attitude change has been previously inferred from the literature. The positive attitudes which support general transfer are more likely to occur in persons who are less seasoned, perhaps less sceptical, than some older workers who have endured countless changes in the work environment. This explanation is again reflective of theories of personality rigidity in some older adults.

The relationship between general transfer and employee attitude is further strengthened by the data from the foundational STD research. Because of the industrial safety training topic, data were collected on the employee's accident experience. The assumption was that the presence of such experience in one's background would add to a person's sense of urgency and interest in the training; accident experience would be a motivator. While such experience did not affect specific transfer, it did predict the extent to which general transfer occurred on the job (see Figure C.10). This type of work experience may reflect the importance of trainee attitudes as a precursor of general transfer of training.

The indirect effects of experiential background on training outcomes

Overview
While one's education, training and work backgrounds appear to directly affect training results, the indirect effects of such experi-

ences are even more substantial. There is evidence of these effects in each of the STD sub-models relating to the various training outcomes (see Figures C.1, C.2, C.4–C.6, C.10 and C.11). However, experiential background is most predominant in the explanations of knowledge retention outcomes (see Figures C.1 and C.2) and general on-the-job behaviour changes (Figures C.10 and C.11).

The greatest indirect impact of the trainee's experiential background is felt primarily through attitudes toward past training and attitudes toward training delivery systems. Moreover, the effects are duplicated in both intensive training programmes, as well as in shorter training seminars. Given the nature of the affected attitudes, it is not surprising that the most critical trainee experiences in this regard relate to the amount of past education and training. The amount of previous participation in training is the most influential experiential factor.

Past experience and training motivation

While trainee age is of great interest to adult educators and instructional designers because of its possible implications for cognitive functioning, trainee experiences have been tied primarily to motivation. Trainers are usually concerned with the motivation of those participating in their programmes. The practitioners' concerns parallel those of many researchers and theorists who also concentrate on factors of adult motivation. Wlodkowski's (1985) work is part of this theory building. He portrays the motivation of an adult learner as a function of 'success + volition + value + enjoyment' (p8). This paradigm is similar to Keller's explanation of motivation as a function of value × expectancy (Keller, cited in Rossett, 1987). At the beginning of a training programme, value and expectancy are greatly determined by the employee's general reactions to other programmes in which he or she has participated in that organization.

Using the more detailed Wlodkowski framework, one can see the enjoyment factor addressed in STD in terms of delivery system preferences and direct measures of the extent to which participants enjoyed past training. The value factor is measured in terms of the perceived utility of information learned in past training programmes. The volition factor is reflected in the employee's inclination to volunteer for additional training. Each of these motivation components is associated with one's past experiences. Enjoyment and value are predicted by more frequent participation in employee training. Volition is predicted by formal education level.

This role of adult background experiences as motivators reflects evidence from other research which links life experiences to adult participation in educational activities. The relationships described in the literature primarily pertain to voluntary educational programmes. The principle is also established here for non-voluntary training programmes.

Pertinent experiences for a training context appear to involve one's background as a learner and as an employee. The relationship between one's level of formal education and one's willingness to voluntarily participate in training parallels past research results relating to active participation in general adult educational activities (Cookson, 1986; Fisher, 1986; Shipp and McKenzie, 1981). However, not only is education level a predictor of adults volunteering for general educational programmes, but such volunteering is also prompted by other personal and family background experiences (Aslanian and Brickell, 1980). These experiences do not seem to influence training, distinguishing it from the more general adult education.

The conclusions presented here are reflective of a group of employees with generally positive reactions to their former training experiences. If the situation were reversed and past training experiences were viewed as unproductive, one could assume that these previous training experiences would inhibit motivation and create barriers to success in any current training.

The conclusions with respect to the role of work experience follow a pattern which differs from that established for education and training experiences. Once again, positive employee attitudes are enhanced by *lack* of experience. This principle applies to both general experience measured by years on the job (see Figure C.10) and by more specific experiences on the job pertinent to the training topic (see Figures C.2, C.4, C.10, and C.11). These linkages play a role in explaining knowledge retention after participation in training (see Figure C.2), and even more so they help explain the transfer of training to general conduct on the job (see Figure C.10).

ADULT BACKGROUND CHARACTERISTICS AND STD PROCEDURES

Instructional design is a combination of both theory and practice. The explanation of STD now turns to a focus on practice. The STD procedural model is inextricably tied to traditional systematic design procedures. As such the new systemic design procedures must be compared to current systematic procedures.

The general method of expanding systematic design into systemic design is similar for all systemic factor categories. Data addressing the new design factors are initially collected in the training needs assessment phase, and then interpreted in the phase 'Analyse employee and organizational characteristics' of the STD procedural model presented in Chapter 2. Usually, systemic factors impact the design in combination with other systemic elements. This is as true for adult background characteristics as it is for trainee attitude and organizational climate variables.

The final chapter in this book synthesizes all systemic design procedures. Here, and in Chapters 4 and 5, each category of systemic design variables will be isolated and discussed in terms of their unique implications for improving design practice.

Emphasizing trainee age and development variables in STD

Most ISD models address learner characteristics. The Dick and Carey model (1990) shown in Figure 1.1 is representative of those with direct reference to learners ('identify entry behaviours, characteristics'). Others, such as Seels and Glasgow (1990), incorporate the 'identify learner characteristics' stage within the problem analysis section. The full explanations of both of these models cite learner age and development as important characteristics.

When designing instruction for pre-adults, the consideration of age and developmental level is essentially an analysis of prerequisite capabilities. For adult learners, age cannot be used for this purpose. This does not imply that all adults have the necessary basic learning and reasoning skills and general knowledge expectations, but only that age is not an indication of who is likely to have the skills and who does not. Age, of course, can suggest the likelihood of some declining physical abilities which often need to be considered when contemplating text design and other aspects of design which rely upon sensory reception.

Nevertheless, with respect to anticipating ultimate learner achievement in a training programme, age is a factor which needs to be addressed. This is not because trainees of differing ages have differing capabilities as learners, but because of the critical interactions between age and attitudes in the learning process. Therefore, age data should be collected in the initial analysis stage. It should be used as a factor in:

- selecting general delivery systems and media;
- determining the extent to which the programme should address motivation issues; and
- interpreting formative and summative evaluation results.

When designers use age-related conclusions as a basis for a particular design tactic, age is seldom the sole basis for the move. Typically, age information is analysed in combination with other learner characteristics. For example, age may be considered in conjunction with work experience or with education level or with learner attitudes.

The difficulties many organizations have in regards to using age information are twofold: 1. there is typically a broad age spectrum of persons in a training programme, and 2. there is a tendency for many training programmes to use group-based rather than individualized delivery techniques. In a training situation characterized by both of these attributes, one is forced to design programmes to target the majority. At best trainee differences are addressed by devising supplementary materials (or sections of materials) for voluntary, individual use.

Special grouping techniques provide one avenue to address the problems. However, homogeneous grouping is not usually possible (or in many cases, desirable) in employee training, unless it is based upon work experience or job title. The group formed on the basis of work experience is an alternative which would tend to address age effects as well as those of work experience itself. Grouping by job title, on the other hand, tends to address the effects of education level, but not work experience or age.

Emphasizing experiential background in STD

Overview
Experiential background characteristics are cited in many ISD models as examples of general learner attributes. In these generic models, background characteristics are usually important because of their implications for learner interest and ability (Dick and Carey, 1990; Kemp, 1985; Seels and Glasgow, 1990).

Adult experiences in the STD model work primarily as factors influencing trainee motivation and competence as a learner. While not altogether different from the roles attributed to background experience in generic ISD models, experiential background characteristics typically have a somewhat unique use in employee training design.

Learner interests usually are identified in the generic design models so that specific learning activities can be built around them. For example, materials used for reading instruction in adult basic literacy programmes can pertain to professional athletics or hobbies, thereby using current interests to foster a desire to persist and complete the programme.

In the generic ISD models pertinent learner experiences commonly cited are educational background, achievement level, professional background and language background. Knowledge of these experiences enables the designer to make more accurate diagnoses of the target population's abilities. Such information can help determine appropriate vocabulary and reading level, and other ability-related decisions which shape the instruction.

In this systemic model for training design, the pertinent experiences are education level, amount of previous training and amount of work experience. Work experience and education and training background all have direct impact on the outcomes a trainer would typically expect. In addition, they have more subtle, indirect effects on outcomes as well. These effects result primarily from interactions between trainee experience and attitude; the implications of these related variable clusters can further shape the design of a programme.

Adult background experience then, in addition to having implications for content-specific prerequisite skills, is also critical to training design in terms of the following specific activities:

- estimating learner interests;
- determining the emphasis and the nature of the motivation design (especially to anticipate the general attitude toward training);
- selecting general delivery system and media;
- determining testing format and constructing test items;
- determining the necessity of testing prerequisite skills, and the scope of such testing if it is deemed necessary; and
- determining the amount of rehearsal and practice required to facilitate transfer to both specific and generalized on-the-job behaviours.

In some respects experiential background influences the same aspects of design as does age, with delivery system selection and motivation design being the most obvious. The link between age effects and experience effects seems to be through their roles in forming areas of interests.

Education and training experience

Experiential background seems to have more implications for adult ability level than does age. This is again reflective of the role of multiple intelligences (especially practical intelligence) in workplace performance. With respect to training as a means of knowledge acquisition and retention, the presence of more formal education would suggest trainees have a greater facility with traditional, objective test items, and a higher level of verbal fluency and learning-to-learn skills. More advanced listening, speaking and writing abilities could also be anticipated, though not necessarily assumed, for those with higher education levels.

The range of education levels among a trainee population also influences the decision to add a pre-training test of entry-level abilities. One may decide it would not be productive to devote time to testing the total group. Moreover, the education level may also suggest whether such testing should encompass only training-related content, or whether component learning skills and attitudes should be addressed. Dick and Carey's (1990) admonition to gather accurate data rather than relying on pre-conceived stereotypes is especially appropriate in this context.

Work experience

Knowing the average work experience of a group of trainees partially indicates the ease with which they will transfer specific skills to the workplace. As one would expect, less practice is necessary for the more experienced group, even though the job skills may be new. This conclusion is independent of the age of the trainee. Practising skills already within one's areas of interest and expertise allows one to build upon existing cognitive structures. In everyday terms, it's easier to understand.

On the other hand, if generalized transfer is the training goal, more work experience can inhibit transfer. These aims are closely related to changing attitudes and for the older, more experienced employee an increased emphasis on motivational learning activities may be warranted in the course of training.

Implications for general organization of training

When the training content can be learned easily on the job, or is more of a refinement and review of things known by the experienced employee, it is not unreasonable to form training groups on the basis of work experience. In this way, the trainers can adapt pre-designed instruction to the particular needs and interests of a group. Groups can vary in terms of the amount of practice or the amount of attention given to motivational activities.

Other trainee background characteristics

The STD model specifically cites three background characteristics as being especially important to training design: age, education and training experience, and work experience. That is not to imply that other traits are unimportant. The instructional systems design process depends upon a clear picture of the pre-requisite skills of the learner. This new systemic model builds upon ISD 'givens' such as this.

Of particular importance in the current training environment are basic learning skills. As training becomes more wide-spread among all employee groups, there is concern at times with language facility, reading and listening competence and mathematical abilities. Hearing problems are also common among older workers and, at times, among those working in plants with high noise levels. It behoves any design team to know the range of prerequisite skills in the target population. Trainee skills not only influence the manner in which complex content is presented, but they have implications for media and delivery system selection. These tactics are fundamental to any design orientation. The age and experiential background design procedures unique to the systemic approach are summarized and presented in a more formal fashion in the STD theory.

EXPANDING STD THEORY: AGE AND EXPERIENTIAL BACKGROUND PROPOSITIONS

In the previous chapter, the STD theory was introduced by identifying two categories of propositions at the first level of generality, a level which speaks to overall training design effectiveness. The first group consisted of propositions describing those factors which seem to predict specific training outcomes. These are oriented toward adult learning and show the role of instructional design in the total learning process. The second set of propositions were those prescriptive statements directed specifically toward training design practice.

The current task is to expand the STD theory by suggesting propositions at a second level of generality. At this point the propositions speak to the effects of the systemic causal factors. These second level propositions are specifically directed to the effects of those trainee background characteristics discussed in this chapter – age and experience. Again, both descriptive theory and prescriptive theory will be formulated.

These propositions are derived from the initial STD conceptual sub-models. As such the findings upon which they are based may or may not have been replicated for a given training outcome. Typically they are supported with empirical relationships which have been duplicated across outcomes. For example, the relationships between age and employee attitudes toward previous training delivery systems have been found in relation to both knowledge acquisition and retention and general transfer of training. These propositions are tentative, even though they have data support. Ideally, they would be tested further in other learning environments.

Descriptions of adult learning in employee training

Age-related propositions
A key factor distinguishing adult learners as a group is their diversity, and age is a typical example of this diversity in most training programmes. This variation alone can create a learner population with many interests, many concerns, and many factors which either facilitate or inhibit behaviour in a learning situation. The following propositions are based upon the learner background data underlying the STD conceptual model. They summarize those conclusions concerning the effects of age on learning in an employee training situation:

- older adults with more work experience may be less motivated to participate in a training programme, thus influencing the extent to which they retain knowledge and apply the general tenets presented in the training;
- older adults are no less likely to achieve intended training outcomes in a well designed programme than are younger or middle-aged adults.

These propositions are seemingly contradictory, perhaps reflecting the confusions which exists relative to age effects in training. Even though at times age appears to influence pre-training attitudes, it does not have an overpowering impact on outcomes, especially for those who are positively motivated. Such conclusions may be influenced by the extent to which trainees are familiar with the subject matter and the extent to which speed of response is an issue in evaluating ultimate trainee performance.

Experience-related propositions
Two general areas of experiential background have been shown to bear upon training outcomes: education and training experience and work experience. This is a narrower range of learner experiences than those which are typically seen as relevant to instructional design and learning in more generic discussions. Their role in the training process is summarized in the following descriptive propositions:

- the more formal schooling an adult has had, the greater the knowledge retention after employee training;
- on-the-job experience does little to enhance work-related knowledge acquisition and retention;
- schooling enhances lateral transfer of training to application in specific on-the-job behaviour, but not transfer to generalized on-the-job behaviours;
- formal schooling does not influence attitude change as a result of training;
- on-the-job experience enhances lateral transfer of training to application in specific workplace behaviours, but not generalized transfer of training or attitude change after training;
- in addition to an accurate knowledge of the task, transfer of training into general workplace behaviour appears to be primarily a function of positive attitude;
- the more formal schooling an adult has had, the more he or she is likely to be motivated to participate in employee training.

The employee's experiential background seems as important in training situations as has been suggested for other adult learning environments, even though the patterns of influence may vary for the training environment. Experience appears to influence not only trainee motivation and attitudes, but perhaps even the trainee's cognitive processing.

Prescriptive propositions for instructional design based upon trainee background

The above descriptive propositions focus upon the learner and the learning process in an employee training context. The most effective instructional design needs to be fundamentally rooted in an understanding of learning rather than the trainer's presentation competency. The following second-level propositions suggest specific design procedures which reflect those portions of the STD theory pertaining to trainee age and experiential background. These prescriptive propositions are grouped below in terms of one of the seven stages of the STD procedural model presented earlier.

'Training needs assessment' propositions
The STD approach demands that increased attention be given to differences among individuals and organizations. Therefore, one additional step must be included in the training needs assessment process:

- The training needs assessment should encompass collecting baseline data on the population targeted for training, including:
  a. age;
  b. educational level;
  c. years on current job (and/or years at company); and
  d. previous training at company and dates of training.

This step does not necessarily involve new efforts in surveying employees. Many personnel offices already have such information, or perhaps these standard demographic data are available from a previous evaluation of a similar population. If there are no such data available, a short survey can be distributed to a random sample of the target group.

'Construct assessment and evaluation procedures' propositions
When planning both the formative and summative evaluation, another data collection step is necessary:

- collect pertinent trainee background data (age, educational level and work experience) from samples of those involved in the tryout of the instructional materials and in the final evaluation of the programme.

This parallels the needs assessment step, allowing designers to continue tracing the trainee background effects on the programme outcomes. This step involves little additional time or effort and should not pose a major problem for the design team, provided formative and summative evaluations are already incorporated into the project. Such data will then be used in the 'try-out' phase by analysing these data and using the information to further modify the instruction. This process is consistent with traditional systematic design procedures.

'Design, contract or select delivery systems and products' propositions
The actual design of the materials in the systemic approach includes modifications to accommodate learner background characteristics. This stage naturally is dependent upon a previous analysis of the learner characteristics. The modifications, however, will vary depending on whether the instructional delivery will be individualized or group-oriented. If the programme will be delivered to groups, the design must accommodate the manner in which the groups will be formed; this topic is discussed in the installation propositions. If groups are going to be formed on a random basis, the designer should incorporate the maximum number of interventions into the programme. If the instruction is to be individualized, modifications are dependent more upon the trainees' attitudes toward that delivery system.

The recommendations listed below encompass both age and experiential background considerations. These are the key steps in the STD procedures relating to learner background issues. Three propositions concern training populations which consist of older, less formally educated employees who tend to have little training experience, but much work experience. The propositions for this group of learners are:

- If the programme's primary objective is knowledge acquisition and retention:
    a. provide increased examples and practice demonstrating the target knowledge (without drill-type exercises);
    b. provide more attention to motivational activites; and
    c. devise creative approaches by which the trainee can demonstrate knowledge, avoiding primary use of objective test item formats.
- If the programme's primary objectives are attitude change or application of generalized skills to workplace behaviour, do not assume these changes will automatically follow knowledge acquisition. Instead, devise special instructional activities especially directed toward these objectives.

- If the programme's primary objective is application of specific skills to workplace behaviour, the same design procedures for producing knowledge outcomes should be adequate given special recognition to the employees' extra work experience and practical knowledge. A concise list of steps used when completing the task on the job may be helpful.

Two additional propositions are directed toward training populations which are younger, more highly educated but possessing less work experience:

- If the programme's primary objectives relate to knowledge retention, attitude change or transfer of *generalized* skills to the workplace, special design procedures are unnecessary.
- If the programme's primary objective is transfer of *specific* skills to the workplace, the instructional design should compensate for the lack of job experience by providing:
  a. more practice of the target skills (simulated or real); and
  b. more discussion of implementation issues.

'Install, evaluate and maintain system' propositions
The key concern in this phase with respect to trainee characteristics involves programme management. These propositions include:

- If instruction is to be delivered with homogeneous groups:
  a. group in terms of the population's most diverse characteristic having the most impact on the primary training outcome; or
  b. group in terms of work experience.
- If instruction is to be delivered with heterogeneous groups:
  a. include the maximum number of instructional events needed to meet the needs of all trainees; and
  b. address the issue of modifying instruction to respond to individual differences in the train-the-trainers programme.

These prescriptive propositions begin the expansion of traditional design practice to accommodate the broader range of factors recognized in STD. They reflect what some may consider common-sense procedures, what others may see as excessive detail. They appear to be unique to training concerns and to both the constraints and the versatility permitted when working with adults as learners. However, these latter points are debatable.

GENERALIZING BACKGROUND CHARACTERISTIC PROPOSITIONS TO OTHER LEARNING CONTEXTS

Throughout the exploration of adult learning in employee training, two questions return to mind: 'is employee training actually a unique form of adult learning?' and 'Is adult learning itself unique?'. The latter question has been answered with an ambivalent 'sometimes'. This less than satisfying answer is probably appropriate for the former question as well.

The potency of the trainee background propositions is determined not only by their utility for training designers, but also by the extent to which these conclusions are likely to apply to other learning situations, for both adults and pre-adults. First, let us briefly examine the role of age and experiential background in other adult learning settings.

The role of background characteristics in other adult learning

The diminished influence of age and ageing on training outcomes appears to be due at least partially to the counterbalancing effects of work experience and experience in other training programmes. When the content of adult learning programmes is new and unrelated to one's previous experiences, one can assume that the older learner will be less likely to succeed without substantial planned intervention. Such a situation seems more apt to occur in programmes which are unrelated to a person's work or avocations. This accounts for attempts which are frequently made to incorporate areas of anticipated learner interest into the instructional activities.

While the importance of work experience is clearly unique to employee training, other content-related life experiences may also serves as a bridge between native intelligence and competence for older adults in other learning environments. For example, travel experiences may help a person in history or certainly geography instruction. Related life experiences appear to have more than motivational value; they may enhance one's abilities to process and make meaningful use of information.

In some respects past experience pertinent to the instructional subject matter may be related to practical intelligence in the same fashion as formal schooling experience is related to fluid intelligence. Both types of experience can develop and strengthen existing capabilities.

However, experience as a participant in other training programmes also seems to serve as a vehicle for enhancing one's intelligence and capabilities as a trainee. Parallel functions may be played by other educational experiences. For example, an older person with previous continuing education experience may demonstrate greater skills as a learner than others without such background.

Age and experiential background also have an indirect effect on adult training outcomes, primarily through their influence on attitudes. Age and experience often have a depressing effect on the attitudes of some. However, experience in training programmes can actually stimulate interest in other programmes, thus serving as a motivator. There is no reason to believe that these relationships would vary for other types of adult education.

It is likely that employee training outcomes are less apt to be affected by other learner background characteristics, in addition to age and education and training experience. A broader range of background variables is usually considered important in most adult education programmes. In these settings, learning outcomes have been associated with factors such as the adult's socio-economic status, family concerns, and other types of life experiences. Training, typically a more directed and less flexible type of learning experience, seems to be influenced by fewer adult background characteristics than does education.

The role of background characteristics in pre-adult learning

The profile characteristics of children and adolescents also play a role in their learning. Age is an important general predictor of achievement for pre-adults because of the strong connection between age and developmental level, especially among young children. Consequently, age becomes a more powerful predictor of many types of achievement for pre-adults than for adult learners. It is more difficult for experience to neutralize the effects of age in this situation, not so much because pre-adults have a smaller experience bank, but because achievement is tempered naturally by the lack of development of the intellect. Piaget's work has been widely influential in this regard.

Multiple intelligences of school-aged young people are also being measured. As with adults, there are multiple ways to measure ability, ways which are dependent upon dealing with different types of symbol systems. However, achievement in formal schooling tends to depend upon linguistic and logical-mathematical symbols rather than the full range of intelligences (Gardner and Hatch, 1989). This differs from adult endeavours which are more comprehensive, tending to rely on a broader range of intelligences.

The use of diverse types of intelligences may produce different roles for background experience in the learning processes of adults and children. For adults, experience can actually develop capabilities which are useful in many learning situations. This supports the importance of work experience in employee training. Since a narrower range of abilities is tapped in most elementary and secondary schooling, experiences may have greater implications for the motivation of children than direct influence on their achievement in school. In other words, experiences may shape interests of pre-adults more than they develop school-relevant abilities.

However, previous educational experiences, both formal and informal, may well serve the same function in pre-adult learning as they do with an older population. Such experience hones learning-to-learn skills, as well as expands the knowledge base. Pre-school education typically increases the potential of a child as a student by developing prerequisites in both subject matter and learning skills. All else being equal, the child with pre-school experience is more likely to succeed in school than the child without a pre-school background. This roughly parallels the influence of both education level and training experience on achievement in an employee training programme for adults.

One difference between the two age groups lies in the greater variation of education and training experiences among adults in a given training programme than there is among pre-adults in a given class. Most formal schooling involves a fairly lock-step sequence of progression which matches the age (and developmental) level of the students. Consequently, educational experience effects tend to be minimized among young people.

Like adults in non-training educational environments, pre-adults appear also to be influenced by background characteristics other than age and educational background. One of the most powerful variables which influences the learning environments of young people is the family's socio-economic status (SES). One of the effects of a higher SES on children is a richer set of background experiences which undoubtedly give added meaning to many formal instructional activities. This is undoubtedly true for adults as well, although an adult's SES is highly correlated with educational level which confounds the issue more so than with children.

Utility of systemic design propositions in non-training environments

Most generic instructional systems design models address learner characteristics, first to determine prerequisite skills and abilities of the learners, and then to identify interests as a key to motivational level. The generic ISD models do not restrict the possibilities of relevant characteristics. Instead, representative variables and their use are cited with the expectation that the designer will apply the general principle in everyday practice.

The STD theory and its matching procedural model are specific to designing instruction for adults in employee training programmes, and only those adult background characteristics linked to trainee achievement have been identified. Could one use any of the prescriptive theory propositions for designing other types of instruction? This question serves as the foundation for the following discussion.

Pre-adult instruction

The variables identified in the STD conceptual model provide one way of addressing individual and organizational differences in an instructional design. However, the very selection of the STD variables emphasized some differences between adults and pre-adults as learners. As such, the theoretical propositions are difficult to apply to children and young adults other than by using the most general interpretation, but this approach is the orientation of most systematic design models.

Kaufman and Thiagarajan's (1987) description of the learner analysis phase of design is representative of the generic ISD approach. They identify five learner characteristics which should be addressed. These are existing relevant knowledge, attitude toward instructional content, language prerequisite skills, learning-to-learn skills and instructional preferences. All represent entering skills and attitudes of the learner, with the emphasis on knowledge and skills which directly influence the selection of teaching/learning objectives and determining the difficulty level of instructional materials.

These general factors are also important to adult learners, including adult trainees. However, by focusing only on adults, not only do additional characteristics become relevant, but other categories of characteristics emerge which more accurately predict instructional outcomes. Thus, generic models seem less precise tools for those designing adult instruction, and the adult model is, in many respects, altogether inappropriate for designing elementary and secondary instruction for children and young people.

Other adult instruction

The question of adaptability to other adult learning environments is more interesting since it poses the challenge of identifying the essential differences between employee training and other adult learning contexts. For purposes of discussion, these learning situations should be separated into two groups: instruction which is occupationally related and that which is not.

Many higher education and continuing education programmes are oriented toward occupational preparation or advancement. For such situations, it is conceivable that those learner background factors identified in the STD model also would be applicable, in addition to those design variables cited by Kaufman and Thiagarajan (1987). Age effects, education and training history and applicable work experience could still logically retain their position as predictors of achievement in occupational education programmes.

For instruction which is not occupational in nature, the role of these background characteristics may be questionable. Those factors which speak directly to work experience are obviously unsuitable. However, it may be possible to identify background descriptions which parallel the function of work experience and training experience in these situations.

Examples which directly parallel employee training are adult education courses in gardening or car-repair. Here avocational experiences in these activities could serve the same function as work experience in employee training. Likewise, other formal learning experiences or personal study experiences could substitute for previous training experience in the proposed model. For situations like these which are closely related to employee training, the analogies could extend beyond knowledge outcomes, pertaining to attitude and behaviour outcomes as well.

With respect to designing instruction for adult general education endeavours (such as a history class), the principles proposed by the sub-model for knowledge acquisition and retention are more likely to be applicable. Here, the critical experience variable for adults is the extent of one's educational background. If the learner had previous experience as a history student, this background would presumably have a role in shaping entering attitudes toward the history instruction. The previous history experience parallels training experience in the model and could thereby affect ultimate retention of the history content.

Conclusions

Can the propositions be generalized? This question can be answered in several ways. First, analysis of learner characteristics in generic ISD models yields conclusions which are generally relevant to all instruction, but typically the interpretation is most appropriate for pre-adult schooling when the emphasis is put on ability level and interests. The background factors in the typical ISD model are also appropriate for adult learning, including employee training, especially those dealing with content-specific prerequisite skills. However, the specific learner background characteristics identified in this research, and the subsequent theory, are most germane to adult learning.

The training design propositions seem directly applicable to adult occupationally-related instruction, especially those relating to trainee background characteristics. For other adult instruction which is performance oriented, the principles also appear to be easily transferred to design practice. Finally, for adult general education, the propositions related to knowledge outcomes can be applied. Therefore, one can reasonably expect that this model would be useful to a skilled designer working with a variety of adult learning settings; pre-adult instructional design may benefit more from use of the generic models with respect to learner background characteristics.

SUMMARY

This chapter has examined those portions of the STD conceptual model and the corresponding STD theory and procedural model which pertain to trainee background characteristics. The critical variables which play a role in determining training outcomes are age, education and training experience and work experience. While they are all important, the weight and the direction of the influence of each varies depending upon the nature of the outcome.

The expansion of the STD conceptual model of design factors

Figure 3.2 provides a very general summary of all relationships empirically identified between significant trainee background factors and two key outcomes of training programmes – increased knowledge and specific behaviour improvement. These outcomes are grouped together because of their similar patterns of pertinent

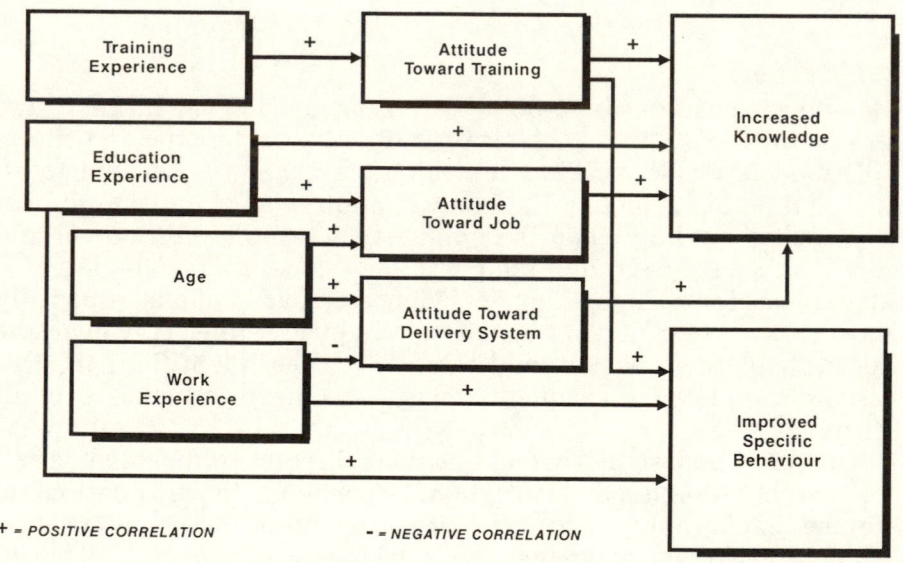

Figure 3.2 *A summary of key background characteristics influencing training outcomes: increased knowledge and improved specific behaviour*

Note:
Both Figure 3.2 and Figure 3.3 reflect the actual relationships among variables. Changes in some correlation signs have been made here to clarify meaning in the data in situations of 'double negatives'.

systemic design factors. The background variables shown here assume both direct and indirect control of the outcomes, with the indirect effects exerted through learner attitudes.

Figure 3.2 shows the specific nature of the relationships between variables (see note below figure), expanding on the STD sub-models presented in Chapter 2. It serves as a synopsis of the detailed explanations of age and experiential background effects presented in this chapter. The connections between many background characteristics and trainee attitudes which have been alluded to in this chapter are also summarized in Figure 3.2.

The dominant role of one's educational level and work experience as predictors of knowledge and specific transfer of training is apparent in this chart. Age and training experience have only subordinate roles in the STD scheme of relationships. It is also clear that background characteristics interact with other dimensions of the total system, making their influence most often less obvious to the casual observer.

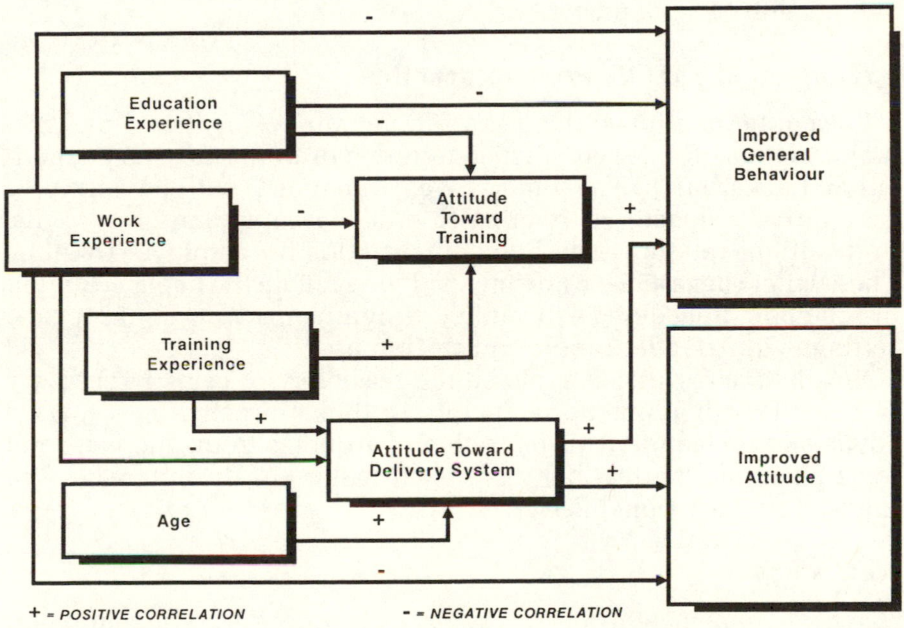

Figure 3.3 *A summary of key background characteristics influencing training outcomes: improved attitude and improved general behaviour*

The two outcomes highlighted in this diagram – knowledge and specific behaviour transfer – typically have the highest priority in an organization, usually receiving the most instructional emphasis. It is interesting that with respect to these critical, but disparate, training goals, there are many similarities in the adult learning process.

The remaining two training outcomes – improvement in attitudes and general on-the-job behaviour – also are clustered together, not only because of their functional interdependence but because of the similar patterns of relationships between these outcomes and the background variables. The summary of these relationships is found in Figure 3.3.

Work experience is again an important predictor of outcomes. It is even more influential with these two outcome measures than with those depicted in Figure 3.2. However, even though the influence of work experience overshadows age, education and training experience, its impact is always shown through a negative correlation. The influence of more work experience, whether direct or indirect, always assumes the role of a barrier to the desired goal.

Again, as with the other two outcomes, the role of trainee age and prior training experience are of a secondary nature. Moreover, the trainee's education level not only has no positive impact, like work experience it actually appears to be a barrier to changing attitudes and general behaviour.

Expansion of STD theory and practice

This chapter continued the task of developing STD theory and recommendations for design practice in terms of trainee age and experiential background. The theory was expanded both in terms of descriptive propositions relating to adult learning and prescriptive propositions relating to designing instruction for employee training. These latter suggestions were intended to facilitate the implementation of systemic procedures by training design teams working in typical settings with standard tools and resources.

Finally, the discussion explored the feasibility of using STD theory in other learning situations, including those directed both toward adults and pre-adults. This reasoning contributes to the more general issue regarding the feasibility of constructing a truly comprehensive theory of instructional design.

Next steps

The next component of the STD approach concerns learner attitudes, specifically attitudes toward past training experiences, and training delivery systems. These elements will be examined in Chapter 4. Attitudes, unlike the trainee background characteristics just examined, are more elusive and sometimes more difficult to identify and measure. However, their impact has already been felt.

Again, research results provide the direction for expansion of the STD conceptual model and sub-models. These models, in turn, will be used to expand both the systemic theory and the design practice model.

4 Attitudes toward Training and Training Delivery

In the previous discussion of trainee background characteristics, age, education and training experience and work experience were frequently shown as interacting with various learner attitudes. Aspects of the adult learning process seem to work, not in isolation, but often as part of an interactive and interdependent system. Hence, the emphasis here on systemic instructional design theory and practice seems to more accurately reflect reality.

This chapter continues delineating the STD conceptual model with an examination of those trainee attitudes which are critical to adult learning in an employee training context. These factors are highlighted in Figure 4.1 which shows the position of trainee attitudes in the total model.

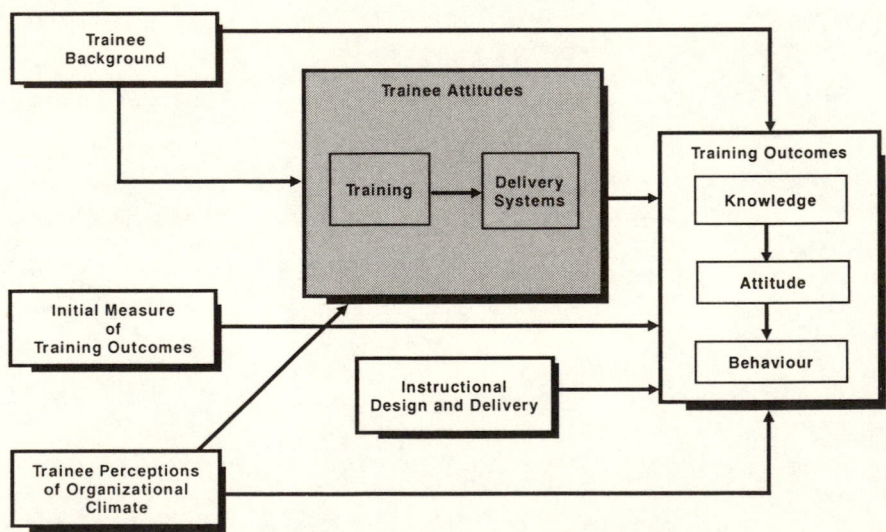

Figure 4.1 *A systemic model of factors predicting employee training outcomes: trainee attitudes emphasis*

There are two major clusters of attitudes which are portrayed in the STD model as predictors of training achievement. The critical attitudes are directed toward:

- previous training programmes; and
- the training delivery system.

Attitudes toward training and toward the delivery system are consistently coupled in a causal relationship, and they are the most important attitudinal predictors of training outcomes. To a lesser extent the data also point to the employees' attitudes toward the training content and their level of job satisfaction as partially influencing training outcomes, but these conclusions are more tenuous and are not presented in the detailed sub-model.

ADULT ATTITUDES AND EMPLOYEE TRAINING

The role of attitudes in training design

Triandis (1971) defines an attitude as 'an idea charged with emotion which predisposes a class of actions to a particular class of social situations' (p2). As such, he notes that attitudes encompass cognitive, affective, and behavioural components. The comprehensive nature of this definition makes it particularly useful in training contexts. Moreover, it is consistent with the STD orientation which also highlights these three types of training outcomes. The Triandis definition is also appropriate because he views attitudes as attributes which are directed toward behaviour – the primary focus of most employee training.

Training designers are concerned, at times, with attitude formation as an end in itself, as well as with the effects of attitudes as inputs to the training environment. These general concerns are manifested in terms of diverse practical training issues such as developing employee motivation, determining 'soft skills' instructional techniques, obtaining management support, and precisely defining and measuring desired attitudes. However, even though most instructional designers have underlying concerns with attitude effects, there is often little incentive to deal directly with them. Many would like to address attitude issues but feel they have insufficient control of the larger situation to be effective in this realm.

The discussion in this chapter focuses on employee attitudes, although it is recognized that attitudes of other groups are also pertinent. Chapter 5 will consider supervisory and management attitudes within the context of organizational climate.

While many attitudes are instrumental in shaping employee behaviours in the workplace, only two are presented here as especially critical to employee training. Personal factors which define a person's general style have not been incorporated into the STD conceptual model. Examples of these characteristics include personality attributes, cultural and religious values, or even one's learning style, a trait more pertinent to many training issues.

It is likely that the target attitudes (those directed toward delivery systems and training) are influenced by these basic aspects of one's personality. There is research which speaks to these relationships. However, amid the 'real world' pressures of training, designers are typically unable to gather extensive trainee data. This is often perceived as conducting basic research. In fact, gathering data directly related to determining training needs of the organization and its employees is often seen as a luxury. Therefore, the STD approach only highlights those attitudes which are closely related to training effectiveness, but this approach accounts for the major portion of the variance in training outcomes.

Attitude formation in work settings

Pre-training employee attitudes form the critical mass of 'emotion-charged ideas' which exert a major influence on subsequent training outcomes. Where do these attitudes originate? Can interventions embedded in a training programme direct employee attitudes into a supportive role? Or are these attitudes resistant to modification?

McGuire (1985) has categorized the origins of human attitudes into two categories: those relating to types of persuasive communications and those emanating from non-communications sources. McGuire's scheme of accounting for attitude formation will be used here to analyse the formation of employee attitudes in the workplace.

Non-communication sources of workplace attitudes

There are four non-communication origins of attitudes: genetic endowment, transient physiological states, direct experience with the attitude object and institutional situations. The first two geneses of attitudes are largely unrelated to workplace attitudes, with the exception of ageing effects which are viewed by some as a physiological phenomenon. However, Murphy and Staples (cited in McGuire, 1985) give evidence for attitude changes over the course of one's life-span as more reflective of social, rather than physiological changes. This research tends to support the notion that work-related attitudes do become more resistant to change with age.

McGuire's third category of non-communication attitude origins, direct experience, is more applicable to work settings. Direct experience includes single significant experiences, exposure effects, and interpersonal contact effects. All can play a significant role in employment attitudes.

There are examples of attitudes stemming from direct experience in the safety training programmes studied here. One example of a single significant experience relates to employees who have had plant accidents. In some cases those with accident histories, or even those with close friends who have experienced a plant accident, were more likely to have positive attitudes toward safety training. Their motivation may have been heightened because of an increased sense of the criticality of the subject matter.

Another example of work-related attitude formation through direct experience is that of the employee who has been previously exposed to training using a given delivery pattern. Being familiar with a delivery system contributes to trainee preferences for learning in that particular manner.

Finally, the social institution can also serve as a source of non-communication attitudes. Some examples of social pressures on attitude formation are reflective of workplace interactions. The most obvious examples are through the roles of peer group norms and ideological schooling, two of McGuire's sub-categories. Work sites can develop an institutional culture based upon peer norms. For example, influence may be exerted by groups of employees formally promoting a common position through collective bargaining. On the other hand, common management positions may be developed through a set of values passed on through collegiate business schools.

Persuasive communications as a source of workplace attitudes. Attitudes and values are also fostered using conscious persuasive techniques. These techniques include tactics such as repetitive expression of an attitude, conformity, group discussion, mass media and intensive indoctrination (McGuire, 1985).

Some of these techniques are used in the workplace to promote institutional values, especially conformity and mass media. One example of the use of conformity is the promulgation of dress codes to convey desired attitudes and values within an organization. In addition, some organizations have purposefully sought to change their image among workers through concentrated media campaigns. These campaigns are sometimes combined with new policy statements, which also have the effect of producing conformity to the preferred organizational value. One current example of this is the conscious move in some corporations toward 'employee empowerment'.

Although there are examples of both persuasive and non-persuasive techniques for forming workplace attitudes, the less intrusive are probably more common. When persuasive techniques are employed, they tend to be more overt than those used in other contexts, such as commercial advertising.

Employee attitudes influence a wide range of workplace behaviours, including training. The more interesting issue concerns the precise attitudes which are relevant and the manner in which these attitudes interact with other factors in the larger instructional system. Since the most critical interaction is with the major training outcomes, one also needs to be aware of the different roles played by trainee attitudes in determining these diverse outcomes.

THE EFFECTS OF INITIAL ATTITUDES TOWARD PREVIOUS TRAINING

An overview of the effects of attitudes toward training on training outcomes

In the previous chapter the importance of one's past experiences was cited. In most situations the employee's previous training experience indirectly affects the outcomes of the present training by shaping one's attitudes toward training (see Figures C.2, C.5, C.6 and C.11). Positive initial attitudes toward training facilitate positive outcomes, and these positive attitudes are encouraged by more extensive training experience. Such relationships can be seen in terms of their contributions to training motivation. Past training contributes to employees' estimations of the potential enjoyment and value they will receive from a prospective training programme.

The role of adult and pre-adult attitudes toward previous learning. The fact that general training attitudes influence performance in current programmes is congruent with much of the adult education literature. This literature commonly cites the important role of adult attitudes toward previous schooling as a predictor of current success in educational endeavours. A typical explanation is Cross's (1981) chain-of-response model which cites not only the learner's attitudes toward education, but also his or her self-confidence, as two factors which predict adult achievement in educational settings. It is logical to see academic self-confidence among adult learners as being dependent upon the success or failure of one's past educational experiences.

The findings concerning adult attitudes toward past education are consistent with Bloom's (1976) classic examination of children's learning in school settings. He concludes that as much as 25 per cent of the variation in school achievement is accounted for by the young person's attitudes toward school. Moreover, he sees the relationship between attitudes and achievement as becoming stronger with age as the learners gain more school experience. It is likely that the influence of these attitudes parallels the role of adult attitudes toward employee training as a predictor of achievement in work-related instructional settings.

The role of attitudes toward training in STD
Employee attitudes toward those training programmes in which they have previously participated were measured in these studies in terms of the degree to which these programmes were enjoyed, were found useful and the degree to which they lead one to volunteer for similar experiences. These measures exemplify Wlodkowski's (1985) notions of enjoyment, value and volition. Consequently, all three factors can be viewed as elements of trainee motivation, elements that can be seen in terms of a continuum based upon the amount of involvement and effort required. One can enjoy training without exerting great effort, even as one would enjoy watching television. Finding training content useful involves actually applying the training principles to one's job, or at least anticipating such an action. This connotes a less passive attitude. Finally, volunteering for future training indicates the most involvement and commitment of the three measures. This graduated scale of involvement and commitment can be used to interpret the precise effects of training attitudes on the learning process.

Training attitudes, in general, have only minimal direct influence on current training effectiveness (see Figure C.6). However, in the STD conceptual model training attitudes are often coupled with attitudes toward training delivery systems creating a pattern of variables with considerable impact on adult achievement in training situations (see Figures C.2, C.4, C.5, C.10 and C.11). Even though training attitudes play a role in each of the four types of major training outcomes, their greatest impression appears to be in terms of facilitating the transfer of *general* behaviours to the workplace (see Figures C.10 and C.11). Simple enjoyment of past training programmes is the most influential aspect of training attitudes, but its effects are felt only in an indirect fashion (see Figures C.2, C.4, C.5, C.10 and C.11). The employees' impressions of the utility of training is also an important factor in successful instruction (see Figures C.2, C.6, C.10 and C.11).

Attitudes toward training are predicted most often by the employees' experiential background and by their perceptions of the climate of the organization in which they work (see Figures C.2, C.4, C.5, C.10 and C.11 for organizational climate involvement). As previously noted, the most important background factors are one's training experience and, to a much lesser extent, one's work experience (see Figure C.10). As such, training attitudes serve as a link between two clusters of systemic design factors – the learners' backgrounds and the nature of the organizational climate – and ultimate achievement in a training programme.

The direct effects of training attitudes on programme outcomes

In summary, the direct influence of employee attitudes toward previous training is from two sources: indications of perceived value and one's willingness to volunteer for training (the volition aspect of motivation). These two factors influence transfer of training to on-the-job behaviour (see Figures C.6 and C.10), but have no *direct* impact on either knowledge retention or on attitude change after training. Once again these conclusions can be interpreted by viewing employee attitudes toward training as expressions of training motivation.

Steers and Porter (1975) identify three components of motivation: forces which energize, direct and maintain behaviour. In effect, these are the functions of motivation. Moreover, Steers and Porter see this conceptualization as a systems orientation, one which emphasizes the interactions between individuals and their environments. This viewpoint is especially compatible with instructional design traditions.

Noe (1986) applied the Steers and Porter motivation framework to training by saying:

> motivation is the force that influences enthusiasm about the program (energizer); a stimulus that directs participants to learn and attempt to master the content of the program (director); and a force that influences the use of newly acquired knowledge and skills even in the presence of criticism and lack of reinforcement for use of the training content (maintenance) (p737).

Noe's interpretation of the Steers and Porter framework can be applied to the STD model. The measures of training attitude which require the most involvement and effort by the trainee (value and volition) relate to the maintenance component of motivation. In other words, those facets of employee training attitudes which directly influence transfer of training demand involvement and effort. This chain of relationships partially explains the effects of motivated behaviour in training programmes. Figure 4.2 graphically describes this phenomenon.

It should be noted here that Wlodkowski's initial model also presented motivation as a function of success, as well as enjoyment, value and volition. This is consistent with the adult learning literature. One's past success or failure in learning situations influences one's enthusiasm for formal learning experiences as an adult. One can assume that the degree of success or failure experienced in past training is highly correlated to the employee's enjoyment of these programmes and desire to volunteer for more. Moreover, it may even be possible to assume that past success influences the value one subsequently assigns to such training. Therefore, the impor-

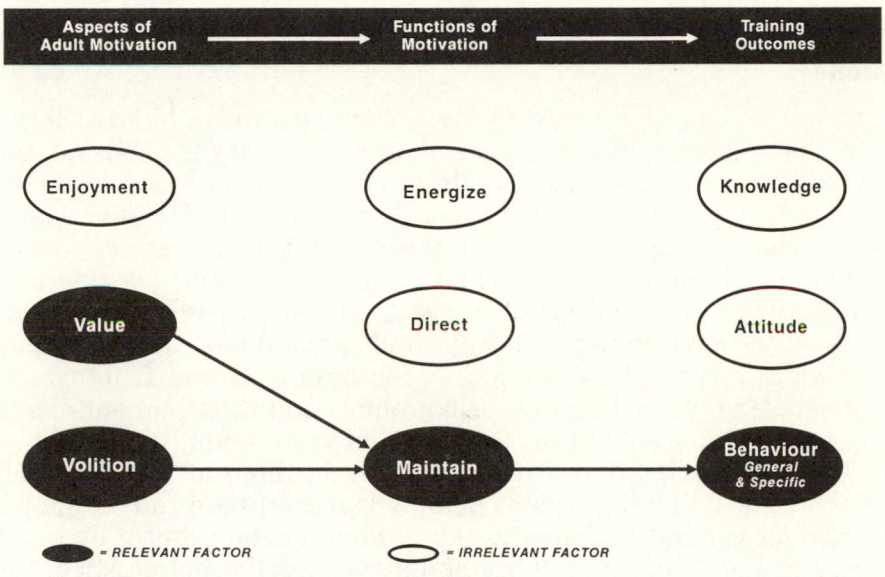

Figure 4.2 *The motivational role of attitudes toward training*

tance of training success is recognized and implied in the other three aspects of adult motivation portrayed in Figure 4.2.

Attitudes impact on-the-job behaviour even when the attitude is related to training processes, rather than directly related to the job. This phenomenon emphasizes the importance of a range of training practices, such as training design, methodology and delivery techniques.

While attitudes do play a role in programme effectiveness, training intensity seems to have a role as well. It appears that in shorter training programmes attitudes toward training which imply the most effort are required to predict transfer of training. In other words, in these short programmes simply enjoying training or thinking it is useful is not enough to actually influence outcomes. However, when the training is longer and more intensive, attitudes which imply less commitment and effort have the same function in terms of promoting workplace behaviour changes as do those attitudes based upon more active involvement. More intensive training can counteract some impact of pre-training attitudes. These specific conclusions are only tentative, but the general notion that training intensity creates varying patterns of factors which affect adult learning seems logical. This is another example of the competition between design and delivery factors and systemic factors as predictors of training outcomes.

The indirect effects of training attitudes on programme outcomes

The role of employee attitude toward training as an *indirect* influence on outcomes of current training programmes is clear-cut and consistently replicated. Those with positive attitudes toward training tend to be positively oriented toward specific training delivery systems. The two attitudes seem to work together and, as previously noted, the chain is often initiated by the presence of considerable training experience in combination with generally positive perceptions of the work environment. Thus, attitude toward past training, functioning as a type of motivation, is the linking factor. It integrates critical elements of trainees' backgrounds and their perceptions of the organization with specific aspects of motivation.

This chain-of-attitude pattern appears in three of the four STD sub-models. It applies to gains in knowledge, attitude and on-the-job behaviour generally related to the training content, but it does not apply to the transfer of those skills specifically addressed in the training programme. Specific skill transfer to the workplace is more profoundly affected by environmental factors which will be examined in Chapter 5.

Employee attitudes toward previous training, thus, are viewed here as factors whose primary function is as a linking or mediating attitude in explaining adult learning in training contexts. It serves as a central part of a set of interrelated attitudes which are promoted by certain experiences. This cluster of systemic design factors (amount of training experience, attitude toward training and attitude toward training delivery systems) can be seen as specific indications of the extent to which an employee values work-related education.

The prevalent pattern of relationships appears to allude to a tendency for individuals to be more positive about those things with which they are most familiar. In addition, these relationships also may reflect a trend in which those with more extensive training backgrounds are not only more positive, but also may be more attentive to instruction. This combination of positive attitudes and attentiveness facilitates comprehension and ultimately the extent to which the training promotes knowledge acquisitions and subsequently influences attitudes and behaviour. This explanation is suggested by the role intelligence plays as a mediating variable in persuasion processes (McGuire, 1985). A person's susceptibility to persuasion is enhanced rather than inhibited by a higher level of intelligence.

This is accounted for by the tendency of brighter people to be more attentive, to comprehend more and to remember a message for a longer period of time. In other words, the more intelligent person exerts more effort to learn, and this effort produces positive results.

Keller (1979) explains effort in instructional situations as a function of the learner's values and expectations and the programme's motivation design. This paradigm can be applied to training contexts in the following manner. To Keller, values are demonstrated by selecting one goal over another. Even though most trainees do not have the choice to volunteer for or to decline a training opportunity, they are always in control of internally choosing to listen and heed the instruction, or not. This decision reflects the extent to which employees value training. These values appear to be the consequence of recent training experiences and employee perceptions of the organization. The nature of one's training values can influence, to a great extent, the amount of effort one exerts during an instructional programme.

Furthermore, Keller (1979) describes 'expectancy' in a learning situation as the anticipation of success or failure, but expectancy can also encompass the perceived utility of the information to be obtained from a training programme. It has been previously argued that this factor can also reflect to some extent one's anticipated success in a programme. This research, however, shows that training attitudes and values incorporate not only general training impressions, but specific attitudes toward the manner in which training is delivered. This link in the attitude chain will be discussed next.

THE EFFECTS OF INITIAL ATTITUDES TOWARD TRAINING DELIVERY SYSTEMS

Delivery systems and employee training

Delivery systems and instructional design
Ellington and Harris (1986) define delivery system as 'a combination of medium and method of usage that is employed to present instructional information to a learner' (p47). The term does not connote the use of any particular technology. It may simply refer to large group instruction, or it may refer to a complex computer and two-way interactive video distance-learning methodology,.

When designing instruction, selection of the general delivery system not only precedes media selection, but the instructional strategy chosen has substantial influence on determining the optimal media for a given situation. These two interrelated selection processes typically are dependent upon the objectives to be taught, the domain of learning to which each objective belongs, the instructional setting and learner ability data (Reiser and Gagne, 1983; Romiszowski, 1988).

The STD models indicate that for employee training one should also consider trainee attitudes toward delivery systems as well as learner abilities. In essence, this means placing an emphasis on learner characteristics in delivery system and media selection equal to the emphases currently placed on content demands, media attributes and practical considerations. In training design, this strategy means one must also be cognizant of the characteristics of adults as learners.

The adult learner and instructional delivery methodology

A traditional part of the 'adult education philosophy' has been an emphasis on self-directed learning. Brookfield (1986) notes that 'the development of self-directed learning capacities is perhaps the most frequently articulated aim of educators and trainers of adults' (p40). He continues to explain that 'this self-directedness is usually defined in terms of externally observable learning activities' (p40). Knowles (1980) takes an even stronger position when he claims that the essence of adulthood is to move toward being self-directed.

Typically, this orientation towards self-directed learning is achieved through either 'group-directed' or 'individual-directed' delivery techniques. Examples of group-directed methodology include the use of small group discussions, role playing and simulations; individual-directed approaches would include computer-assisted instruction or programmed instruction. These are contrasted to 'instructor-directed' methods, lectures being the most common example.

These observations are interesting in light of the common approaches to instructional delivery in corporate training. *Training* magazine's 1990 industry-wide survey showed that videotapes (used by 88.7 per cent of responding companies) and lectures (used by 84.1 per cent) were by far the most common vehicle for delivering instruction in the corporate training milieu. These are instructor-directed delivery systems. Group-directed methodologies were commonly used, but to a lesser extent: 54.4 per cent used role playing; 46.4 per cent used games and simulations in their training. In addition to these group-oriented delivery systems, a smaller percentage used individualized techniques: 38 per cent of the organizations with more than 100 employees engaged in computer-based training; 25.9 per cent used non-computerized self-study programmes; 15 per cent used interactive video for training ('Industry Report', 1990).

These figures reflect typical instructional delivery patterns which are totally oriented to one approach. For example, there was either all instructor-directed training, or all individualized. Hiemstra and Sisco (1990) also point to the value of blending delivery patterns.

There can be an 'operational mix for the instructor, trainer, or leader between an expert (instructor-directed) role and a facilitator (learner-directed) role' (p13). Moreover, they describe possibilities for individualized instruction only in terms of certain components of the instructional process, such as needs identification, pacing or evaluation.

Whether adult learners actually prefer those methodologies which rely on self-direction either wholly or in part has not been empirically proven; nor is there confirmation of the assumption that self-direction is beneficial to the learning process (Caffarella and O'Donnell, 1987). This research seems to suggest that self-direction in itself is not always beneficial to learners. Its value depends at least partially on the person's attitudes toward the particular delivery technique.

The effects of attitudes toward delivery systems in the model of STD concepts

Overview

Even though the most common training delivery systems are group-oriented, many companies, especially the larger corporations, are turning toward individually-oriented strategies, especially computer-based instruction. In this research trainees were asked to rate the extent to which they enjoyed four different delivery strategies: instructor with videotape, lecture/discussion, individualized instruction by computer and self-instructional workbooks. Consequently, it is possible to use this information about trainees' delivery system attitudes in a further interpretation of Wlodkowski's (1985) structure of motivation; adult preferences for certain approaches to training can be viewed as elements of enjoyment.

According to the STD conceptual model, trainees' perceptions of the delivery system seem to affect more than whether they are simply pleased with the training experience; they contribute to the overall effects of the training programmes. In general, if adults enjoy learning in the manner in which their training is primarily delivered or enjoy a similar strategy, they tend not only to learn more (see Figures C.1 and C.2), but are more likely to make a general transfer of the training content to their jobs (see Figure C.10) and to modify their workplace attitudes as well (see Figures C.4 and C.5). However, perceptions of delivery systems appear to have no effect on transferring specific skills and knowledge to the workplace.

The direct effects of delivery system preferences on training outcomes

Employee preferences for the manner in which training programmes are delivered seem to exert direct influence on the outcomes of the instruction. The exact nature of the influence, while not always consistent, can be summarized in the same fashion as training attitude effects were portrayed in Figure 4.2. This chart relates Wlodkowski's aspects of motivation and Steers and Porter's functions of motivation to training outcomes. While attitudes toward training highlighted value and volition as precursors of behaviour maintenance, delivery system preferences affect other components of motivation. These are shown in Figure 4.3. Here, enjoyment (of delivery techniques) is shown as promoting the energizing, directing and maintaining effects of motivation. Thus, delivery system attitudes acting as motivators have a comprehensive impact on the ultimate outcomes of a training experience.

Figure 4.3 speaks to the ability of a delivery system to generate or inhibit enthusiasm as well as to guide learners through a sequence of instructional activities. Both functions can affect the degree of trainee effort expended and, in turn, the amount learned. Moreover, the delivery system attitudes also seem to serve the maintenance functions since they impact on-the-job transfer of training.

Clark and Salomon (1986) note the effects of the current emphasis on a cognitive learning paradigm with respect to media research and theory. The STD model is consistent with this trend by recognizing that learners react to instructional stimuli in light of their own interests and expectations. Furthermore, it is likely that this phenomenon is

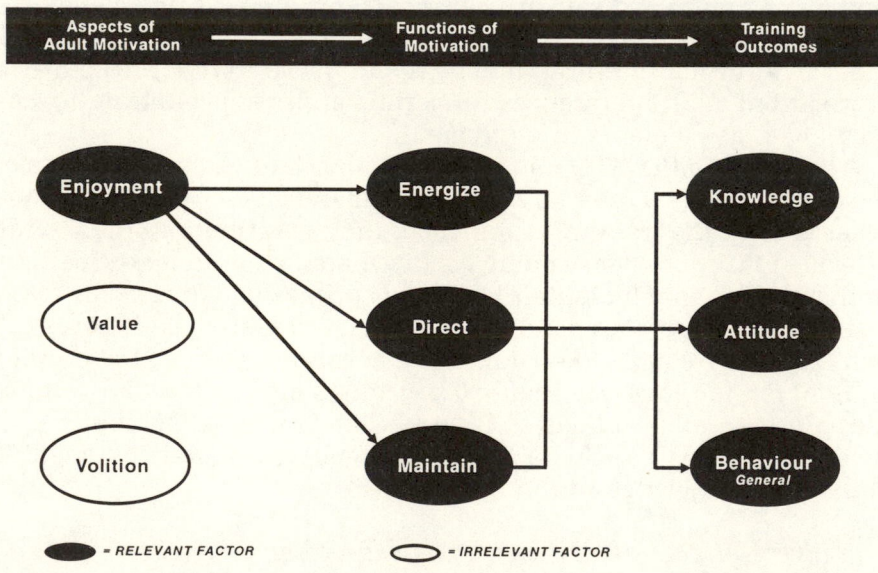

Figure 4.3 *The motivational role of attitudes toward delivery systems*

more pronounced with adult learners since their attitudes are typically more firmly established.

Trainee delivery system preferences
The delivery system incorporated into each of the three training programmes studied involved use of an instructor-led group with heavy reliance on professionally prepared videotapes. The trainees had, for the most part, previous experience with this training format. This training strategy is not atypical of much employee training as noted in the 1990 *Training* magazine survey of the industry.

The participants in the target research overwhelmingly endorsed the group-based and instructor-directed delivery methodology. These preferences are clear in Figure 4.4. Moreover, the preference for either instructors with videotape or the traditional lecture and discussion was common not only to the trainees as a whole, but also to sub-groups based upon age, education level, or job type (Richey, 1991).

The strong preferences for group-oriented instruction over more individualized instruction can be interpreted in several ways. First, they reflect the appeal of the social aspects of many learning situations. Most individualized delivery strategies not only provide for self-pacing and variations in the amount of instruction, but also call for learners to work alone. While such tactics permit adaptation of

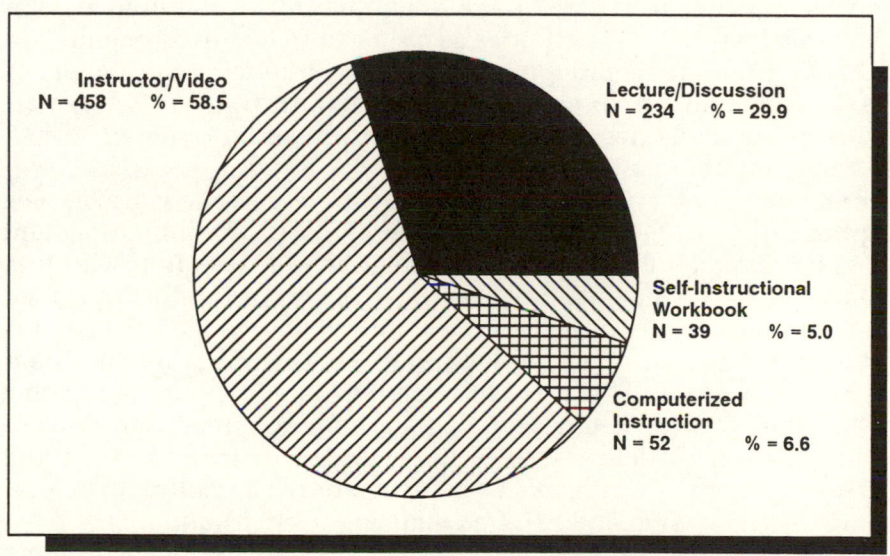

Figure 4.4 *Most preferred training delivery systems* (N = 783)

the instruction to the abilities and background of the individual, they also impose social isolation.

Such isolation establishes educational barriers for many adults if one acknowledges the conclusions of those who have studied the reasons adults voluntarily participate in formal learning. An important contribution to this area has been made by Boshier (1989) who, after extensive international research, still supports Houle's theoretical typology for explaining adult motivation to participate in learning activities. This framework includes a need for social contact as one of the six primary factors which explain participation. Essentially, Houle and Boshier assert that a key reason people choose to participate in adult education is because of their need for group activities and friendships.

This rationale is consistent with the overwhelming preferences of trainees for group instruction over individualized formats. They welcome the opportunity to meet with their colleagues in class settings where typically more interaction is possible than is frequently practical on the job. In addition, individualized instruction usually relegates all reinforcement and initial modelling of desired behaviour to the instructional materials. There is no opportunity for feedback and reinforcement from peers until the group returns to the work site. This reinforcement, then, is not controlled by the instructional leaders, but rather it is left to the chance responses of co-workers, which may be either positive or negative.

Another explanation of trainee preferences for group instruction may be preconceptions that greater mental effort is required to complete self-instructional activities as opposed to the effort required to learn via traditional classroom instruction. Preferring the avenue of least effort is not an unreasonable approach for trainees whose participation is mandated, or for adults who have not been in formal learning environments for some time.

Cennamo *et al.* (1991) conclude that for college-age learners perceptions of increased difficulty with a given instructional medium were correlated with lower achievement after instruction with that medium. These students, however, saw the more tightly controlled instructional media (individualized interactive videodisc, in this case) to be easier than media with more of an entertainment orientation (television). These results can be compared to Salomon's (1983) studies with younger students which conclude that perceptions of lesser difficulty lead to lower levels of mental effort and correspondingly lower levels of achievement. The Salomon studies compared television and print as vehicles of instruction.

Even though there are some differences, adult trainees are more like the older subjects of Cennamo *et al.* The industrial trainees in this research performed better with respect to most types of learning when confronted with delivery systems which they enjoyed and presumably thought to be less strenuous. However, if trainees were given the same choice as the college student subjects, one would expect their preferences would not be for a computer-based medium since their experiences with this delivery system are far less extensive than the experiences of current college students.

An alternative explanation for delivery system preferences is one's recognition of one's own cognitive style. One might expect current full-time college students to be more aware of their best learning medium than are adults who have not been in formal schooling situations for some time. However, even though active students may be more knowledgeable with respect to their own learning skills, one can not be certain that older adults would be any less sure of their opinions regarding themselves as learners. This is often the nature of attitudes of older persons. Therefore, the corresponding effects of delivery system preferences may be similar for both older and younger adults because of attitudes with similar intensity.

Adult attitudes toward technology in training delivery

Overview
Special emphasis is warranted in relation to adult attitudes toward the new technologies used in employee training. Many training programmes, especially in the larger organizations, are turning to the use of more advanced delivery systems, typically those which are computer-based. Interactive video instruction, expert systems and computer-based simulations are representative of these new technologies. The advantages of these new delivery systems are numerous. There is usually management support for their use, primarily due to the cost of training an individual. In a large organization these costs are typically reduced, largely because there is no need to pay for trainee travel. In addition, flexible scheduling of work sessions permits training with minimum disruption to work.

The organizational advantages often coincide with a firm theoretical basis for selecting technology-based delivery systems. For example, instruction can be adapted to the abilities of each trainee, providing variable amounts of explanation, practice and feedback. Pacing can be individually determined. Interest can be heightened through the use of advanced visual designs.

However, there can be problems when using technology-based training delivery. Even though the instruction may be effective in terms of both cost and learning outcomes, many trainees and training facilitators alike have had little experience with the new media, or even with individually directed training. Given the important role of delivery system preferences in determining training outcomes, such inexperience and the poor attitudes which often accompany novel approaches to training can prove detrimental in spite of the advantages the new technologies offer.

Trainee attitudes toward computers

As training prorammes begin to look to computers as a delivery medium, the issue of 'computerphobia' emerges. Does this term reflect real concerns or simply the natural uneasiness of beginners?

The trainees in this research were not particularly fond of computer-based instruction. While it was not as odious as self-instructional print material, 25 per cent of the sample found working with computers as their *least* preferred methodology, as shown in Figure 4.5. Moreover, Figure 4.4 showed that only 7 per cent of the trainees cited computerized instruction as the delivery system they preferred over all other techniques.

Predictors of computer anxiety

Neither the source of negative computer attitudes nor the extent to which these attitudes toward learning by computer leads to a generalized sense of computer anxiety has been firmly established. Morris (1988–9) found in his study that negative attitudes toward computers were correlated with both age and education level. However, the younger people in his study were also more highly educated, and he concluded that the more significant characteristic was education level rather than age. This research was conducted with a large sample

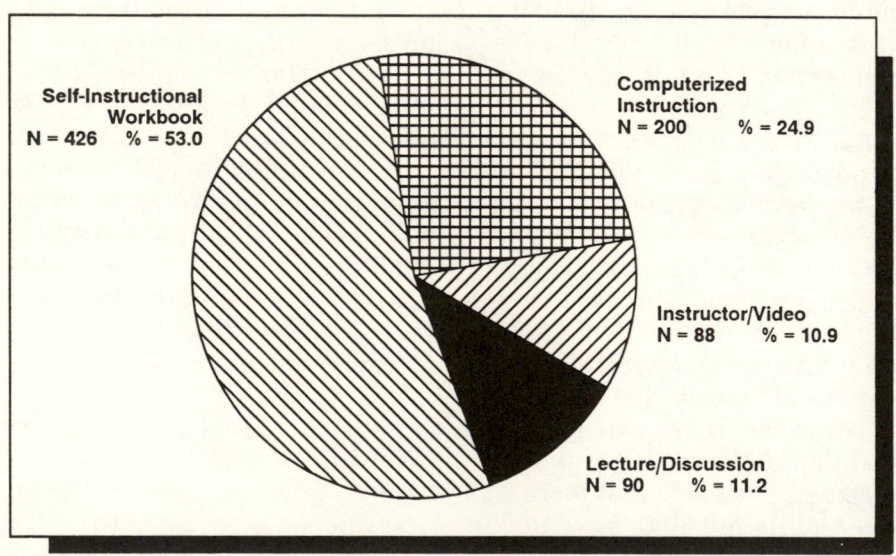

Figure 4.5 *Least preferred training delivery systems*

with ages ranging between 17 and 90. The results are predictable, conforming with popular notions of adults as computer users.

Three other studies of dissimilar adult populations, however, present some variations in the popular notion of adults and computers. These each pertain to the critical role of computer experience as the more important predictor of computer use or computer anxiety. First, there is Loyd and Gressard's (1984) research into the computer use patterns of high school and college-age students. The subjects here were not only younger than the Morris subjects, but they were active students. Here, age was a significant factor in explaining whether one liked computers, but it did not explain whether they felt confident or anxious when using one. The one factor which consistently contributed to each of these computer attitudes was the amount of computer experience possessed by the individual.

The Flynn (1988–9) study concerned a large group of older adults, aged 40–86, who were economically disadvantaged. The sample was approximately 50 per cent minority, 60 per cent female, and 84 per cent unemployed; however, 25 per cent did have a college degree. In summary, Flynn found that 'older people can be satisfied, enthusiastic computer users irrespective of education or other socio-economic variables' (p239). Guided experience facilitated positive computer attitudes even for this older group. The effects of facilitator biases toward older computer users, however, were reported.

There was no evidence in any of these studies that negative computer attitudes were associated with gender or with socio-economic status, nor were age and education level consistently found to be factors in determining computer attitudes.

Computer experience alone, however, may not be the sole factor affecting computer anxieties. Mahmood and Medewitz (1989) have developed a model showing the relationship between adult computer literacy and attitudes and values toward information technology. Their subjects were also college students, but they consisted entirely of business students. The attitudes of these young people changed as they became more computer literate. The changes, however, affected attitudes toward technology applications, but not the basic values themselves. Mahmood and Medewitz conclude that while training in computer usage does aid the attitude change process, the larger issue of computer anxiety is more complex. In the business setting it is also impacted by other ramifications of computer technology, such as human jobs being assumed by computers with subsequent employee layoff. They would suggest that the sources of computer anxiety are multi-faceted and complex in work settings.

The role of trainee attitudes toward computers in the STD model
Trainee attitudes toward learning by computer played an insignificant

role in the STD model of adult learning. This is most likely attributed to the lack of general experience with computers as a learning medium among these workers. There was only one situation in which computer attitudes were relevant to training outcomes (see Figure C.2).

It is difficult to characterize those persons who enjoy learning by computers in the training programmes studied here. While there may be some tendency for the younger trainees to be more inclined toward computerized instruction, even this conclusion is weak at best. In some situations those with less work experience at the company are more likely to enjoy learning with a computer. This is not unusual, implying the younger workers are more inclined toward computer-based learning. However, there were significant groups of older workers with similar positive attitudes toward computers.

Attitudes toward computers can not be attributed to age, nor education level, nor training experience with any real assurance, even though there is limited evidence that these factors may play some role in isolated situations. With respect to computer attitudes, it seems that trainees are similar to other groups of adult learners.

The more interesting conclusion relates to the nature of the attitude toward computers and knowledge retention after training. If trainees have more favourable pre-training reactions toward computers, but this medium was *not* used in their assigned training, positive computer attitudes can actually be detrimental to the learning process. Positive attitudes toward the target delivery system may enhance learning, and positive attitudes toward other delivery patterns may inhibit learning. Computer attitudes are one of the prime examples of this phenomenon.

The relationships between attitudes toward training delivery systems and training content

Given the interactions between general attitudes toward training and the more specific attitudes toward training delivery systems, it is reasonable to explore relationships that delivery attitudes might have with other training-related attitudes. Based upon pre-adult learning research, one attitude which logically could have substantial impact on trainee motivation is the employee's attitude toward the content of the training programme.

Attitude toward training content can be seen in at least two ways. First, attitudes can be measured in terms of observable behaviours which provide evidence of these convictions. For example, in the training programmes studied here, pre-training attitudes toward the content can be defined in terms of the consideration employees give to safety on a daily basis in the workplace.

Why is this issue important? A person's motivation to participate in a training programme on a given topic would be likely to correspond with the degree of criticality assigned to that topic by the employee. In the Wlodkowski motivation framework, one's orientation toward content could reflect expressions of value.

A second way of viewing training content attitudes is in terms of the expectancy of success a person has when approaching a training programme on a given topic. Previous success in academic activities can create a sense of self-confidence for learners. This position has been frequently supported, and Shavelson and Bolus (1982) extended it to subject-specific interpretations. They argue that achievement in a particular area is highly related to one's self-concept in that same area. In addition, they conclude that achievement in a specific area is not correlated with one's self-concept in other subject areas, and it is certainly not correlated with non-academic self-concept.

Trainee attitude toward content, thus, can fit perfectly into Wlodkowski's concept of motivation. It has implications for success, for enjoyment, for value and for volition. As a motivator, attitude toward content would serve to energize and activate the learner.

What role, if any, does this attitude play in employee training? Content attitudes do impact training outcomes, but in a limited fashion. It serves as an indirect influence, partially predicting trainee attitudes toward the delivery system (see Figures C.1 and C.5.) However, this relationship does not influence all types of training outcomes. Its effects are seen only with respect to knowledge acquisition and attitude change and not to transfer of training to the job. Moreover, even the two relationships identified appear to be isolated instances. The impact which has been demonstrated is described in Figure 4.6 in terms of its motivational role.

This diagram summarizes a plausible hypothesis regarding the role of this particular attitude in the training process. Because one's attitude toward the training content has no impact on workplace behaviour, direct or indirect, it appears to play no part in behaviour maintenance. However, when the content is valued, trainees are likely not only to be energized to learn, but also to direct their attention to the instruction. Positive attitudes toward the training's subject matter seem to create a generally positive predisposition as evidenced in the positive attitudes toward the delivery system which seem to match to trainee's content attitudes.

The validity of this hypothesis is unclear. It seems reasonable, and may be particularly pertinent to some training situations.

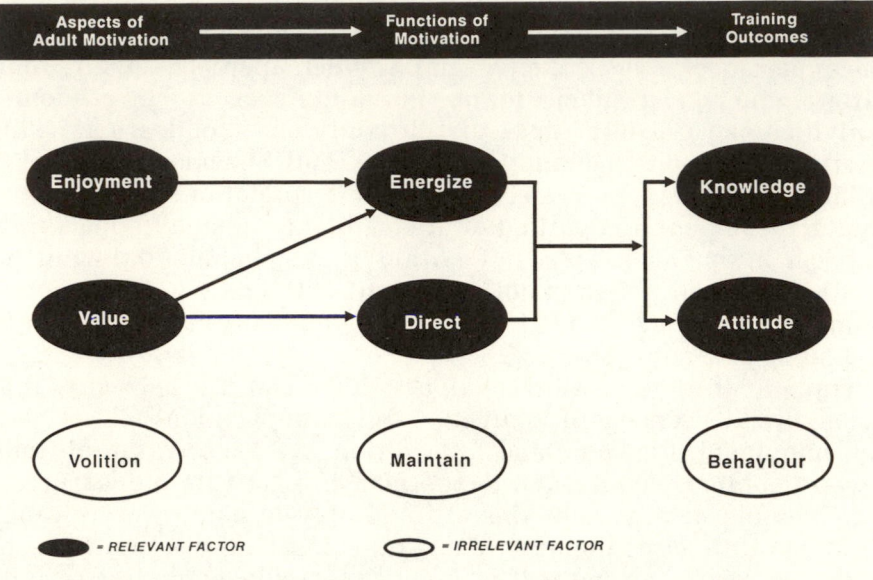

Figure 4.6 *The motivational role of attitudes toward training content*

THE IMPLICATIONS OF JOB SATISFACTION

Job satisfaction and workplace behaviour

It seems natural to believe that a person's job satisfaction has important effects on his or her job performance. This common sense viewpoint is also supported in the research literature. Consequently, this position merits consideration as a facet of training performance within the general context of trainee attitudes. Job satisfaction is distinguished here from perceptions of satisfaction or dissatisfaction with the work environment. These factors are discussed in detail in Chapter 5 within the context of organizational climate.

Typically, job satisfaction is seen as the precursor of performance and effort on the job. As such, it is viewed as an element of motivation. This notion, however, has been disputed on two grounds (Schwab and Cummings, 1975). First, some see both satisfaction and performance as results of other factors such as organizational effectiveness. This conclusion suggests that there is not a causal relationship between satisfaction and performance. Instead, they are both influenced by other variables, variables which may have a more powerful impact on performance in the workplace than job satisfaction.

Second, Schwab and Cummings (1975) cite other researchers who *reverse* the traditional causal relationship between satisfaction and performance, proposing now that performance precedes satisfaction. These positions support a relationship between the two variables but espouse a different explanation of the process. It is now posited that satisfaction is a function of: 1. individual efforts precipitated initially on valued rewards, and 2. one's own performance which is rewarded in a manner which is perceived as both predictable and equitable.

These diverse positions both contradict popular presumptions about workplace behaviour and, furthermore, cast doubt upon the hypothesized relationships between the motivational aspects of job satisfaction and its relationship to increased employee effort.

Job satisfaction and employee training outcomes

Caution in assigning a causal relationship between job satisfaction and workplace performance also appears warranted with respect to performance after participation in a training programme. While this research showed some evidence of this causal pattern, it was not generally replicated, nor are the conclusions particularly consistent with popular notions of organizational behaviour. The limited evidence shows a tendency for those who are *less* satisfied with their jobs to be more likely to retain knowledge (see Figure C.1) and modify training-related attitudes as well (see Figure C.3). There are no effects on transfer of training.

Can this be explained logically or is it a spurious effect evident in the data? Perhaps dissatisfied employees look to training programmes as somewhat of an escape from their jobs, and the attention they give to the instruction results in some improvement. If job satisfaction did play a consistent role in determining training outcomes, one could picture its part in the motivation process similar to that of the trainees' attitudes toward content shown in Figure 4.6. It would tend to energize and direct behaviour in a training programme with the likely results evident in terms of new knowledge or attitude change.

This is not entirely implausible, especially in terms of knowledge retention since those employees who did demonstrate a relationship between diminished job satisfaction and improvement after training also tended to have a higher education level. However, it is intriguing that neither one's work experience nor job type influenced job satisfaction or dissatisfaction. On the whole, job satisfaction is more dependent upon the nature of the work environment than the background of the employee or the nature of the job itself. This latter conclusion is made recognizing that those who were most dissatisfied with their jobs are likely to have already resigned.

In summary, employee job satisfaction seems to be of questionable value as an element of training effectiveness. Moreover, the worth it does have is felt more in terms of cognitive and affective outcomes rather than on-the-job performance. The STD model then, in effect, provides some support for those theorists who have contradicted commonly held views that job satisfaction is an important determinant of workplace performance. The larger lesson seems to be that while pre-training learner attitudes are very important, the more critical motivation factors are those with a direct relationship to the training process itself.

ADULT ATTITUDES AND STD PROCEDURES

The most important instructional role of employee attitudes is in terms of their motivational function. As motivators, they influence the extent to which one attends to the principles being taught during instruction and even after the training has been completed. In the context of STD, motivators are seen as essential to comprehensive employee training achievement.

A comparison of the roles of attitudes in STD procedures and ISD procedures

The varying conceptions of motivation as a prerequisite to learning
In the classic ISD approach to instructional design, Gagne (1991) presents learner attitudes as supportive, but not essential, prerequisites to each of the five types of learning outcomes in his taxonomy. Prerequisite skills in this context are the results of previous learning which *must* be brought to mind and incorporated in the current learning activity to ensure success. They are essentially cognitive in nature. Positive attitudes are supportive because they create an environment more favourable to learning the particular task at hand. For example, if you enjoy gardening, learning horticultural concepts would probably be accomplished more quickly than if you would rather spend your time watching a football game.

On the other hand, the STD model presents pre-training attitudes as foundational elements of adult learning processes, rather than simply aspects of situations which are more conducive to learning. Certain positive attitudes are prerequisite conditions required for learning just as certain intellectual skills are prerequisite to each learning task. Thus, instruction designed using STD principles may encompass learning activities which are intended to facilitate attitude formation as well as skill development.

This approach expands the traditional ISD approach in a manner consistent with Keller's (1987b) ARCS model of motivational design. This model emphasizes attention, relevance, confidence and satisfaction. It incorporates motivation design into instructional design through the phases of: 1. audience analysis, 2. writing motivational objectives and matching test items, 3. designing motivational strategies and integrating them into the instructional design and 4. pilot-testing the final product.

It is one of the most direct approaches to emphasizing motivation within an ISD context; for other ISD models motivation is a less predominant component. However, the goal, even for the ARCS model, is primarily the creation of appealing instruction as a vehicle to obtaining effective instruction. In contrast, the goal of systemic motivation design is to address specific factors in employee motivation which directly affect knowledge retention, attitude change and performance changes on the job. Instructional appeal is a secondary benefit. The goals are ultimately the same for the ARCS and the STD approaches. However, the training data upon which the STD model is built provide additional support for the work of Keller and others who emphasize the motivational aspects of instructional design.

Motivation and attitude as a means to instructional ends
Martin and Briggs (1986), in providing direction for integrating the cognitive and affective domains, clearly distinguish between incorporating affective elements into instruction as a means and as an end of instruction. While the STD approach does address affective ends of instruction by recognizing attitude change as one of the four major types of training outcomes, this discussion focuses upon affective topics as elements of the *means* through which adults can achieve all types of training outcomes – cognitive, affective and psychomotor. There is no attempt here to 'address the whole person' or expand training objectives. The goal is simple: to influence and, hopefully, to ensure adult learning in employee training programmes by building upon existing trainee attitudes.

When one addresses the learners' attitudes as one means of attaining instructional goals, the instructional designer is sometimes restricted by the discipline's behavioural ancestry. Many design conventions are based upon notions of feedback, reinforcement and rewards as external motivators. However, while there is 'hope that extrinsic rewards will eventually result in intrinsic motivation . . . there is little evidence to support this transfer' (Knirk and Gustafson, 1986, p129).

The STD approach, on the other hand, establishes instructional direction and shapes motivation based upon existing internal attributes of the learner, rather than solely depending upon external events to change internal states. This approach seems particularly appropriate for adult learners, especially in short-term employee training pro-grammes, given the tendency for attitudes of the older person to be at times more firmly established and more resistant to change.

Emphasizing attitudes in STD using attitude data in instructional development

Attitude identification and use in the STD approach parallels the manner in which learner background characteristics were utilized. Only those specific attitudes which have been shown to affect training outcomes are addressed; other attitudes which have no empirical support, even though they may be interesting, are not considered in the design process. This is especially appropriate given the more limited occupational nature of training goals.

Learner interests are the most common attitudes addressed in ISD models. The Dick and Carey (1990) model is again representative. However, the Seels and Glasgow (1990) model also includes attitude toward subject matter when analysing potential learners, and Romiszowski (1981) suggests using learning styles when making media decisions. The two critical attitudes here are those directed toward training in general and training delivery systems. These are both dependent to a great extent upon the previous training experi-ences of the target employees.

The use of these attitude variables impinges upon the following training design activities:

- selection of delivery strategies;
- selection of media;
- determining the need for media orientation and guidance; and
- determining the emphasis and nature of the motivation design.

Essentially, attitude factors are used as a basis for decisions relating to the design of delivery strategies and instructional activities.

Use of these factors points to the importance of maintaining records of employees' participation in training programmes and their general reactions to these experiences. Data can be simply collected after each programme; even the quick 'smiling face' formats are appro-priate for this purpose. Such data can be useful to make inferences about training and delivery attitudes rather than collecting new data with each programme design. Therefore, even though prerequisite attitude data initially may seem difficult to acquire, it is among the easiest of the systemic data to collect.

Using attitude toward training data

The employees' attitudes toward past training directly affects general transfer of training and also influences trainees' attitudes toward specific delivery systems. Positive attitudes are greatly affected by the amount of training each person has completed, as well as the quality of these programmes. If the quality has varied among programmes offered by a given organization, a wider range of attitudes can naturally be expected. In these situations further analysis may be warranted in terms of job titles, age or perhaps employee education level.

Obviously, the easiest way to avoid great variation in employee attitudes toward training is to have consistently well designed training. However, homogenous grouping can also make it possible to address those with similar attitudes as well as allow some cost-efficient individualization even in those programmes using large group instructional strategies. The trends in this research continue to point to the wisdom of using work experience as a reasonable basis of grouping.

Using delivery system attitude data

While much of the literature ties delivery system attitudes to learning styles, there also seems to be a close relationship between delivery preferences and familiarity with those teaching techniques. This supports the notion that people are simply more comfortable with what is known and are usually resistant to change. These preferences, however, are important aspects of the learning process; they directly affect cognitive, affective and psychomotor training outcomes. This speaks to the power of established patterns of learning for adults.

Two key delivery decisions for the adult learner relate to individualization of instruction and selection of novel delivery methodologies. Both decisions often carry the advantage of being cost effective, and consequently there is often pressure to accommodate the advantages of both. Individualized instruction facilitates learning when the training must adjust to a wide range of abilities and skills, a common characteristic of many of today's trainee populations; however, it typically creates an isolated environment which can be detrimental to learning.

Designers must also weigh the advantages of changing standard delivery patterns against the inhibiting effects on the learning process of using new methodologies. These decisions are especially critical if the change involves using computers or other newer delivery systems with a technology-naïve population; then one must allow more time for instruction. Much of this additional time should be given to orienting both learners and instructors to the technology and providing opportunities for using the equipment in a practice setting without the concurrent pressures of unfamiliar content. Testing adult learners within the context of the new technology can create even more anxiety, and should not be attempted without practice time given to this task as well.

EXPANDING STD THEORY: ATTITUDES TOWARD TRAINING AND TRAINING DELIVERY

This section continues to expand STD theory to the second level of generality with respect to trainee attitudes. The descriptive propositions focus on adult learning processes. The prescriptive propositions expand the STD procedural model and provide detailed guidelines for instructional designers concerned with employee training.

Descriptions of adult learning in employee training

Propositions related to attitudes toward training
The following statements summarize the findings relative to training attitudes and their role in effective instruction:

- positive general attitudes toward training contribute to trainee motivation;
- those persons with positive attitudes toward training are likely to have participated in more training programmes or more educational programmes than other employees;
- positive attitudes toward previous training experiences directly facilitate transfer of current instruction to the workplace;
- positive attitudes toward previous training experiences do not directly influence knowledge acquisition and retention or changes in work-related attitudes; and
- employees with positive attitudes toward previous training experiences are also more likely to have positive attitudes toward training methodologies even if they had not been used in their previous training.

There is some relationship between these propositions and those generated from the trainee background characteristic data, especially those relating to the education and training background of the employee. Both sets of propositions have implications for the motivational level of the trainee. These explanations of trainee motivation will be further expanded in terms of delivery system attitude. Learner age, however, has no role in explaining training attitudes. Older adults are as likely as younger to be positive (or negative) about employee training.

Propositions related to delivery system attitudes
Employee reactions to the manner in which training is presented

proved to be an important influence on learning. The role of these attitudes is summarized in the following theoretical propositions:

- the more trainees expect to enjoy the manner in which a programme is taught, the greater the improvement in knowledge retention, attitudes and generalized on-the-job behaviour after training;
- delivery system attitudes do not affect transfer of training with respect to workplace behaviours specifically taught in the training programme;
- trainee motivation is a function, in part, of positive attitudes toward training delivery patterns combined with positive general attitudes toward training;
- computer-based instruction and other individualized methods are initially less attractive to trainees of all ages than are group-oriented strategies; and
- trainees of all ages and education levels can enjoy computer-based learning given experience with the medium as an instructional delivery system, although computer use may be more attractive to those who are younger and have more formal education.

It is difficult to make generalizations about the attitudes of particular sub-groups of adult trainees with respect to how they like to learn. The degree of similarity among all trainees is at times remarkable. Older workers often like what the younger ones do. Educational background makes some difference, but it does not explain great deals of variance. Gender is unimportant. What are important, in most situations, are one's feelings about other training programmes one had been a part of and how one has been taught. These attitudes are commonly called motivation.

Prescriptive propositions for instructional design based upon trainee attitudes

The prescriptive propositions relative to trainee attitudes follow the same pattern as the second-level prescriptive propositions concerning trainee background. Using the STD model of procedures as a framework (see Figure 2.7), these propositions provide designers with specific direction for applying theory to training design practice.

'Training needs assessment' propositions
As previously suggested the STD approach relies heavily on more learner data than are usually needed in systematic design approaches. Even so, the goal is to collect minimum amounts of information for efficiency's sake, using one detail for multiple purposes whenever possible. For example, it was previously recommended that data on trainee background characteristics be collected. All of these data

are useful in terms of interpreting trainee attitudes. The background information which is most useful in terms of determining trainee attitudes is the amount and type of training experience each person has had. In addition:

- the training needs assessment should use data previously collected on trainee delivery system preferences and reactions to previous training.

'Determine goals and objectives' propositions

In addition to the content-related goals, process goals may be necessary depending upon the nature of the population.

- Develop goals and objectives directed toward orienting trainees to the delivery system chosen if that strategy is novel to a large part of the target population.

Initial consideration should be given to whether the instruction will be individualized or delivered to groups. There are seldom difficulties with large group delivery strategies because they are so commonly used in both formal education and training. However, some populations may be unfamiliar with small group strategies, such as case study analyses, games or simulations. Individualized instruction may create even more difficulties for some persons depending upon the amount of structure and guidance built into the particular plan.

- Develop goals and objectives directed toward orienting trainees to the instructional media selected for the programme if the target population is inexperienced in learning with that media.

Even if the general delivery strategy is familiar, the media may not be well known. For example, while large group instruction is commonplace, trainees may not have experienced two-way interactive television with the instructor and part of the class a considerable distance away. Others may have worked in an individualized learning situation using printed materials and workbooks but have never been involved with computer-based learning. In each of these situations, orientation to the media may be necessary rather than to the general strategy. Preferences for new delivery systems and new media can be cultivated, rather than only relying on familiar approaches in a training design.

Propositions related to 'Construct assessment and evaluation procedures'

If the typical employee's attitudes toward training and training delivery had not been known and had been estimated during the needs assessment phase, then it is appropriate to collect such data as part of the programme evaluation. The relevant proposition is:

- Using either pre-training or post-training surveys, identify the average reaction toward:
  a. past training programmes attended;
  b. a range of training delivery systems; and
  c. a range of available instructional media.

If these data are general in nature, rather than relating only to the delivery and media of a given training programme, such information can be used for designing other training programmes. If time is available, it may be useful to analyse these attitude data in terms of smaller, more distinctive groups of employees. The groups may vary depending upon the nature of the organization or the training needs. For example, groups may be formed in terms of major job titles, or departments or years of work experience.

Propositions related to 'Design, contract or select delivery systems and products'
The STD model has implications for selecting both media and delivery systems.

- When making media and delivery system decisions, learner attitudes toward the delivery system and the media, in addition to learner abilities, should contribute to the decisions.

This step can sometimes be difficult for designers who deal with adult training populations given the similar attitudes of many adult learners. Sometimes this situation leads to a tendency toward repeated use of the same media and delivery strategies rather than experimenting with the newer technologies and benefiting from their advantages. However, if unfamiliar training methodologies are selected, the following steps should also be incorporated into the design:

- If the trainees are unfamiliar with, or if they do not enjoy learning with the selected training methodology:
  a. provide detailed step-by-step directions in the correct use of the learning media, or the manner in which the learning activity should be conducted;
  b. provide frequent feedback which is process-related as well as content-related;
  c. have process-related feedback available from a training

facilitator, in addition to the programme, when using computer-based instruction;

d. provide opportunities for discussion, even with individualized methodologies; and

e. incorporate a variety of learning activities and media into the total programme, if possible.

- If trainees find the training methodologies unfamiliar or unenjoyable, assume the trainers may also share this attitude and provide special orientation and guidance for these persons as well.

Gaining support from those persons who will be supervising the training is as important as gaining trainee support. These persons must be comfortable with any new equipment so that they can help trainees with mechanical problems, in addition to managing content issues.

- Construct job aids for use by both trainees and trainers to provide assistance in the use of new media or methodology.

'Try out instructional system' propositions
While trainee attitudes can be used as one basis of interpreting summative evaluation data, it seems more critical to use such information, especially attitudes toward delivery systems, as a part of the formative evaluation of instructional materials.

- If try-out data show that the instructional materials are not as effective as expected and yet the design seems appropriate, consider the effects of trainee or trainer attitudes toward the media or delivery strategy as a source of difficulty.

'Install, evaluate and maintain system' propositions
As with other learner characteristics, trainee attitudes also have implications for programme management and systems maintenance. One must be sensitive not only to initial learner attitudes, but also to the implications of changing attitudes during the course of instruction. The key proposition related to these issues follows:

- If instruction is to be delivered in an individualized format:
  a. maintain records of trainee activity to identify difficulties in persistence or pacing;
  b. schedule work sessions so that they conform to both the trainee's learning style, as well as constraints within the organization;

c. provide more frequent formal feedback than would normally be necessary in group instruction; and

d. establish clear programme completion targets.

GENERALIZING TRAINEE ATTITUDE PROPOSITIONS TO OTHER LEARNING CONTEXTS

The STD model has two interrelated emphases: 1. adult learning in training contexts, and 2. instructional design principles. The working assumption is that consistently effective design is impossible without using knowledge of the learning process. The previous chapter initiated a discussion of the extent to which STD learning concepts are applicable to other adult-oriented instructional situations, and correspondingly the extent to which the STD design procedures are realistic in pre-adult teaching and learning settings. These same issues will be examined here with respect to specific learner attitudes.

A comparison of the role of attitudes in training and in other adult learning contexts

Research shows attitudes have an important influence on adult as well as pre-adult learning. Those particular attitudes which contribute to one's motivation as a learner have been emphasized here, and it seems likely that attitudes with similar targets are important for any adult learning situation.

Adult motivation towards learning has been frequently studied in relation to areas such as:

- adult participation in educational programmes;
- facilitating self-directed learning;
- exerting effort and maintaining attention; and
- adult instructional techniques.

Using a pre-adult learning context, Carroll (1963) simply defined motivation in terms of the perseverance with which the individual attacked a learning activity. This is not unrelated to the Steers and Porter (1975) view of the functions of motivation in terms of energizing, directing and maintaining behaviour.

The effort here has been to operationally define motivation in terms of specific attitudes which have been shown to influence learning in a training context. The general conclusions are: 1. positive attitudes toward past training are facilitated by increased training experience, 2. these training attitudes contribute to positive attitudes toward training delivery techniques, and 3. the extent to which one enjoys the manner in which one is taught plays an important role in determining one's achievement. Thus, those attitudes brought to the instructional setting relating directly to training and training processes exert considerable influence on the success of that programme.

Training and training delivery attitudes can be characterized as intrinsic motivators, even though they are reactions to external events rather than internal needs. Keller (1983) identified four components of motivation: interest, relevance, expectancy and outcomes (the satisfaction of goal accomplishment). The explanations suggested here share more in common with two of Keller's notions – relevance and expectancy. Attitudes toward training encompass both of these concepts, while attitudes toward delivery systems coincide only with the concept of expectancy. Yet each of these attitudes interact to influence one's general motivation for learning.

The question remains whether these same conclusions can be generalized to other learning situations which are not influenced by job considerations and the work environment. The educational experiences accumulated by an adult influence each person's expectations and values, and any learning situation can be shaped by one's expectations. The anticipated relevance of the instruction or one's hopes and apprehensions of a given teaching method are all logical parts of these expectations.

In non-training settings, however, personal interests may exert more influence on educational attitudes than they do in work-related training where the content is always pertinent to daily activities. A person's natural interest in a subject or in the manner in which it is taught may command more influence in voluntary learning than in mandatory training. Likewise, Keller's (1983) fourth component of motivation – satisfaction with outcomes – may also be more important in voluntary forms of adult learning. Attaining certain prized goals may be reward in itself and worthy of sustained effort in a learning situation. Many older adults pursue advanced degrees, not because of their vocational value, but simply because they want to complete a college degree.

There may be common motivational elements in all adult learning situations, but it seems premature to conclude that the precise same attitudes are critical and, if so, that they exert the same magnitude of influence in all contexts. Even in employee training situations, different attitudes have varying amounts of influence. For example, training attitudes are most important in predicting knowledge retention and least important in transfer of specific skill knowledge to on-the-job use. It is not known whether this same pattern would exist in an adult education class on completing home repairs or in a patient education class on diabetes control, for example. In these situations other affective considerations might prove more critical. It is conceivable that the relevance of the content to personal needs might overshadow the influence of other attitudes.

The role of attitude characteristics in pre-adult learning

While there is some certainty that attitudes play an important role in pre-adult learning, the nature of that role appears to vary considerably from adult learning contexts. With respect to motivation, relevant attitudes appear to interact with the child's level of academic maturity. Therefore, issues such as academic self-concept and the young person's mastery of learning-to-learn skills interact greatly with general motivation in learning environments. Aspects of interest and curiosity are important for individual lessons, probably more important for pre-adults than for adults with greater attention spans.

Those attitudes influencing adult learning in training contexts appear to be dependent upon one's experience as a learner. It is logical to conclude that these same attitudes (those directed toward instructional delivery methods and past instruction) exert *less* influence on pre-adult learning processes because of the more limited educational backgrounds of children.

This lack of experience as a learner may also explain the different effects of delivery system preferences of adults and pre-adults. The adult's preference makes a great deal of difference in ultimate achievement; however, Clark's research (cited in Clark and Salomon, 1986) has shown negative correlations between achievement and children's enjoyment of particular media. This appears to be one situation in which learning patterns of adults and pre-adults can differ.

If one assumes that delivery attitudes of older learners are not only important but are also relatively stable (as are other adult attitudes), interventions may be necessary to facilitate effective use of unfamiliar delivery strategies and media. New media are usually less problematic for younger learners; consequently, using new technologies seldom poses significant barriers for pre-adults. On the contrary, the novelty of the newer media often stimulates interest and curiosity among many young learners. This often results in the computer expertise, for example, being controlled by the younger members of a family.

The attitudes which may function in a similar fashion for both adults and pre-adults are attitudes toward previous training, or previous educational experiences for the younger learners. The measures of previous enjoyment, estimations of value and desire to volunteer for additional training can be compared to Bloom's (1976) school-related affect and academic self-concept. He has concluded that such factors alone account for up to one quarter of the variance in cognitive achievement of elementary level children.

This position compares favourably to the emphasis Wlodkowski (1985) places on the influence of one's past success as a learner on an adult's current motivation to learn. If one also uses Carroll's

(1963) concept of motivation as instructional perseverance, the importance of attitudes toward past education or training can be seen for both adults and pre-adults.

However, Bloom's (1976) position is that quality instruction partially counteracts the effects of negative attitudes of children, especially if they possess the essential cognitive skills. 'Favorable school conditions can enable most students to learn well and to get satisfaction from their learning' (Bloom, 1976, p106). For adults, at least for those in fairly short training programmes, attitudes seem to affect outcomes regardless of the quality of the instructional design.

The utility of systemic design propositions in non-training environments

Based upon the previous discussion, it seems likely that at least a portion of the descriptive propositions relative to learner attitudes are appropriate for non-training instructional environments. Correspondingly, some prescriptive propositions recommending specific design steps should also be relevant, at least for adults. The parallels with pre-adult learning seem too tenuous to suggest design tactics in addition to those which are commonly recommended in the ISD models. General attention to student interests, academic attitudes and levels of motivation, in addition to the young person's cognitive prerequisite skills is appropriate for the average learner. Special situations, such as those with students who are consistently under-achieving, may demand more emphasis on motivating activities and materials.

Alternative schools often exemplify education which stresses affective characteristics and corresponding design procedures which emphasize affective concerns (Beauchamp, 1990). However, these procedures incorporate general attention to the affective domain. While Swisher *et al.*'s, (1983) review of pertinent research literature does show that programmes which emphasize clear affective goals and strategies show corresponding gains in both student self-esteem and academic achievement, the utility of a similar general emphasis on affective variables has not been shown for the adult learner. Instead, a selective emphasis on particular attitudes is suggested here for adults.

The design procedures particularly pertinent to learner attitudes emphasize:

- collection and use of attitude data;
- delivery system and media selection; and
- delivery system and media orientation and guidance.

One difficulty encountered when designing for the typical adult learning situation is that the actual students are frequently not accessible prior to instruction. Designers then must rely on estimations of expected learner characteristics based upon previous students' profiles. Unsubstantiated predictions can lead to the use of erroneous design tactics. Moreover, there is another danger – designing instruction based upon stereotypes and personal biases. These hazards are less likely in training design because accessibility to trainee populations is usually possible (at least for in-house training designers), even though one may be inhibited by time or organizational constraints.

In spite of possible difficulties obtaining accurate base data, it is likely that the STD attitude propositions can be useful for designing adult-oriented instruction in non-training environments. The minor influence of job satisfaction demonstrates the minimal role of factors which concern the work setting in this facet of adult learning. Minimally, designers should recognize the benefits of learners being familiar with the chosen delivery techniques and compensate for the barriers posed by new delivery processes, especially when using individualized instructional strategies and the newer technologies. In addition, designers might provide more structure and direction for those with less extensive schooling or training backgrounds.

When designers attend to issues such as these, instead of totally concentrating on content presentation and learner abilities, they are addressing critical elements of motivation by taking a more systemic approach to the design task. As a consequence, they are interjecting steps in the learning process which not only will energize and activate learners, but will also provide direction for learning. The ultimate objective is for learners to maintain interest in the topic and adhere to its principles *after* the instruction has ended. These are the functions of motivation as well as the purpose of instruction.

SUMMARY

The expansion of the STD model of concepts

Chapter 4 has continued to explore the STD conceptual model emphasizing the contributions of trainee attitudes to learner achievement and programme effectiveness. The thrust of this discussion has been on the function of attitudes as aspects of motivation in adult learning. The critical variables are attitudes toward past training and toward training delivery systems. Both the employees' degree of job satisfaction and their attitudes toward the content of the training programme have negligible effects on the outcomes of training and are, therefore, not included in this diagram. Figure 4.7, thus, summarizes the role of adult attitudes as predictors of learning in training environments (see note below figure).

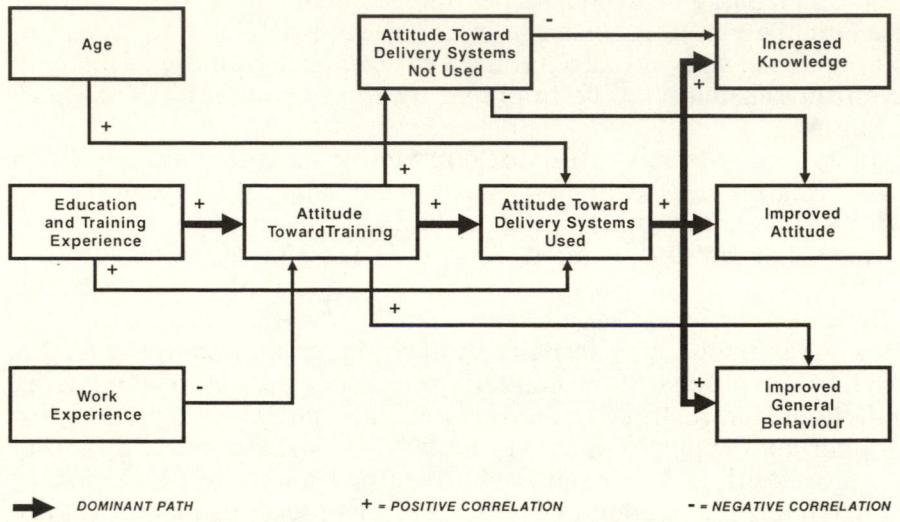

Figure 4.7 *A summary of key attitudes influencing training outcomes*

Note:
This diagram reflects the actual relationships among variables. Changes in some correlation signs have been made here to clarify meaning in the data in situations of 'double negatives'.

While trainee attitudes are emphasized in Figure 4.7, they are also linked with pertinent trainee background characteristics. This demonstrates the truly interactive nature of the STD model. Moreover, this interaction will be further emphasized in the following chapter when trainee perceptions of the organizational climate are also integrated into the model.

Attitudes impact training effectiveness in a more consistent fashion among the various outcomes than was the case with trainee background variables. There were two major patterns for background characteristic effects – one for knowledge retention and specific behaviour improvements, and a second for attitude changes and general behaviour improvements. On the other hand, attitude affects all training outcomes in basically the same manner, with the exception of transfer of specific behaviours to the workplace. Even though there are minor variations within the diagram shown in Figure 4.7, the general pattern shown in the dominant path applies to the three key training goals. This path shows that the amount of one's education and training experience serves as a consistent influence on one's training attitudes which, in turn, influence an employee's attitudes toward the training delivery systems. As a whole, these factors have a major influence on the ultimate impact of a training programme.

The expansion of STD theory and the STD procedural model

The STD conceptual model paved the way for theory construction, including propositions descriptive of the adult learning process as well as prescriptive propositions addressing design practice. Since the attitude component was directly related to training issues and almost totally unrelated to elements of the workplace, the theoretical principles appear generally applicable to designing instruction for other types of adult learning programmes. On the other hand, these propositions are mostly *inappropriate* for designing instruction for pre-adult learners. This is primarily due to the academic immaturity of most children, even though it is beneficial to incorporate motivation design principles into any instructional programme.

The last major cluster of systemic design factors relates to employees' perceptions of the atmosphere in which they work. These effects will be examined in Chapter 5, and this discussion will complete the detailed presentation of the major facets of the STD approach.

5 Perceptions of the Organizational Climate

The STD conceptual model as described to this point has emphasized trainee characteristics – background and attitudes. The STD approach recommends that designers explore more learner attributes than only basic ability and knowledge and skill prerequisites as is usually the case. Designers are encouraged to expand the training needs assessment and to use their knowledge of the pertinent trainee attributes not only to shape the initial design, but also to evaluate and manage the instruction. This systemic approach to design also places equal importance on another major category of variables which impinge on the learning process: the environment in which the training takes place.

The notion of emphasizing the organizational environment is unique to a systemic orientation to instructional design. It expands the boundaries of the instructional system beyond the instructional materials, beyond the learner and beyond the instructor to encompass other elements in the workplace which influence employees' behaviour. The geneses of the prevailing climate in an organization are typically outside traditional training concerns. However, the STD model relates the atmosphere of a particular job setting to the design process and describes its impact on adult learning in the workplace. Figure 5.1 fits employee perceptions of the organizational climate into the STD conceptual model and shows the first level of detail discussed in this chapter.

Organizational climate encompasses a myriad of details pertinent to a given company, as well as a given type of training. This mass of specifics is grouped in three categories:

- factors which describe the general environment of the institution;
- factors which are related in a general manner to the subject matter in the training programme; and
- factors which are specifically related to the training's topic.

These three categories of variables are themselves intertwined: the global environment controls to a certain extent those aspects of the workplace which are generally related to the training, and both sets

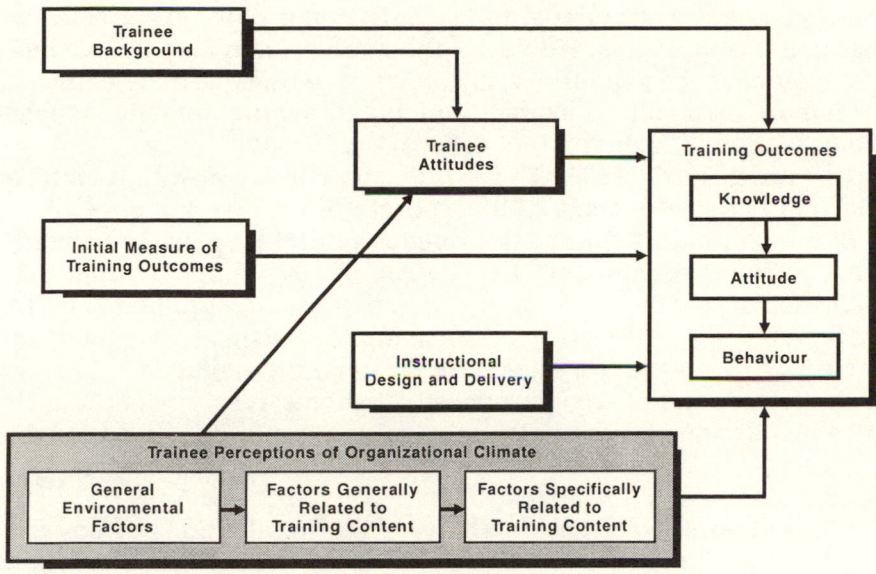

Figure 5.1 *A systemic model of factors predicting employee training outcomes: organizational climate emphasis*

of factors exert great influence on the most specific descriptors of the environment. The most important role of these factors in the learning process is in terms of affecting transfer of knowledge and skills to the job. However, they also influence attitude formation and training motivation.

ORGANIZATIONAL CLIMATE AND EMPLOYEE TRAINING

Environment and learning

Environment and traditional instructional design
Environment, as an instructional design factor, has typically referred to physical facilities and attributes: lighting, class size, room arrangement, equipment. These features are inherently important in media selection decisions and aspects of instructional delivery, although, as Tessmer (1990) points out, an analysis of such characteristics is seldom systematically completed in a design project, and consequently their instructional impact is usually uncontrolled.

Tessmer (1990) defines environment analysis as an effort 'to describe where an instructional product will be used, how it will be used, and how it will be sustained' (p57). The focus is primarily on the immediate instructional environment and more specifically on instructional products. However, the analysis can also be extended to encompass the support environment, in which case the emphasis is on those elements which facilitate the dissemination and management factors related to the use of the product (Tessmer, 1990; Tessmer and Harris, 1990). This is perfectly consistent with traditional ISD and is a useful stage to incorporate in an ISD model.

In the context of needs assessment, Rossett (1987) takes a somewhat different approach to environmental support when she identifies it as the root of some performance problems in the workplace. She stresses the relationships between environment and performance incentives, especially the need for management to consistently practice desired performances themselves. In addition, she cites the effects of other personnel, company policies and available tools on job performance. These are all elements of organizational climate.

While Rossett's discussion analyses the implications of environment on workplace performance, Streibel (1991) directly relates environment to learning. He describes the standard cognitive approach to instructional design which generates instructional activities aimed at controlling the environmental stimuli and interactions. These should produce cognitive changes in the learner and ultimately behavioural responses. The difficulty lies in the fact that instructional plans cannot control many aspects of the 'life-world' which consists of responses to particular, concrete circumstances. Streibel (1991) calls for a shift in standard design practice: 'An instructional system that is sensitive to the situated learning paradigm, has to respect and encourage the very social-linguistic processes by which rationality is constructed' (p131).

This is a complex charge, difficult to translate into usable design procedures. However, the STD approach provides one attempt to respond to this challenge to the extent that it incorporates detailed elements of organizational climate into the design process.

The systemic orientation
The primary concern of the STD approach is always learning; instruction and instructional products are intermediate steps. This approach is more consistent with Streibel's orientation as opposed to that of many instructional designers. This stance encourages alternative ways of conceptualizing 'environment', ways which differ from the approach historically taken by most designers. This broader approach to environment is more in keeping with the orien-

tation in many studies of school environments but it is not antithetical to Rossett's orientation. For example, Anderson (1982) used Tagiuri's taxonomy as a basis of reviewing the school climate literature. These major approaches to the research were in terms of ecology (physical surroundings), milieu (profiles of individuals), social system (interaction characteristics) and culture (norms and beliefs). Within this framework, the STD organizational climate variables stress social system and cultural elements, although the role of one's physical surroundings are also recognized. The pertinent aspects of an organizational climate are *not* elements within the instructional setting; rather, they are descriptors of the larger organization in which the trainees work.

In general, few critical interactions between environmental elements such as these and adult learning have been empirically demonstrated. Cookson (1986) notes that 'external context variables have been largely ignored in the adult education literature' (p133). In spite of this, many believe in the general proposition that 'learning is not just a psychological process that happens in splendid isolation from the world in which the learner lives, but that it is intimately related to that world and affected by it' (Jarvis, 1987, p11). The STD model provides empirical support for this notion within the context of an organization viewed as a place of employment.

Organizational behaviour and training

Given the emphasis here on employee training, understanding the nature of general behaviour within an organization is useful as a guide to understanding training behaviour. Pfeffer (1985) summarizes the alternative theoretical perspectives of action within organizations:

a. Action is seen as purposive, rational or boundedly rational and prospective.
b. Action is seen as externally constrained or situationally determined.
c. Action is seen as being somewhat more random and dependent on an emergent, unfolding process, with rationality being constructed after the fact to make sense of behaviors that have already occurred (pp383–4).

Each of these orientations can be useful as aids in interpreting and understanding trainee behaviour.

Planned organizational behaviour
The first position reflects a view that organizational actions are goal-directed and consciously chosen. Pfeffer (1985) emphasizes the relationship between this position and needs theory of job design

and expectancy theory. Such explanations emphasize the role of management decisions, even though they may be restrained by the nature of the organization.

With respect to training performance, the position which views organizational behaviour as essentially goal-directed is consistent with a systematic approach to training design. The similarities are apparent not only because instruction which is designed according to ISD tenets is directed to specific goals and objectives but also because of the underlying faith placed in step-by-step planning and careful, rational decision-making. The expectation, then, is that if training addresses one's job needs as well as the needs of the larger organization, one would be motivated to participate and to learn.

Constrained organizational behaviour

Bowers calls the second explanation of organizational behaviour 'situationalism' (cited in Pfeffer, 1985). From this theoretical vantage point, external stimuli have the greatest impact on behaviour, with external constraints exerting more influence than conscious decisions. On the surface this seems antagonistic to systematic instructional design principles but somewhat supportive of the systemic approach which is more sensitive to environmental influence.

Of particular interest to training designers is the related line of research which highlights social influence and social information processing. These studies speak to the influence other people within an organization have on one's attitudes and behaviour. Within the training context, this encompasses the influence of behaviour modelling by supervisors and co-workers. These aspects of organizational behaviour are prominent within the STD model of learning-relevant concepts. This view of work behaviour also reflects a traditional behaviourist orientation since the actions of others in the workplace provide or withhold reinforcement for using those principles espoused in a training programme. In addition, this position speaks to the importance of one's established role in an organization as a factor in determining transfer of training. The more firmly entrenched the trainee is in the company and its philosophy, the more likely it is that his or her workplace behaviour will be affected by training.

Reactive organizational behaviour

The third explanation of organizational behaviour summarizes theories which 'stress the sequential, unfolding nature of activity in organizations' (Pfeffer, 1985, p385). The emphasis is on process rather than particular outcomes, primarily because it is felt that outcomes are caused neither by the people nor the environment of the organization. Rather, organizational behaviour is caused by a combination of people, problems and solutions. This position is somewhat reminiscent of the theory that attitudes are an outgrowth of behaviour rather than rational causes of behaviour.

A proponent of this latter stance might see training primarily as a retrospective reaction to a series of events within the organization designed to assure fulfillment of the organization's mission. Trainee success would be essential to this end, and therefore necessary resources would be allocated for the training. While management exerts some control in this orientation, the employee trainee has less. Once again motivation as a learner then appears dependent upon the extent to which the trainee supports the organization and its goals. This conclusion seems to pertain to each of the three theoretical orientations to organizational behaviour.

Undoubtedly, many can identify with scenarios that support each of these positions with respect to training, perhaps even within the same organization. Like so many types of behaviour, the behaviour of trainees as learners, as well as employees, is multi-faceted. All of these perceptions of organizational behaviour, however, show an integration between aspects of the larger institution and the behaviour of the persons who are a part of that establishment.

THE OVERALL EFFECTS OF TRAINEE PERCEPTIONS OF ORGANIZATIONAL CLIMATE

The STD organizational climate framework

The work environment from which trainees come and to which they return is described in the STD model in terms of a three-level taxonomy of factors. The first level divides the factors in three groups depending upon not only the particular nature of a climate being discussed, but also upon the function it serves in the STD model. The first group, general environmental factors, includes general characteristics of the work environment. For example, one general environmental factor would be employee's evaluations of their supervisor's performance. Another example would be the general morale of the employees. These types of factors, as a whole, provide an overall description of the trainees' work environment from their point of view.

The other two categories in this first level of the taxonomy identify workplace descriptors which are related either generally, or specifically, to the subject matter of the target training programme. An example of a factor generally related to the subject of the training programmes studied here is the supervisor's enforcement of plant safety rules. This would generally relate to a training programme which presents rules for safe pedestrian travel in a manufacturing plant. On the other hand, an example of a specific training-related factor on this same topic would be the supervisor's enforcement of those same pedestrian rules presented in the programme.

The second level of the taxonomy identifies four distinct aspects of a work climate which can be used to describe any organization. These sub-categories are perceptions of:

- management behaviour;
- co-worker behaviour;
- physical working conditions; and
- employee empowerment.

These categories can be applied to each of the three types of climate descriptors. The specific measures of these aspects of an organizational climate comprise the third level of the taxonomy. To exemplify this level, one can examine the physical working conditions in an organization. Physical conditions can be perceived generally, such as 'We have start-of-the-art equipment in this plant'. On the other hand, they can be viewed very specifically, such as 'The equipment we use makes it very easy to lock-out'.

The taxonomy which serves as the framework for describing an organizational climate in the STD model is visualized in Figure 5.2. An examination of the highlighted section of the cube in Figure 5.2 provides another example of the STD approach to portraying an organizational climate. 'Co-workers always follow the truck operation rules'. This is a specific measure of co-worker behaviour. It is also an example of a factor specifically related to a target training programme. This scheme may seem particularly burdensome; however, it provides a process by which one can analyse any environment with respect to any training programme in a comparable fashion. (The precise measures used in the research foundation of the STD Model are found in Appendix B).

An overview of the relationships among organizational climate factors and their roles in training outcomes

The direct effects of climate
Organizational climate plays an important role as both a direct influence and an indirect influence on the outcomes of a training programme. The most *direct* impact, however, is on specific transfer of training (see Figures C.7 and C.8 in the Appendix). However, a more generalized application of training is also directly influenced by the employees' perceptions of the organizational climate as well (see Figures C.10 and C.11). Each of the three major types of climate attributes can directly explain on-the-job behaviour after the employee's participation in a training programme. In summary, one could conclude that those employees who work in an atmosphere

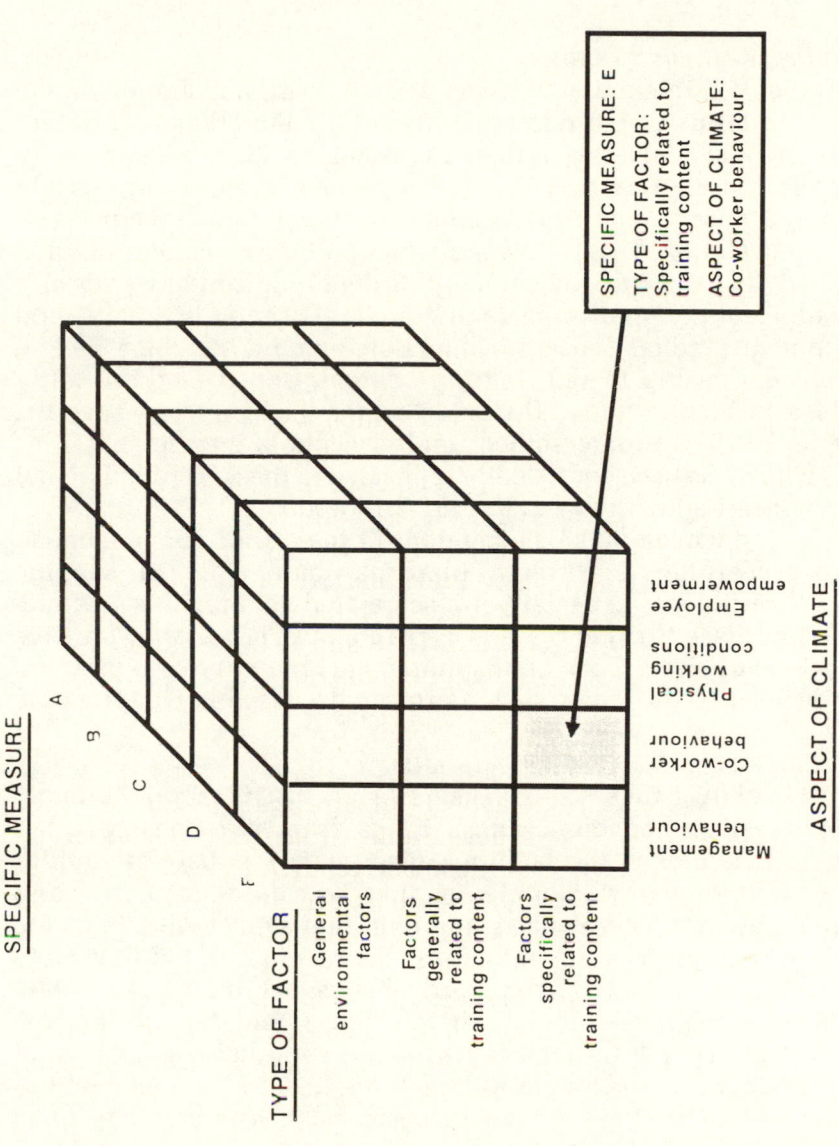

SPECIFIC MEASURE: E

TYPE OF FACTOR:
Specifically related to
training content

ASPECT OF CLIMATE:
Co-worker behaviour

SPECIFIC MEASURE

A
B
C
D
F

TYPE OF FACTOR

General
environmental
factors

Factors
generally
related to
training content

Factors
specifically
related to
training content

Management
behaviour

Co-worker
behaviour

Physical
working
conditions

Employee
empowerment

ASPECT OF CLIMATE

Figure 5.2 *A framework for analysing organizational climate*

which they consider more supportive and, generally speaking, a better place to work, are those who are more likely to apply those principles taught in the programme to their jobs. Moreover, training goals which centre on changing employees' attitudes are also affected by their perceptions of the organization, but the major impact is not of a direct nature (see Figures C.3, C.4 and C.5).

The indirect effects of climate

One can look at the indirect effects of organizational climate in two ways: 1. in terms of the relationships among the climate variables themselves, and 2. in terms of their connections with another category of systemic design factors: trainee attitudes. First, as one might expect, the various measures of climate interact among themselves. These interrelationships follow a distinct pattern which is shown in Figure 5.1. The general environment of the organization serves as a foundation for the other aspects of climate. Essentially, the general environment predicts those attributes of the climate which have a general relationship to the training content, and then these latter variables influence those attributes which have a very specific, direct tie to the training subject matter. This is another chain of effects which has been consistently replicated in the STD foundational research (see Figures C.1 – C.5, C.8, C.10 and C.11).

The second way in which perceptions of the organizational climate influence learning is through their particular role in shaping employee attitudes, especially those related to previous training programmes (see Figures C.1 – C.5, C.10 and C.11). Again, positive perceptions of one's work atmosphere contribute to the expression of other positive attitudes, such as those discussed in Chapter 4.

The critical aspects of a work climate

Figure 5.2 shows those four aspects of an organization's climate which are addressed here. These range from reactions to other people to reactions to the facilities. The relative impact of each of these aspects of a work climate are shown in the four charts comprising Figure 5.3. These charts highlight that aspect which has the most influence on training outcomes: the reaction of employees to management's on-the-job behaviour. This aspect of a work climate not only has the greatest direct role in achievement, but also has the greatest indirect role through its influence on other organizational climate perceptions and trainee attitudes. Figure 5.3 shows all relationships identified throughout the research base whether they have replicated or not. The charts are useful for presenting a general impression of the relative influence of the various critical aspects of a work environment on adult learning.

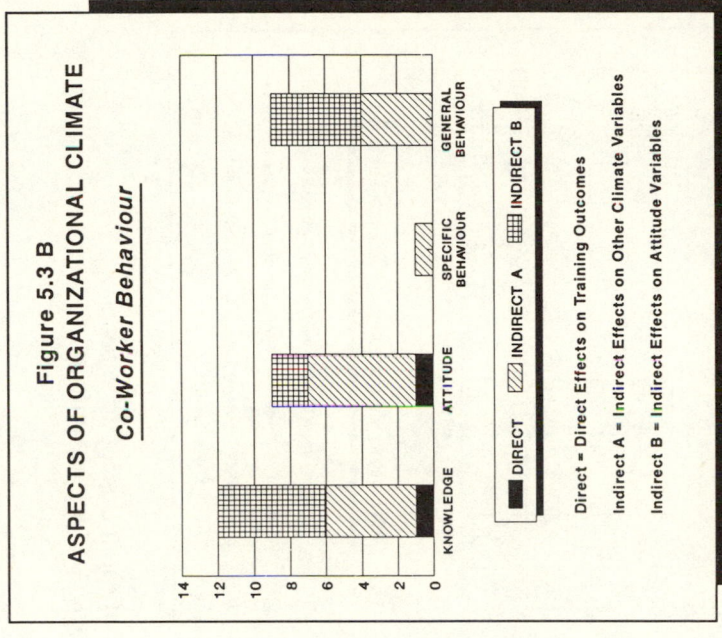

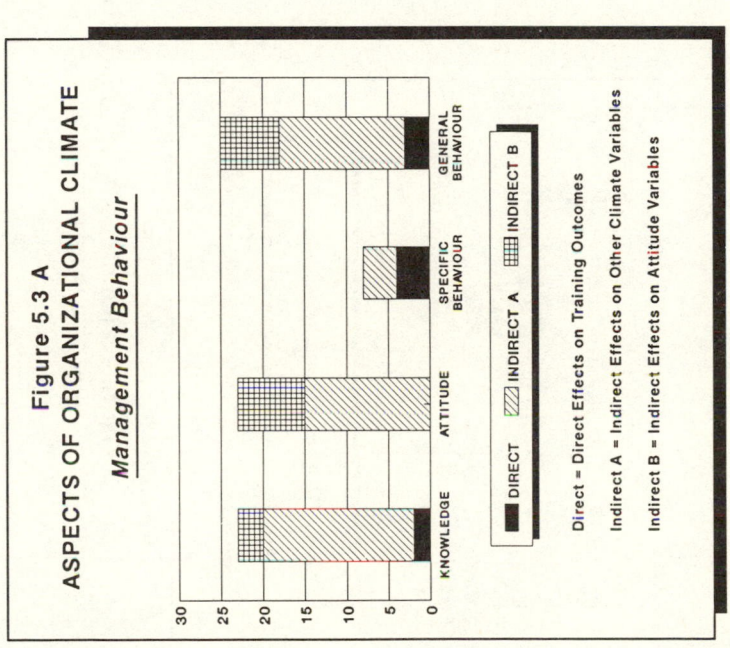

Figure 5.3   *A comparison of the influence of aspects of organizational climate on various types of training outcomes*

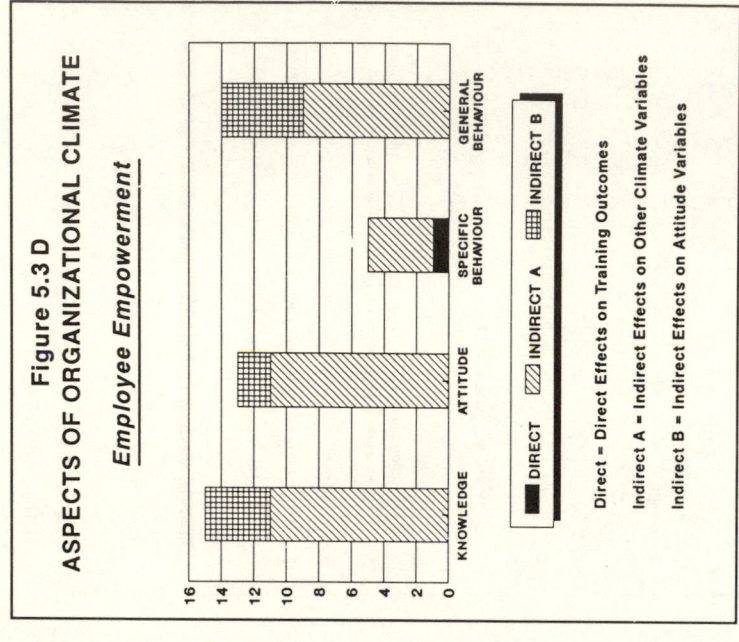

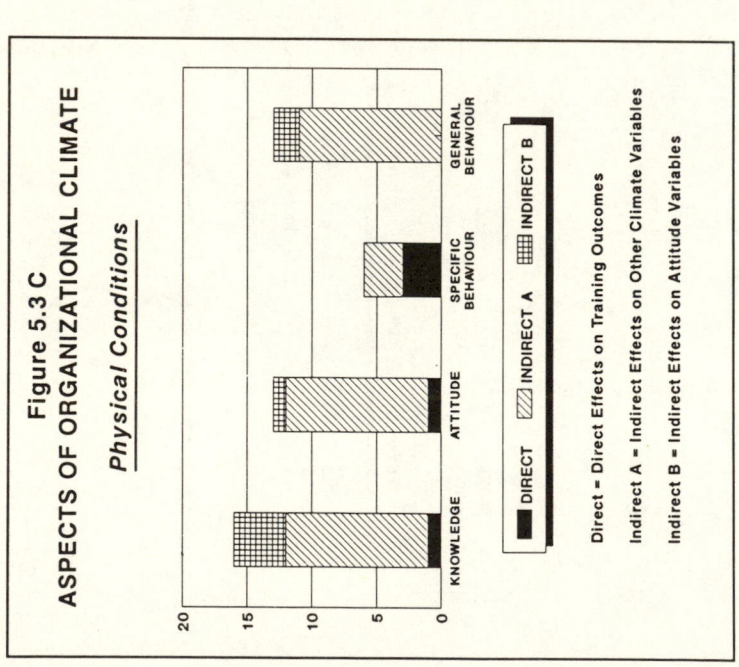

Figure 5.3 (continued) *A comparison of the influence of aspects of organizational climate on various types of training outcomes*

Figure 5.3 also shows that while supervisors and management exert much influence in terms of shaping employee opinions, peer influence is less meaningful with respect to training outcomes. Aspects of employee empowerment and perceptions of the physical working conditions have similar overall influence, even though trainees' opinions regarding the physical aspects of their work environment play more of a direct role in determining training outcomes. Each of these four areas of concern, however, represents facets of a systemic design model which have typically been ignored as components of the adult learning process in a training context.

THE EFFECTS OF SOCIAL SUPPORT AND BEHAVIOUR MODELLING IN THE WORKPLACE

Evidence of social support and behaviour modelling

Noe and Schmitt (1986) expand upon previous definitions of 'trainability' by adding an environmental component. This results in the following equation: trainability = f (ability, motivation, environmental favourability). Their concept of environmental favourability speaks to three of the four aspects of organizational climate addressed here: perceptions of management behaviour, co-worker behaviour and physical working conditions. With respect to the first two, Noe and Schmitt (1986) state:

> Of particular importance are the climate of the organization concerning change and the extent to which the social context (supervisors, co-workers) of the work setting provides reinforcement and feedback. A supportive work climate in which reinforcement and feedback from co-workers are obtained is more likely to result in transfer of skills from the training environment to the work environment (p498).

While Noe and Schmitt emphasize the importance of environmental favourability for transferring skills to the workplace, the STD model reinforces its importance in relation to both transfer and attitude change as well.

Social support, however, implies more than reinforcement and feedback. In the strongest sense it implies modelling of the intended workplace behaviour. Behaviour modelling can take many forms. Using the data base of the STD approach, pertinent workplace behaviours are both training-specific and also more generalized applications of those principles taught in the training programme. Consequently, a favourable social environment is defined and measured in terms of a range of factors, including an atmosphere in which:

- the supervisor is highly rated and co-workers cooperate on the job (general environmental factors);
- supervisors, co-workers, union and management support safety and follow general safety rules (factors generally related to training); and
- all employees follow the specifically targeted rules, and supervisory staff hold employees accountable if they do not follow these rules (factors specifically related to training).

These behaviours provide evidence of a positive work environment and the assumption that the training principles are generally modelled in the workplace. They provide a favourable environment for successful training.

The direct effects of social support and behaviour modelling

The factors encompassed in Noe and Schmitt's (1986) definition of environmental favourability account for essentially all of the *direct* effects of an employee's organizational climate perceptions on training outcomes in the STD foundational research. The major thrust of the influence, however, can be attributed here to the worker's social context rather than the physical facilities and resources in the workplace. This is evident in Figure 5.3.

While elements of the organizational climate seem to affect all types of training outcomes, the only direct effects replicated across studies were in terms of transferring training principles to the workplace. Furthermore, all organizational climate impact on transfer of training (be it specific transfer or general transfer) can be credited to the influence of management and supervisory personnel rather than co-workers, although the nature of the influence is not consistent (see Figures C.7, C.8, C.10 and C.11).

The direct impact of the supervisors' behaviour is most apparent as a factor which encourages an employee's use of those exact skills presented in a training programme, even though their behaviour also impacts a more generalized transfer of skills. It seems that if supervisors demonstrate any type of training-related behaviour, this encourages employees to apply what they learned in the training programmes to their jobs (see Figures C.10 and C.11). However, supervisors need not demonstrate only the exact behaviour stressed in the training workshop to be effective; even general support and concern for the subject area is useful and influential in promoting the application of newly acquired skills and knowledge. Minimal supervisory encouragement and support for the training principles in the workplace have powerful effects on employee performance. This exemplifies Noe and Schmitt's concept of 'environmental favourability'.

The indirect effects of social support and behaviour modelling

Impact on other organizational climate perceptions

The behaviour of management and supervisory staff also exerts the most important *indirect* influence on training outcomes as well as having the most important direct influence. Moreover, this particular type of impact appears to permeate all types of training outcomes (see Figures C.1 – C.4, C.7, C.8, C.10 and C.11).

The web of interrelated factors which describes the indirect effects of management behaviour on training perfectly exemplifies the logic of a systemic approach for instructional design as well as for understanding adult learning processes. The effective atmosphere seems to be one in which employees give high marks to their supervisors, supervisors who appear to be good models of those behaviours (general and specific) which have been presented in the training programme (see Figures C.3, C.4, C.7, C.8, C.10 and C.11).

Knowledge acquisition and retention is less affected by this atmosphere than are the other types of outcomes. However, knowledge acquisition is less affected by organizational climate in general than are those outcomes of training more directly related to workplace behaviour.

The second major aspect of social support comes from one's colleagues in the workplace. Collegial aspects of social support, while unimportant in terms of their direct role in determining training outcomes, do exert some influence in an indirect fashion. In all situations cooperation among employees tends to be related to desirable management behaviour (see Figures C.1, C.2, C.3, C.5, C.7, C.10 and C.11). General collegial modelling of the training skills and principles provides some contribution to successful training, but the influence is far outweighed by the role of employee perceptions of management behaviour.

Impact on trainee attitudes

Aspects of social support and behaviour modelling also have other indirect effects on training outcomes. There is some evidence that they influence attitudes toward training, and through this route affect generalized transfer (see Figures C.10 and C.11) and attitude improvement (see Figures C.4 and C.5) and even knowledge retention (see Figure C.2). This relationship between current behaviour modelling and attitudes toward previous training may seem odd. However, it may reflect the human tendency to form attitudes, even retrospective opinions, based upon current stimuli and reinforcement.

The stimuli in this situation come not only from supervisory behaviour but also from co-worker behaviour. If supervisors or co-workers model the desirable behaviours, employee attitudes are more likely to be positive. However, the impact of supervisory behaviour is more pronounced by indirectly affecting all training outcomes, except specific transfer of skills to the workplace. Behaviour modelling is crucial; general support of management is not.

Overall impact of elements of social support and behaviour modelling

Ajzen and Fishbein's (1980) Behavioral Intention model shows the interactions between a person's attitude toward a given behaviour and his or her perceptions of what others believe. In other words, attitudes are shaped in part by whether a person's social contacts support a given type of behaviour. Depending upon the relative importance of the attitudinal considerations and the subjective norms, one forms intentions and consequently behaves in a rational manner. The elements of social support and behaviour modelling addressed here correspond with the development of subjective norms in the Behavioral Intention model.

The STD model supports the role of subjective norms in shaping training outcomes, but even more so it supports the role of subjective norms in predicting behaviour. This is also consistent with the Behavioral Intention model. However, the STD model further defines the roots of such norms in terms of both co-worker and supervisory influence. The predominant source of the organizational norms in this context are employees' perceptions of a prevailing management position as reflected in their daily on-the-job behaviour.

Logically, the major effects of these views of management behaviour are felt in terms of employees' changes in their on-the-job behaviour. Indirectly, social support and behaviour modelling also affect attitude change, as well as a more generalized transfer of training. The more precise summary of these findings is portrayed in Figure 5.4.

This diagram highlights several aspects of the research findings which constitute the basis of the STD model:

- management and supervisory modelling of training-related behaviour is more influential than behaviour modelling by co-workers;
- behaviour modelling is more critical to training success than is a climate in which employees have general support for their supervisors, although the two situations are typically combined; and
- social norms and mores in an organization exert more influence on specific transfer of training principles than on other types of training goals.

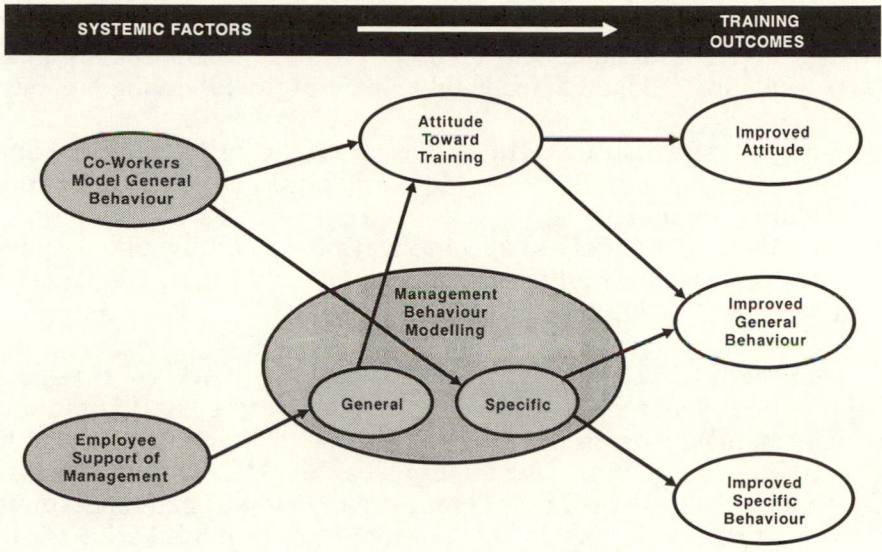

Figure 5.4 *The role of social support and behaviour modelling in determining training outcomes*

THE EFFECTS OF PHYSICAL CONDITIONS IN THE WORKPLACE

Evidence of physical support and constraints

The second part of Noe and Schmitt's (1986) concept of environmental favourability focuses upon those constraints imposed within an environment which affect one's accomplishment of a task. They cite lack of equipment or financial resources as examples of task constraints. The question centres on the extent to which the physical aspects of a work situation inhibit or facilitate employees' on-the-job behaviour after participation in a training programme.

Many have seen environment as one of the important constructs for understanding organizational behaviour, and it has also been proposed in non-training contexts that environment is a primary determinant of performance in the workplace (Porter, cited in Prescott, 1986). For example, Peters *et al.* (1980) concluded from their research that inhibiting conditions in the workplace 'tend to both "lower the ceiling" on performance among better performers *and* "lower the floor" among poorer performers' (p93).

Typically, physical working conditions are seen as a key part of this array of environmental considerations (they constituted the majority of the relevant conditions in the Peters *et al.* research.) Within the STD foundational research, physical conditions are analysed as a part of the organizational climate in the following manner:

- employee satisfaction with physical working conditions and agreement that conditions promote productivity (general environmental factors); and
- perceptions of a variety of specific ways in which the plant equipment or physical layout permit the employee to follow the targeted rule (factors specifically related to training).

These descriptions of the physical nature of a work environment capture both general impressions as well as very specific opinions which can influence on-the-job use of those principles presented in the training programme. One example of this latter category would be 'There is a shortage of locks in my area'. Peters *et al.* (1980) found that situational variables of this nature not only inhibited or facilitated performance in the workplace but also influenced affective reactions, such as degrees of frustration and satisfaction with the task at hand.

The effects of physical conditions on training outcomes

Direct effects
Even though workplace performance is commonly accounted for in some respects by the situation's physical attributes, these variables have no consistent direct role in training-related performance of any type. While this might be expected in regard to knowledge retention, and perhaps in regard to attitude change, it is unexpected with respect to on-the-job behaviour. Even more surprising is the trend for those working in conditions that they saw as *less* than desirable to learn more and apply more of what they learned to the job. Perhaps physical conditions, which some would see as inhibiting good behaviour, actually contributed to success by forcing close attention to the content of the training.

Nonetheless, the STD model's interpretation of environmental favourability emphasizes only the social aspects of Noe and Schmitt's (1986) definition rather than task conditions. Social support and behaviour modelling are the key elements.

Indirect effects
Physical working conditions, however, do seem to play an indirect role in determining training effectiveness. These characteristics of

the work environment appear to contribute to a general atmosphere which shapes other employee perceptions of the organizational climate.

The most important way in which physical conditions can affect training outcomes is by contributing to an environment which is conducive to behaviour modelling, especially by supervisory staff. Here only general impressions of beneficial physical conditions are pertinent, but this general atmosphere leads directly to management modelling of targeted behaviours and the effects of this atmosphere are fairly widespread. Physical condition factors contribute to knowledge improvement (see Figures C.1 and C.2), attitude improvement (see Figures C.3, C.4 and C.5), and to transfer of general behaviours to the job (see Figures C.10 and C.11). There was even one instance of physical conditions influencing specific behaviour change in this manner (see Figure C.8).

One example of the way in which physical aspects of the work climate influence behaviour is through the use of cues in the environment. For instance, in some plants signs were placed on the equipment, or in the work areas, to serve as cues to information recall. These signs served as job aids and were also concrete evidence of the supervisors' support of the target rules.

Cues are an integral part of Hochbaum, Leventhal, Kegeles and Rosenstock's Health Belief model (Becker and Maiman, 1975). In this model, cues are necessary to precipitate appropriate action. While they can be internal cues, often external cues in the physical environment are effective.

The physical elements of an organizational climate also influence employee attitudes, although these relationships are not always as predictable as with the factors relating to social support and behaviour modelling. As might be expected, physical conditions exert some influence on the employees' job satisfaction (see Figures C.1 and C.3). In addition there is some evidence of impact on attitudes toward previous training (see Figures C.4 and C.10). However, one can not consistently attribute these relationships to any particular training outcome.

THE EFFECTS OF EMPLOYEE EMPOWERMENT

Evidence of the individual's influence in an organization

As important as it is, the mere presence of model behaviour may be insufficient in itself to promote training effectiveness. The modelling provides external stimulation, but internal motivation also seems dependent upon the trainee's perception that he or she has a role of some importance in the organization. Many organizations are emphasizing employee involvement and union-management cooperation as an avenue toward improved production quality. It appears that these same goals directed toward employee empowerment also encourage employee performance in training programmes.

There are two elements of employee empowerment in the STD models – the extent to which the trainee feels, 1. involved in decision making, and 2. encouraged to devise new work methods. Both elements play an indirect role in shaping other trainee attitudes and in contributing to other perceptions of the organizational climate.

It is a long-accepted principle of professional development of teachers and other school-based personnel that success is not likely unless the participants 'buy into' the activity. Without a sense of ownership and dedication to the objectives of the training, there can be little hope of lasting effect. This approach is consistent with two diverse paths of thought – the management orientation of participative decision making and the andragological approach to adult education.

Bowers (1977) notes that one of the critical parts of participative decision making is the ability of all parties in a work organization to exercise some influence over outcomes. This approach is presented as an alternative to classical management theory, which has been described by Likert as relying,

> 'primarily upon the economic motives of buying a man's time and then telling him precisely what to do, how to do it, and at what level to produce'. . . . It is one of the anomalies of our time that research shows that it is in the low-producing organization, far more often than in the high, that these injunctions are most closely followed. It is where performance is less stellar that managers and supervisors tend to concentrate on keeping their subordinates busily engaged in going through a specified work cycle in a prescribed way and at a satisfactory rate as determined by company standards (Bowers, 1977, pp17–18).

Participatory management philosophy also parallels training practices based upon the commonly espoused principle of andragogy which states that 'adults both desire and enact a tendency toward self-directedness as they mature, though they may be dependent in certain situations' (Knowles, 1980, p43). One implication of this conviction is the notion that instructors should be facilitators rather than teachers or trainers. According to Brookfield (1986),

> facilitators do not direct; rather, they assist adults to attain a state of self-actualization or to become fully functioning persons. . . . This view emphasizes the primacy of the learner, grants a substantial measure of control to learners, and places learning directly in the context of learners' own experiences (pp123–4).

The two measures of employee empowerment pertinent to training design are compatible with both of these philosophies. The fact that these two variables contribute to training effectiveness provides some support for a more open approach to training design and implementation as well as for a more open general atmosphere in the organization.

The effects of employee empowerment on training outcomes

Empowerment characteristics, like the physical aspects of the organizational climate, are important because of the indirect manner in which they influence training results. Their role is easily overlooked because their influence is but one part of a complex network of variables, even though the network pattern is consistently duplicated in various situations. Empowerment characteristics contribute to the formation of learner attitudes toward training and of other climate perceptions as well.

The major thrust of the impact of the empowerment variables is on perceptions of social support and behaviour modelling in the work environment; and the vast majority of this influence is in terms of effects on employee perceptions of management actions. Thus, there is an interaction between trainees' feelings of empowerment and their views of management and supervisors. Those employees who feel they are more involved in company operations are more likely to be aware of the model behaviour of management and supervisors in their work areas (see Figures C.1–C.5, C.8, C.10 and C.11).

In addition, there is limited evidence of employee involvement in organizational decision making as a factor in moulding positive attitudes toward training itself (see Figures C.2, C.5 and C.11). This may be one example of Pfeffer's (1985) explanation of employee action in an organization which is seen primarily as a process of making sense of behaviours after they have already occurred. In other words, current feelings of involvement and participation in an organization encourage employees to view previous training in a positive light.

In each of these situations the positive attitudes associated with empowerment appear to generalize to other aspects of the organization with secondary effects on training outcomes. All types of training outcomes seem to be affected by this good will, although its effects on transferring specific skills to the workplace seem minimal. Once again, the impact of organizational climate perceptions on specific transfer is essentially the direct result of behaviour modelling. Indirect influence is negligible.

ORGANIZATIONAL CLIMATE AND STD PROCEDURES

The essence of a systemic approach to instructional design as compared to a systematic aproach is redefining the instructional system so that it encompasses the larger environment in which the instruction is delivered and will be used. It is likely that most designers will find it easier to accommodate a broader definition of learner characteristics than to accept responsibility for addressing aspects of organizational climate such as those just considered. These factors constitute a major departure from issues normally included in traditional ISD. The first question then is of the propriety of these attributes within a design model.

The appropriate environment for an instructional system

Both systematic instructional design and systemic design are rooted in general systems theory. Environment assumes an important position in this philosophical and theoretical orientation. For example, Hall and Fagen (1975) describe the environment of a system as 'the set of all objects, a change in which attributes affect the system and also those objects whose attributes are changed by the behavior of the system' (p56).

Using this definition, the data presented here support the inclusion of organizational environment as part of a training system. The question can still be posed as to whether the organization is, in fact, the supra-system of which the training is a part rather than an integral part of the target system. Miller (1978) describes the relationship between a system and its total environment in the following manner:

> In order to survive, the system must interact with and adjust to its environment, the other parts of the supra-system. These processes alter both the system and its environment. It is not surprising that characteristically living systems adapt to their environment and, in return, mold it. The result is that, after some period of interaction, each in some sense becomes a mirror of the other (pp29–30).

Miller emphasizes the nature of feedback and self-adjusting properties of systems as they interact with their environment. The more immediate the environment, the more quickly this interaction occurs. The nature of the interaction between the components of a training instructional system and the organization in which it resides is at times overt and obvious, as with the effects of management decisions to support the training goals. At other times the effects are subtle, with more of a psychological character as with the effects of employee empowerment.

In both cases, however, the organizational environment directly and indirectly affects the operation of the instructional process. The question is whether designers should assume responsibility for addressing these issues or allow the interactions to occur randomly or as a consequence of the decisions of others in the organization. It seems both valid and wise for designers to accommodate elements of the organizational climate in their training programmes to the extent that they in turn are held accountable for the success of these programmes. Therefore, it appears appropriate for the organizational environment to be considered an immediate and legitimate part of a training system. Systemic design procedures are built upon this premise.

Organizational climate and motivation design

Chapter 4 discusses those trainee attitudes which serve a motivation function within STD. In this chapter the roles of employee perceptions of an organizational climate are being examined in terms of their effects on training outcomes. To some extent some aspects of climate also can be seen as performance motivators similar to the functions of trainee attitudes. Rather than expressing individual likes and dislikes, however, the elements of climate are external stimuli which provide information to the employee which either encourages or discourages performing the targeted behaviours on the job.

Typically, worker motivation is explained in terms of two things: 1. assurance that the organization will be successful in the market place, thus insuring the employee's economic needs, and 2. a sense of accomplishment, fulfillment, satisfaction and pleasure which is attained by participating in the successful venture (Bowers, 1977). This explanation can also be related to one's motivation to apply training principles on the job by viewing motivation in terms of the impact of organizational climate.

The extent to which management and co-workers support and model the targeted behaviour reflects their estimations of that behaviour's worth in terms of the primary business of the company. If these people do not think the behaviour significantly contributes to the company's success in the market place, they usually will not give it their full support regardless of the time and resources allocated to the training effort. The practical-minded employee, regardless of job title or rank, is supportive of actions which contribute to the company's profit and indirectly to their own pockets.

However, even if the behaviour is likely to lead to increased earnings, one would not expect full compliance if such actions, or the responses of others to these actions, do not meet employees' personal needs for job satisfaction. When transfer of training is viewed within the framework of job satisfaction, it is possible to understand the added roles of both employee empowerment and physical facility issues as performance motivators.

Within this context, addressing elements of organizational climate in training design becomes a facet of the overall motivation design of the programme. These issues correspond with some aspects of the relevance and satisfaction components of Keller's (1987b) ARCS model of motivation design. Relevance impinges on organizational climate issues in terms of the extent to which the training goals meet employee needs, especially those needs implied by impressions of the physical facilities as well as by the interest and support of others in the workplace.

Satisfaction is gauged in terms of the natural consequences of using the target behaviours on the job, especially the reinforcement received or frustrations encountered for such actions. However, fully addressing organizational climate in the design of a training programme goes beyond these aspects of motivation.

Emphasizing organizational climate in STD

Organizational climate considerations have their primary direct effects on the extent to which knowledge is transferred to on-the-job behaviour. However, their indirect effects also contribute to the other types of training outcomes. Consequently, designers should address these issues in all training programmes, regardless of the nature of their goals. Climate concerns have less influence on the selection of learning activities and delivery processes than did trainee background characteristics and attitudes; their major impact is on goal definition, evaluation processes and the specification of plans for programme installation and maintenance.

Andrews and Goodson (1991) primarily attribute the proliferation of ISD models to a need to adapt to the peculiarities of specific learning environments. The STD model is another example of this phenomenon in its specific concern with employee training. In a sense the existence of many instructional design models is a response to organizational climate concerns. This type of adaptation, however, typically results in only a very general reflection of differences among the various organizational settings. For example, school settings might use models which emphasize development of different instructional tracts; military models might emphasize evaluation and product control; medical models may incorporate aspects of the health belief or health behaviour models.

The major ISD models do not incorporate procedures for addressing specific organizational characteristics which directly reflect a particular subject matter or a particular social climate since their intent is usually generic use. The models which do address the nature of the organization typically do so within a needs assessment framework as a step in identifying the source of a problem. For example, Rossett (1987) suggests analysing the organization to determine if the problem involves the absence of environmental support and incentives. Seels and Glasgow (1990) suggest using Kaufman and English's Organizational Elements model to determine the nature of discrepancies between the actual behaviour and the desired behaviour in an organization; this approach emphasizes the organizational inputs and training processes as compared to the products and outcomes of instruction. Romiszowski (1981) views the environment of an instructional system from the orientation of general systems theory and analyses the effects of the system and supra-system on sub-system operation. This is essentially a type of problem analysis emphasizing inputs.

STD builds upon these more general approaches to addressing the organizational environment by identifying those specific attributes of the organizational climate which have demonstrated effects on training outcomes. It recognizes and endorses the use of environmental data as just discussed; however, it expands the use of such data beyond needs assessment and goal definition.

EXPANDING STD THEORY: PERCEPTIONS OF THE ORGANIZATIONAL CLIMATE

Previously, theoretical propositions have been directed toward specific categories of variables such as work experience or attitudes toward training delivery systems. The elements of organizational climate pertinent to effective training are typically interrelated and propositions pertaining to certain types of employees are difficult to isolate. Consequently, the theoretical propositions relative to organizational climate are presented here as a total group. The descriptive propositions summarize the tentative conclusions regarding the role of employee perceptions of organizational climate on the learning process; the prescriptive propositions give initial direction to design practice.

Descriptions of adult learning in employee training

The additional propositions given here appear to describe the unique aspects of adult learning as it occurs in an employee training context. They concentrate on what many believe to be the most critical aspect of a training programme – on-the-job application – and as such tend to distinguish training from other types of adult learning:

- trainee motivation is a function, in part, of a supportive social environment in the workplace;
- those training principles which have the strong support of supervisors and management throughout the organization are more likely to be used on the job, regardless of the extent and quality of the training;

- when supervisors model behaviour to any extent, even behaviour which is only generally related to the training, employee performance is likely to improve;
- supervisor support and behaviour modelling are more influential than peer support and behaviour modelling;
- peer support appears influential in terms of its role in creating an atmosphere conducive to fostering management support and behaviour modelling;
- management support and modelling of the targeted behaviours is facilitated by a work environment with good physical conditions;
- management support and modelling of the targeted behaviours is more likely to occur in an environment with employees participating in decisions which affect their work; and
- social support and behaviour modelling promote more effective training programmes through their part in shaping positive employee attitudes toward previous training, even though these behaviours have little impact on specific transfer of training.

Organizational climate plays its most important role as either a facilitator or an inhibitor of transfer of training. In the case of the more generalized transfer, perceptions of the organization appear to have an even greater impact in those programmes which are less intense or in which the instructional design is of a lower quality. This phenomenon is exacerbated with respect to specific transfer of training.

If one is interested in transfer of training, the most important aspect of an organizational climate is the extent to which supervisors and management not only support but model those behaviours espoused in the training programme. Other elements of the environment: peer support, employee empowerment and the physical conditions, may tend to either encourage or discourage this support.

While designers may at times feel frustration with the extensive influence of these variables, the quality of their work can significantly alter such environmental effects. The next section speaks to ways in which the design itself can address the characteristics of the larger organizational setting.

Prescriptive propositions for instructional design based upon organizational climate

A 'Training needs assessment' proposition
Existing ISD models often emphasize environmental considerations when determining the problems to be addressed in training. These procedures are sound, and systemic design incorporates such tactics. Kaufman and English's (1979) Organizational Elements model is one example of an existing approach which is still useful. Here five

categories of needs are cited: inputs, processes, products, outputs and outcomes. This model is adaptable to many ISD orientations. For example, it easily fits into the Seels and Glasgow (1990) approach. However, to be consistent with STD, the Organizational Elements model (or other similar tactics) should be supplemented in the following manner:

- When determining the 'inputs' as part of a problem analysis, identify the extent to which:
  a. supervisors support and/or use the behaviours required to resolve the difficulty targeted in the problem analysis;
  b. co-workers support and/or use the behaviours required to resolve the difficulty targeted in the problem analysis;
  c. employees are satisfied with their physical working conditions, especially those pertinent to solving the targeted problem; and
  d. employees participate in key decisions relative to their jobs.

Such information can be used in three ways: 1. as an aid to further defining and understanding the problem, and/or 2. as an aid to interpreting evaluation data, and/or 3. as a basis for designing the installation and maintenance parts of a training programme.

The challenge is to establish routine procedures for collecting necessary data. The first two categories of data cited in the above propositions are project-specific and must be embedded into a needs assessment. The latter two groups are general and can be used across projects, thus negating the need to collect new data with each training design.

A proposition related to 'Construct assessment and evaluation procedures'

It has been shown that organizational climate can have profound but easily overlooked influence on the apparent effectiveness of a training programme, especially in relation to the programme's impact on everyday job performance. It is easy to attribute deficiencies to the basic instructional design or to the delivery process, when many of the problems may lie in the work environment.

Carey and Dick's (1991) recommended structure for a summative evaluation provides a way to address this pitfall. They divide a summative evaluation into six phases – outcomes analysis is one of these six phases which involves field testing of the programme with target learners in the prescribed setting. As such, the instruction is viewed in both the immediate and larger contextual situation. This orientation allows one to examine the training effects in light of the organizational climate. However, the STD approach again suggests supplementing existing procedures by incorporating the following steps:

- The outcomes analysis stage of the summative evaluation should provide for the possibility of partially explaining a training programme's impact on job performance in terms of organizational climate characteristics with the primary focus on:
  a. management and supervisor's support and behaviour modelling;
  b. levels of employee empowerment; and
  c. satisfaction with the physical facilities, especially those pertinent to the target behaviour.

A proposition related to 'Design, contract or select delivery systems and products'
Given the role of organizational climate in trainee motivation, it may be important to address these issues in the programme's motivation design.

- If the organizational climate is characterized by a management and supervisory staff which does not clearly support the training's target behaviours, stress the instruction's relevance by:
  a. emphasizing positive role models and concrete examples related to the workplace; and
  b. stressing the positive consequences of behaving in the recommended manner on the job.

This proposition corresponds with Keller's (1987a) tactics explained in the ARCS model of motivation design. If the feedback and reinforcement is not likely to occur in the workplace naturally, then the responsible designer will create an intervention which attempts to establish reinforcement during instruction. While on-the-job feedback is preferable, this technique is warranted in some circumstances.

'Install, evaluate and maintain system' propositions
Sometimes designers can address the pertinent organizational climate issues through the programme's installation and maintenance procedures, rather than through the instruction itself. These tactics emerge when using the broader systemic orientation, instead of traditional systematic procedures which typically concentrate on instructional materials or programme delivery.

The systemic approach, especially with respect to organizational climate concerns, extends Cash's concept of external efficiency (cited in Morgan, 1987). This refers to the extent to which educational experiences relate to students' daily lives after graduation. Morgan (1987) incorporates this notion into an eight-step 'macro-systems analysis' which includes consideration of the non-instructional, supra-system environment. By expanding this process, one could logically address work environment demands in a similar fashion and thereby establish external efficiency in a training programme. In this vein, the following STD implementation and maintenance principles are suggested:

- For each major training programme, construct a brief orientation for all management personnel which would:
  - a. describe the rationale and significance of the training and the consequences of non-compliance;
  - b. summarize the principles employees are being told to follow;
  - c. provide practice opportunities when appropriate;
  - d. emphasize the physical facilities and conditions necessary for full application of the training principles to the job; and
  - e. discuss the impact on the organization if the training principles are consistently used and the corresponding return on investment.
- Include both employees and their immediate supervisors in the same training programmes.
- Provide periodic review and refresher follow-up sessions for employees and their immediate supervisors alike to reinforce the content in the original training programme.
- Create cues and/or job aids in the workplace designed to remind both employees and supervisors of the appropriate behaviour and to stimulate recall of the training principles.

These steps can begin to address the larger issues in the receiving environment which influence the use of training principles on the job. They are important regardless of the quality of the instructional materials and their use in a training programme.

GENERALIZING ORGANIZATIONAL CLIMATE PROPOSITIONS TO OTHER LEARNING CONTEXTS

The role of organizational factors in adult learning in non-training contexts

The fact that organizational climate plays such a large role in transfer of training easily leads to the assumption that such a phenomenon is unique to employee training. Not only is transfer a primary goal of most training programmes, but training is a key type of formal adult learning that is embedded within a particular organizational setting. However, Merriam and Caffarella (1991) point out that most adult educators believe that the people, the structure and the culture of an organization either inhibits or facilitates learning. Their reference here is not to employee training, but rather to any formal adult learning situation. The important distinctions to consider are the nature of the physical boundaries of the target environment and the influence of mandatory versus voluntary participation.

The nature of the environment

The STD model is oriented toward a view of context as the larger organization. This can also be seen as the supra-system or the receiving environment. For training programmes, this environment is always the company in which the learners work. The boundaries extend beyond the physical classroom in which training is delivered to encompass the setting in which training is used. In most general adult education literature, the environment is the educational institution with primary emphasis placed on the classroom environment. This highlights the distinction between the immediate and the extended organizational setting.

Knox's (1986) description of a supportive learning environment includes both physical aspects of the facilities and interpersonal support, such as helping participants get acquainted, reducing their apprehension and encouraging participation. This is a good example of those who view educational environment in the more immediate sense. The effects of these aspects of environment have also been documented in employee training programmes, as well as the more general adult education (Lick, 1989).

The question still remains as to the comparability of the effects of an extended organizational setting in general adult education and employee training. In this respect designers of non-training adult learning may have a problem defining the supra-system, or the receiving environment. This obstacle has implications for Morgan's (1987) concerns with external efficiency, or measuring the relevance of education in one's everyday life outside the school. It is an issue of relevancy in a particular setting.

For training designers relevance should be reasonably well assured if the instruction is predicted on an accurate training needs assessment. Adult education designers must predict the typical environment to which learners return after participation in the programme. This is easier in some situations than others. In higher education programmes with occupational goals, the typical work environment can be predicted and described. For adult literacy programmes, the needs analysis must identify common uses of basic skills in everyday lives. For continuing education programmes, the needs and interests of persons in a given community must be predicted. The objective in each situation, however, is to define the receiving environment that is pertinent to the target programme's content in a fashion which parallels the training designers' needs to describe pertinent elements of their organizations' environments.

Once the appropriate environment is identified and described for non-training adult learning situations, it is likely that the receiving environment would play a role in application and transfer similar to the role of organizational climate in employee training. The specific aspects which exert the most influence, however, may vary between different learning contexts.

The larger, receiving environment is important for any teaching/learning endeavour (adult or pre-adult) in which quality assurance is an issue. Branson (1991) cites two aspects of quality control and assurance which relate to the environment outside of the immediate classroom. The first is determining the degree to which the learners meet performance expectations after instruction. The critical performance is that which is apparent in the larger environment.

The second aspect is one of technical and political fitness. Technical quality encompasses all instructional dimensions, such as the integrity of the design specifications (eg, test item construction, sequencing patterns, delivery techniques), the amount learned and efficiency. Political quality, however, relates to the extent to which the programme is compatible with the needs and expectations of the receiving community. For example, a high quality individualized instructional programme with little or no instructor input would be unacceptable in most higher education environments. Thus, programme quality judgements are often based upon contextual characteristics rather than elements of the immediate instructional environment.

The effects of mandatory and voluntary participation

The impact of this larger environment, however, may be moderated in some circumstances by the initiative and energy of the learners. Participation in an employee training programme is typically required; participation in most other forms of adult learning is usually voluntary. It is possible this distinction may exacerbate the impact of organizational climate as an aspect of motivation within a training framework. Correspondingly, in non-training settings inherent interest and enthusiasm for a topic may overshadow situational constraints resulting in both knowledge gains and consistent use of the content in everyday life.

Interjecting motivation into the picture of organizational climate effects expands the dimensions of the issue. Courtney (as cited in Merriam and Caffarella, 1991) says:

> Those who appear eager and willing to participate in organized learning activities are distinguishable from those who are not by an underlying attitude which sees education as a positive force, to be equated with happiness, and finds in it also a mechanism for solving 'acute' problems. However . . . the person must be in a situation calling for the solution of a particular problem (p83).

The workplace provides an immediate environment in which one can easily find situations appropriate for using training principles.

In this respect, training programmes, by the very fact that they take place within a specific organization, often have settings which facilitate motivation, and subsequently transfer, even though the learning experience is not voluntary. Adults in other types of education experiences which probably are voluntary, need to identify their own sources of problems, their own arenas for application.

This does not negate, however, the power of an individual's drive to offset the impact of a negative environment, and in a positive environment the interest and support of the individual may make transfer of training virtually assured. The participation question once again highlights the value of learner motivation and strengthens the argument for employing all means available to cultivate such attitudes, esepecially in training situations. If participant motivation is not clearly present (as is more likely the case in voluntary learning), then designers should increase the attention given to the receiving environment and other types of motivators.

The role of the larger environment in pre-adult learning

For children, the family and the community environment may have a role analogous to that of organizational climate. Behaviour modelling and peer influence have long been recognized as critical variables in predicting educational outcomes. The influence of feelings of self-worth, comparable to employee empowerment characteristics, are well-documented. In fact, it is possible that the receiving environment, positive or negative, may exert more control over pre-adult learning than that of the mature adult. The best instruction may be overshadowed by environments which do not show evidence of valuing education and learning and conversely, the worst instruction may still be effective when children return to supportive family and community settings.

The question of the relative impact of quality instruction and environment for pre-adults has not been fully answered. However, it seems clear that established interests and goals of adults can withstand situational influences and facilitate learning. While pre-adults' interests can serve the same purpose, it is often more difficult for interests and goals to sustain young people who lack environmental support.

The utility of systemic design propositions in non-training environments

It is likely that the systemic propositions which describe the learning process are also applicable, in principle, to other learning contexts, even though modifications may be needed to make them fully relevant. Most notable would be the need to identify comparable authority figures to substitute for the role of management and supervisory staff. However, this should not negate the importance of the general principle of social support and behaviour modelling as an influence on transfer of training. Likewise, a concept parallel to employee empowerment needs to be identified for each context. Involvement, recognition and resulting self-worth have been suggested.

Since there is little research on the role of the larger environment in non-training learning situations, one can not verify its part in predicting achievement. It is logical that the same principles apply in all adult learning, once an appropriate receiving environment has been identified. However, there is also the persistent problem of accurately anticipating the target learner population, let alone the nature of the environments in which they work and live. These dilemmas speak to the continued need for a bank of typical learner characteristics for designer use in a given setting.

Design of traditional group-based learning in these non-training settings is difficult if the receiving environments vary for persons in a given class. Here is a situation in which the use of advanced computer technologies can facilitate instruction which is tailored to accommodate different areas of application and use. However, even without these capabilities, it is possible to emphasize the positive consequences of regular use in everyday life of the training principles. A range of relevant situations at home, at work and in the community can be analysed to foster application of the target behaviours.

It is more difficult to incorporate installation and maintenance approaches into instructional design plans. Activities which parallel supervisor orientation are at times difficult to construct, although the aims of parent education programmes can have a similar function in instructional programmes for young children. Another example may be some adult literacy programmes in which orientation programmes are provided for spouses to help them anticipate changes in their partners' behaviour. However, most adult and continuing education programmes have no comparable phase. In such cases, further attempts would be necessary to expand the instruction to provide alternative approaches to garnering support from the important people in the learner's environment.

In some circumstances it is possible to provide learners with job aids which serve as cues and memory aids to help them apply the formal instruction to their daily lives. These devices can thereby substitute for human support in the receiving environment.

All of these tactics presuppose that knowledge has been obtained so that it can be used. This is usually the case in adult learning, but not always. Knowledge may be acquired for its own sake rather than for use in vocational or avocational situations. In these cases recall and attitudes toward the learning process itself have more immediate importance than application. However, all knowledge becomes part of the storehouse of information which can be combined and used in subsequent problem-solving given the proper conditions. In this light, as organizational climate is important for employee training, the receiving environment is important to other learning situations, although the essence of the theoretical propositions may require new interpretation to accommodate those conditions which are unique to each programme.

SUMMARY

Expanding the STD conceptual model to encompass the organizational climate

Organizational climate factors serve as a major source of input to an instructional situation. Combined with the basic trainee background

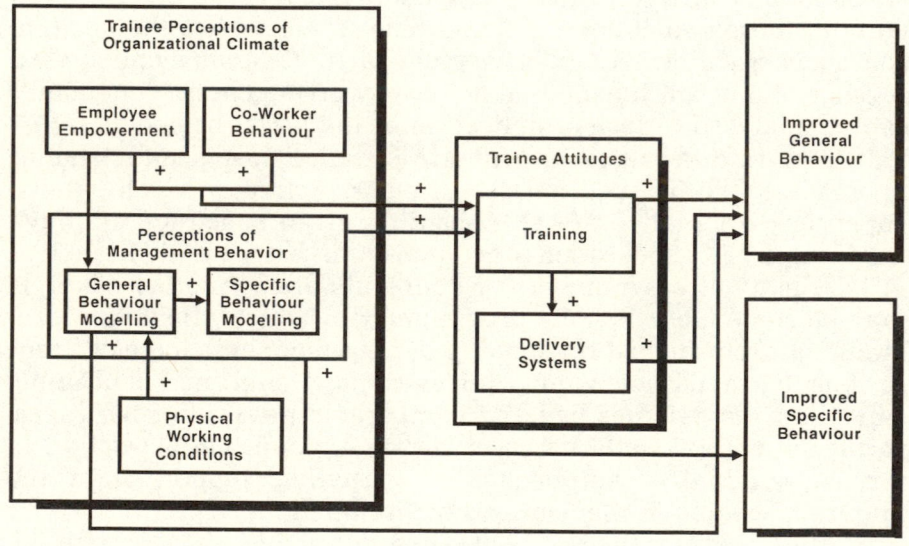

Figure 5.5 *A summary of the effects of organizational climate on transfer of training*

Note:
Both this diagram and Figure 5.6 reflect the actual relationships among variables. Changes in some correlation signs have been made here to clarify meaning in the data as has been the practice in previous chapters' summary charts.

characteristics and attitudes, the work climate serves as either a barrier to or an expeditor of adult learning in training contexts. In addition to the direct impact of design strategies, these three major categories of systemic design factors allow one to predict an overwhelming portion of the outcomes of an employee training programme.

Aspects of the work climate primarily affect changes in on-the-job performance as well as improvement in employee attitudes after training. Climate variables have their most direct influence on the extent to which trainees use those behaviours upon which the training focused. However, they also form a network of interrelationships among themselves creating an atmosphere which indirectly impacts training effectiveness.

The hypotheses suggested in this chapter are summarized in Figures 5.5 and 5.6. They show two different patterns of influence similar to the two patterns which emerged with respect to trainee background characteristics. The first, Figure 5.5, shows the effects of organizational climate on transfer of training to the workplace (see note below figure)

The pattern which has been used throughout the STD model distinguishes between transfer of general and specific behaviours. Specific behaviour transfer involves what is called lateral transfer of the same exact principles from classroom to workplace. The alternative is a generalized application of these principles. The environmental effects of the organization on specific transfer are almost entirely attributable to the extent to which management and supervisors model that behaviour on the job.

General behaviour transfer, on the other hand, is determined by the indirect effects of both management and co-workers modelling these general behaviours and evidence of employee empowerment. These climate factors are felt through their influence on attitudes toward previous training. Both of these transfer effects are shown in Figure 5.5.

Figure 5.6 portrays a very different picture. This diagram summarizes the manner in which organizational climate factors influence the extent to which training programmes result in attitude changes pertinent to the training topic. The effects are indirect, working again through their influence on training attitudes.

The environmental focus is still upon the extent to which management models the target behaviour on the job. Specific behaviour modelling is influenced by the general support provided by the workers. General behaviour modelling is again influenced by perceptions of physical conditions and employee empowerment.

Overall, organizational climate has an important role in determining the effects of a training programme; however, it has less significance if the view of training effectiveness is confined to only knowledge

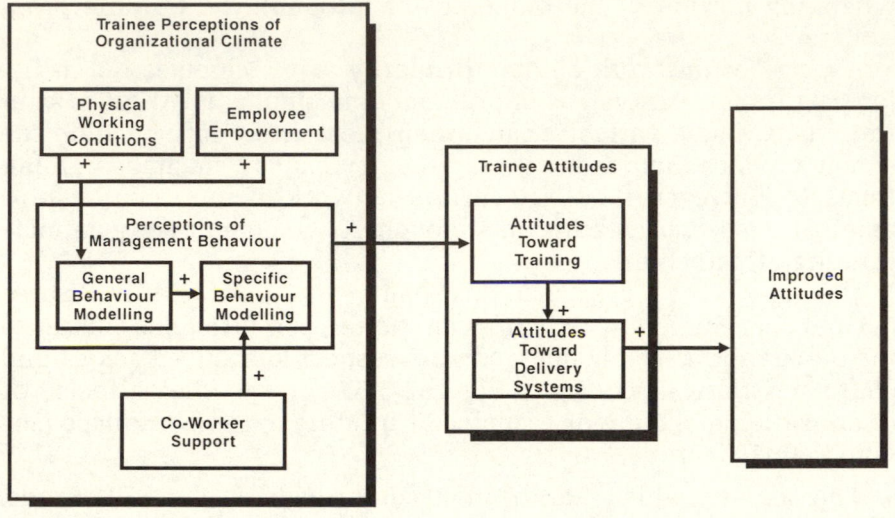

Figure 5.6   *A summary of the effects of organizational climate on attitude*

gains even though some evidence of such impact has been noted. The more isolated effects on knowledge retention which have been identified parallel the attitude patterns shown in Figure 5.6. However, it is clear that these are not replicated and will not withstand rigorous standards for final inclusion in the STD model.

An argument has been made for the relevance of these conclusions in designing instructional programmes for both adult and pre-adult learning situations. This can be accomplished by recognizing the role of the larger, receiving environment in addition to the immediate classroom environment. Given this premise, one can modify both the descriptive and prescriptive organizational climate propositions to adapt to these settings.

Applying knowledge of the organizational climate to instructional design procedures

Designers who make use of information they have about the trainees' work environment will be orienting their programmes toward on-the-job application. To a great extent this information is used in designing the summative evaluation and the implementation and control procedures. These are programme components that are often neglected in favour of concentrating on delivery procedures and instructional materials.

In situations with a climate which does not promote transfer of training or foster improved attitudes, designers may include additional learning activities which provide role models and emphasize the positive consequences of the desired behaviour. This approach attempts to create a substitute environment to serve as internal support for the employee back on the job.

Next steps

This chapter completes the full explanation of the major parts of the two STD models, conceptual and procedural. As such, the models address both theory and practice. Integration of the STD propositions is still a problem.

A training designer is faced with problems not only of analysis but also of synthesis of a new, coordinated programme. These programmes usually are directed toward one or more of the four major training outcomes: knowledge retention, attitude change, general behaviour improvement, specific behaviour improvement. Consequently, one must combine a large number of propositions relevant to each target outcome.

This task can be complicated, at best. Chapter 6 will sythesize the STD propositions into coordinated procedures directed toward attaining each of these four training outcomes. Simply – what do I need to do if my programme is only to lead to knowledge retention? How can I be assured of changing attitudes? If the most important outcome is having people behave differently on the job, what kind of programme should I put together?

6 A Synthesis of Systemic Training Design Procedures

The explanation of STD to this point has been driven by the results of quantitative research and a more qualitative analysis of practice. The conclusions have been transformed into an organized theoretical structure as well as a set of design procedures. The very nature of this ordered arrangement and the genesis of the tenets would distress some who view systemic design as the antithesis of systematic design rather than a complementary approach. Moreover, using flowchart-like diagrams would surely symbolize, to those with this orientation, a rigidity typically associated with commitment to scientific method and positivism.

STD is a departure from traditional design, but one which still relies on the systematic roots. This position is especially apparent at the point one synthesizes the many details into a more cohesive set of procedures. The question then surfaces of the philosophical and theoretical compatibility of the systemic and systematic approaches. Can there be a true overlap?

Since the primary aim of this chapter is to synthesize the various descriptive and prescriptive propositions into a coherent approach to designing instruction, the propriety of merging two seemingly divergent orientations will be addressed once again. The focus of this argument is primarily philosophical, addressing the underlying tensions between those who view instructional design fundamentally in the scientific tradition and those who view it as essentially art. Indirectly, these alignments can affect the manner in which one synthesizes design procedures and evaluates the results.

REVISITING THE DICHOTOMY BETWEEN SYSTEMIC AND SYSTEMATIC DESIGN

The intrinsic nature of instructional design

Science and art
Davies (1991) distinguishes between the systemic approach as an art and the systematic approach as a craft, emphasizing the different roots in the two words. ('Systematic' has a Latin root referring to

order; 'systemic' has a Greek root meaning organized whole). Davies sees science and craft as two similar elements stressing clarity, replication and planning. Conversely, the exercise of art involves spontaneity, abstraction and creativity. While concluding that instructional development encompasses all three–art, craft and science–Davies opts for an art emphasis.

These comparisons are similar to Hlynka and Nelson's (1991) contrast of engineering and orchestration views of the instructional design process. The systematic approach is engineered and efficient based upon an organized plan of production. The systemic approach is a strategy which accounts for many players involved in simultaneous performances. There is 'no one best move'.

The dispute may parallel the distinctions some make between theory and practice, description and prescription. On the one hand, the concerns are with knowledge for the sake of knowledge. On the other, the emphasis is on imaginative and inventive applications in social settings.

Practical sciences

The science/art controversy can be expanded by considering the implications of a particular class of sciences, the practical sciences. Wallace (1979) defines a practical science (or the practical disciplines) as those devoted to the investigation of 'what is to be done to make the world a better place to live in' (p263). Theoretical sciences, rooted in theoretical knowledge, are typically unconcerned with everyday application. Instructional design is by this definition a practical discipline rather than primarily a theoretical discipline. Moreover, since instructional design's sources of knowledge relate to a great extent to causal inferences, it can also be considered a practical science. This argument is supported by instructional design's extensive research foundation in the areas of communication theory, behavioural and cognitive learning theory and instructional theory (Richey, 1986). While design is also rooted in general systems theory, this knowledge base is not typically viewed as rooted in research; therefore, its influence does not contribute to design's position as a practical science.

Wallace (1979) also compares science to art. Art, in his mind, covers those situations in which 'the knower' seeks knowledge only for the purpose of practice, with no theoretical intentions at all. While such an explanation may apply to some practitioners, it does not accurately characterize the instructional design field as a whole which is also interested in the sources of effective design and the nature of human learning. Some may be primarily interested in practice and secondarily in theory; others are equally interested in both. These situations still warrant classification, according to Wallace, as a practical science.

Classifying instructional design in this fashion is important to the central discussion of the propriety of joining systematic and systemic design procedures. Wallace (1979) discusses the relationship between theoretical and practical knowledge in a manner which can be directly applied to a relationship between systematic and systemic orientations:

> But theoretical and practical are not necessarily spoken of in a mutually exclusive way. The intellect that is perfected by these two types of knowledge is one and the same, and there are degrees of both theoretical and practical knowledge. So it is possible to differentiate between the actually practical and the formally practical, and between the completely theoretical and the formally theoretical. Likewise there can be some overlapping: we can have theoretical knowledge of something performable or doable, and we can even make our theories in some sense practical. In the former case, such theoretical knowledge is not of great value unless it is actually ordered to operation, and hence it is said to be primarily practical and only secondarily theoretical; in the latter case, the theoretical knowledge is worth having even if it is never ordered to operation, and thus it is said to be primarily theoretical and only secondarily practical. And even in purely practical knowledge we still theorize, which means that in a certain sense practical knowledge presupposes theoretical knowledge, although the reverse is not necessarily true (p264).

The role of systemic and systematic orientations in a practical science framework

If one adopts the position that 1. instructional design is a practical science, and 2. practical knowledge is based upon theoretical knowledge, then certain conclusions can also be made relative to the role of systemic orientations. First, if the systemic orientation is more of an art form than systematic design which is more scientific, one could logically assume the prominence of practical knowledge in the systemic approach. Practical knowledge has more reliance upon what Wallace calls a compositive methodology. The ultimate aim is to apply universal principles to complex operations. The purely systematic approach, on the other hand, relies more upon analytic methods. These either lean toward a theoretical bias or stress the equality of theoretical and practical knowledge.

It could be argued that the best training design requires both compositive and analytical methodologies and as such requires an integration of practical and theoretical knowledge. Therefore, another premise can be formulated. Not only is it possible for systemic and systematic oreintations to co-exist, but their merger is desirable from a philosophical point of view. Practically, it seems that merging the two orientations encourages the benefits of both and correspondingly offsets each of their limitations.

Analysis and synthesis in the STD models and theory

It has been suggested that the STD approach presented here enhances the major phases of traditional instructional systems design procedures. As such, this systemic approach, in the very process of addressing all elements of the larger system in terms of a broader set of variables, encompasses art and science, theory and practice, analysis and synthesis. The fact that it is data-based reflects the fact that the most robust practical sciences are rooted in theoretical knowledge rather than the more subjective interpretation of one's experiences. However, it also avoids the artificial constraints sometimes created when being aligned with a rigid methodology which does not permit speculation and creativity.

The STD approach, however, assumes skilful use of the propositions in each setting to which it is applied. Its use depends upon wisdom and insight, as well as data and logic. This involves integrating the relevant propositions from the various major components (ie, trainee background characteristics, attitudes and perceptions of organizational climate). Likewise using the STD approach involves an application of the individual propositions in a manner which varies with respect to each major type of training outcome. The topic of Chapter 6 is the synthesis of this approach from the details previously presented.

REFINING THE STD CONCEPTUAL SUB-MODELS

Model building and the subsequent theory construction is a complex task when one adheres to the direction provided by data from actual training programmes. The approach taken here is one of analysing all causal relationships identified in light of current research and then refining the models to reflect only those relationships which were precisely replicated. Thus, the initial conceptual sub-models presented in Chapter 2 showed all those relationships among systemic design variables and training outcomes which occurred in the STD foundational research. The in-depth analysis of particular clusters of variables in Chapters 3–5 also considered all observed relationships. At this point the final sub-models are being constructed by eliminating non-replicated relationships and emphasizing those variables which can be supported with the most confidence.

The advantages of this approach are twofold. From a theoretical orientation one strives for replicated results. There is always danger in placing confidence in isolated findings which could be spurious results. Furthermore, practitioners appreciate the ease of dealing with more streamlined models whenever possible.

However, insights can be developed by examining all possible effects of the systemic factors. While it can be risky giving too much credence to a single statistical conclusion, it is nevertheless possible for single findings to direct attention to a potential trend. Consequently, the fuller models shown in Chapter 2 can be useful nonetheless.

The larger issue concerns the heavy (almost exclusive) reliance on data as a basis for design practice. Does this approach characterize an over-reliance on statistical aberrations? Has the STD theory and model development process created a structure even more rigid than the typical ISD orientation?

Data should be used with caution. This is the rationale for emphasizing replicated findings. However, empirical observations are useful as a means of devising explanations for human behaviour, explanations which may not be readily apparent and which are free from the biases and limitations imposed by one's subjectivity.

The remaining sections of this chapter will present the final synthesized versions of the four sub-models which provide the framework for the STD approach and discuss their use in everyday training design practice.

CREATING TRAINING PROGRAMMES DIRECTED TOWARD KNOWLEDGE RETENTION

Knowledge outcomes in training

The nature of knowledge
Greeno (cited in Kozma, 1991) suggests an alternative view of knowledge, defining it as the relationship between an individual and a given situation, either physical or social. This orientation focuses not only on the internal condition of the learner (as is more typical of design theory) but also on the larger environment in which the learner operates. This definition is particularly useful within the context of the STD approach which highlights trainee characteristics and attitudes as well as the nature of the work environment.

This definition can be contrasted to that of Dijkstra (1991) who sees knowledge as 'the internal or external representation of objects and their lawful relationships' (p20). Dijkstra's and Greeno's viewpoints highlight the different positions on the influence of context on one's knowledge. For Greeno, contextual elements shape knowledge; for Dijkstra, knowledge is an extension of objects regardless of their context.

These two stances are reflective of the distinctions between the objectivist and constructivist traditions. The former pictures the world as a place which is 'completely and correctly structured in terms of entities, properties, and relations' (Lakoff, cited in Duffy and Jonassen, 1991, pp7–8). Duffy and Jonassen further explain objectivism as including a notion that meaning is imposed upon us by the nature of this structure. Constructivists, on the other hand, assert that meaning is rooted in experience and in context: 'Each experience with an idea–and the environment of which that idea is a part–becomes part of the meaning of that idea' (Duffy and Jonassen, 1991, p8).

These two conceptions of knowledge have the potential for shaping one's view of instruction and learning. Many instructional designers, if pressed, would have a tendency to reflect Dijkstra's view. The flexibility resulting from Greeno's definition, however, is very compatible with STD theory, even though this theory and its underlying models are conceptualized in a rule-bound format.

Speaking in a more general manner, the notion of changing one's knowledge level (whatever the philosophical orientation) is so commonplace when thinking of education or training programmes that it is typically considered synonymous with 'learning'. Even so, knowledge changes can encompass a range of instructional objectives. Howe (1988) identifies five general areas in which training technology has been applied in industry, three of which are usually included in the knowledge category. These are conceptual knowledge (eg, the knowledge of medical topics required by pharmaceutical representatives), physical knowledge (eg, how to perform a specific physical skill), and process understanding (eg, supervisory decision making). Using Gagne's (1985) classic taxonomy of learned capabilities, the term 'knowledge' would relate to intellectual skills, verbal information, and cognitive strategies.

These 'definitions' of knowledge are descriptions of the types of content encountered. Knowledge, in this light, is a comprehensive category which includes virtually all types of training content, with the exception of attitudinal and performance outcomes, and many would argue that even these types of content emanate from the knowledge category.

Knowledge acquisition and retention
Often it is unclear whether knowledge outcomes refer simply to immediate knowledge acquisition or whether long-term retention of knowledge is implied. The two are considerably different. The speed with which we forget newly learned information is widely known.

Murray and Mosberg (1982) cite classic research which shows 90 per cent of the subjects forgetting nonsense material only 18 seconds after its initial presentation. This was without any practice or rehearsal of the information. With active rehearsal, there are corresponding effects on long-term retention. Moreover, when the rehearsal is varied and the information is encoded into meaningful associations it is more probable that the information will be stored in one long-term memory. However, the general principle of forgetting large amounts of abstract information is still valid for people of all ages.

Memory has been a particularly fertile area of study within the context of adult development. While memory can become more problematic for older adults, the decline varies depending on the type of memory task. Hultsch and Dixon (1990) cite various reasons for such differentiation, including whether the task requires explicit or implicit memory and whether the information is meaningful or related to real-life events.

Adults, even older adults, are more likely to remember information that does not involve conscious recall (Howard and Light, as cited by Hultsch and Dixon, 1990). Typically these implicit memory tasks are most influenced by prior related experiences (Hultsch and Dixon, 1990). While meaningful material is always easier to remember than nonsense, research has shown that for adults information related to everyday activities is more resistant to ageing effects than is one's memory of verbal prose (Blackman, as cited by Hultsch and Dixon, 1990). This seems to be the case regardless of one's ability level. Therefore, for most trainees acquisition of knowledge is enhanced by the fact that the content of the typical training programme is meaningful and directly relevant to their daily work activities.

However, knowledge retention involves more than memory; it also demands recall. It has been documented that often the problems of older adults attributed to memory defects are actually difficulties in information retrieval. The information is stored in long-term memory but not quickly retrieved (Schaie and Willis, cited in Merriam and Caffarella, 1991). Knox (1977) explains this phenomenon in terms of the need to make more connections and cross-references between new and stored information, primarily because over the years more information has been stored.

Knowledge outcomes in the STD approach

In the foundational STD research, knowledge outcomes are gains in knowledge after participation in the training programme. The content represents the range of training knowledge according to Howe (1988)–knowledge of conceptual information, physical skills and processes. Moreover, because these gains represent long-term retention of training information, the adult trainee is exhibiting information retrieval capabilities, as well as giving evidence of long-term storage.

Knowledge acquisition and retention, in this context, always has verbal implications. The knowledge has been demonstrated via paper-and-pencil testing. The information has been acquired through reading and listening.

Even though there were only limited opportunities for practice in retrieving the information during training, one can assume there have been opportunities for reinforcement of the content on the job. To a certain extent this also provides a kind of review of the content. It also reaffirms the relationship between knowledge acquired in a training programme and the trainees' work environment and job experiences.

This pattern of knowledge acquisition and retrieval demonstration is typical of the vast majority of employee training situations. Therefore, the research conclusions drawn from these training programmes should be applicable to the design of many other programmes.

The major factors affecting knowledge outcomes in training

Improving trainees' knowledge level is the easiest outcome to achieve in a training programme–even when viewing knowledge as a reflection of long-term retention rather than immediate acquisition. Of course, few outcomes are really easy to achieve, but knowledge gains appear somewhat simpler because the relevant factors are more under the control of the instructional designer.

The various techniques for influencing knowledge acquisition and retention have been discussed throughout this book. It is possible for many trainee background and attitude factors to influence this process. Likewise, organizational climate variables can also play a role, even though these relationships seem more tenuous. However, when design quality and training intensity are taken into consideration, the number of factors which repeatedly affect knowledge outcomes is reduced. This, of course, is a primary goal of the purposeful design of instruction: to create an effective intervention which mitigates the wide range of factors which can obstruct learning.

Based upon the replicated research findings, knowledge improvement is *directly* influenced by:

- the quality of the instructional design;
- the learner's pre-training knowledge of the target topic; and
- the trainee's attitude toward the delivery system used in the instruction.

Indirectly, gains in trainee knowledge are also influenced by another category of variables:

- the trainee's attitude toward his or her past training experiences.

The final sub-model showing the manner in which these variables explain knowledge gains in a training programme is given in Figure 6.1.

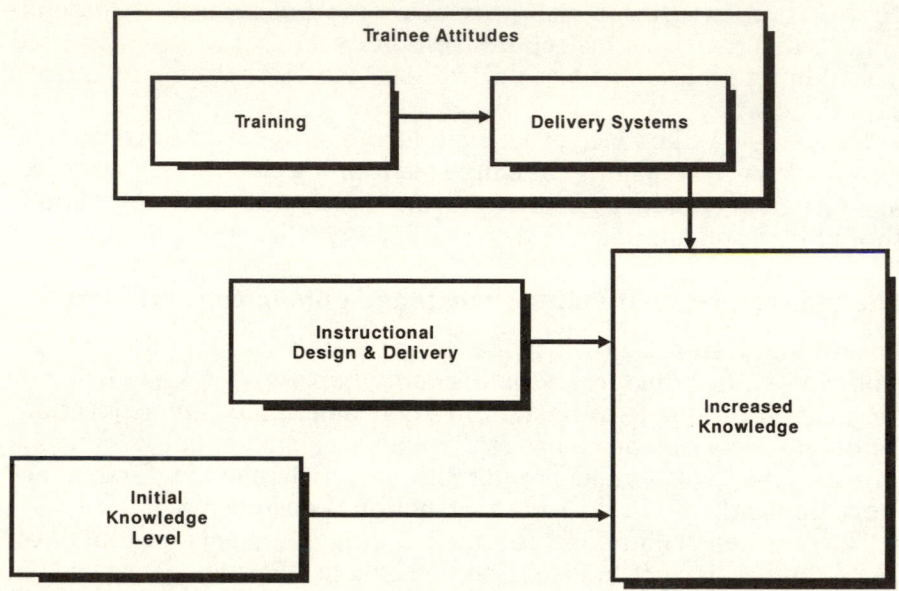

Figure 6.1 *The STD model of replicated factors predicting increased knowledge after training*

While one might argue designers have little control over three of these four factors, it is possible to create interventions which partially counteract the predictable negative effects of unfavourable attitudes toward a chosen delivery system. Moreover, increased attention to motivation design can address unfavourable training attitudes. While the problems with minimal prerequisite skills related to the training content are well-documented in the literature, the remedies are also well documented.

Thus, it is fairly easy, given time and attention, to greatly improve expected training knowledge outcomes. This is shown by the fact that in programmes with the very best designs, 40 per cent of the variance in knowledge was accounted for by non-design factors and 60 per cent by the design features (see Figure C.1 in Appendix C).

Many have assumed that by scrupulously following existing design principles, they would be accounting for far more than 60 per cent of the variance in learning outcomes. This initial influence level, however, seems commendable. The task is complicated. Designers who follow traditional approaches are able to exert more influence over knowledge acquisition than other types of training goals by conscientiously adhering to what we already know about design and learning.

Using the STD approach to expand traditional instructional design to promote knowledge retention

STD provides alternatives which will help designers gain even more control over knowledge acquisition and retention outcomes. These new directions stem primarily from attending to the influence of selected attitudes on trainee motivation: attitudes toward training and attitudes toward the delivery system. There is no indication that these trainee attitudes affect one type of knowledge acquisition more than another; conceptual knowledge, physical knowledge and process knowledge all seem to be influenced by pre-training attitudes.

Addressing learner attitudes in a knowledge-oriented training design
Kozma (1991) offers new evidence pointing to the interactive effects of delivery methodology and delivery media on learner cognitive processes. He argues that micro-level media decisions should be made for specific sections of content and individual learners. Such decisions would be made utilizing information such as the learner's prior knowledge and the structure of the knowledge.

This research and the STD approach are also stressing the importance of whether the trainees simply want to learn in a given manner. This may be more critical for adults than pre-adults. It may also be more critical for shorter-term learning experiences. Regardless of the rationale, media and methodology decisions are critical to the success of a training programme. However, it seems possible that most training delivery systems can be used successfully, even with unsympathetic trainees, if the training directly addresses issues related to learning with that system. A process for accomplishing this task is outlined in the STD prescriptive propositions. These procedures include activities such as: 1. reviewing the advantages of the chosen methods and media in light of the trainees' attitudes, or 2. including provisions for small group interaction, even when using self-instructional media.

Trainees' general attitudes toward training also influence their motivation as well as their opinions of learning with a certain type of training delivery pattern. If the attitudes are favourable, the designer need not worry. If the attitudes are negative, the problem should be tackled to avoid easily hidden influences on knowledge acquisition and retention. These issues can also be seen as motivation design problems.

Addressing trainee differences

The employees' pre-training knowledge level exerts at least as much influence on knowledge outcomes as does the quality of the instructional design. Subsequent gains in knowledge will appear to be less for those with higher amounts of content-relevant information, larger for those with lower entry levels, especially if those lower prerequisite skills are addressed during the course of the training programme.

Trainee prerequisite deficiencies can relate to a number of causes, including:

- a lack of the necessary basic skills;
- an inability to interpret training principles due to a lack of job experience; and
- a lack of recent practice using one's learning skills.

All of these situations can create problems in terms of traditional knowledge acquisition and retention. Moreover, it is not unusual for a lack of ability and experience prerequisites to contribute to motivational and attitudinal prerequisites which also exert major influence on achievement.

Basic skill and learning skill deficiencies especially affect knowledge acquisition tasks which demand verbal abilities: listening, reading and writing. These are primary concerns if the training content is conceptual knowledge. Lack of experience on the job often greatly influences acquisition of physical knowledge and the ability to understand job process subject matter.

On the other hand, a breadth of experience is typically advantageous for the adult trainee. Knowledge retention and retrieval skills are enhanced in training situations for those with considerable work experience because one's memory is more automatic in relation to topics routinely reinforced on the job. For employees with substantial education and training background, this experience also tends to increase their facility as learners.

Dealing with these variations in prerequisite skills should be fairly routine to a skilled designer. Sequencing of content, the use of examples and non-examples, practice, feedback, mnemonics, advance organizers–all exemplify areas in which behavioural and cognitive-based design techniques are used to promote adult learning and information processing. These traditional routes are appropriate for addressing the needs of individual learners based upon their entering knowledge levels, thereby alleviating many individual differences in knowledge acquisition and retention.

When the effects of these background differences are not successfully counteracted, other learner characteristics also may emerge as additional barriers to the learning process. For example, elements of organizational climate can exert a greater influence on trainee attitudes and motivation than would be typical and indirectly deter knowledge acquisition and retention.

CREATING TRAINING PROGRAMMES DIRECTED TOWARD ATTITUDE IMPROVEMENT

Attitude outcomes in training

Attitudes are of interest at times as a factor which influences training outcomes and, at other times, as a type of outcome itself. The focus now is upon the latter orientation. The 'learning' has little to do with facts and figures, but a lot to do with beliefs and feelings. Instruction is not totally independent of factual information, but is more concerned with employee behaviour which reflects a particular attitude. Howe (1988) cites interpersonal skills training as a major area which has traditionally been viewed as an attitude change problem.

Attitudes are typically resistant to change, especially as a result of a short-term intervention unless there has been a cataclysmic event. Nonetheless, training is often directed toward attitude change and its behavioural consequences, and sometimes the anticipated changes are fundamental. For example, receptionists may need to be more polite on the telephone, or employees may need to be more safety-conscious (as was the case in those programmes studied prior to the development of the STD approach).

The nature of attitudinal learning objectives
As an object of learning, attitudes are more than vague feelings. In Chapter 4 Triandis' view of attitudes was presented; he sees attitudes as having cognitive and behavioural components as well as an effective component. Gagne (1985) has also built upon this orientation in his discussion of attitudinal outcomes of learning. He stresses the tendency of individuals to adjust a given attitude to make it consistent with their other attitudes and understandings. This provides some evidence of the cognitive, rational component of an attitude. The affective, more emotional component is shown in the presence of feelings, and the behavioural component is shown by those actions precipitated by the attitude.

The more pertinent questions relate to attitude change rather than definition. Gagne (1985) summarized this literature by identifying three kinds of learning situations which produce attitude changes. The first situation resembles classical conditioning in which emotional reactions are produced by accidental pairing of two stimulus conditions, such as hearing a favourable word with certain first names and unfavourable words with others.

Attitudes can also be changed through reinforcement, such as developing positive attitudes toward school if one is successful. Finally, attitudes are changed through human behaviour modelling. In these situations, learning is demonstrated by imitating the actions and the choices of other people who are respected, admired, or have a great deal of credibility. The most common example of attitude change via behaviour modelling is the manner in which young children are influenced by their parents' actions and values.

Gagne (1985) has used these views of attitude change when identifying the internal and external conditions of learning necessary to achieve attitude objectives. Internal conditions include the learner understanding the necessary prerequisite concepts and remembering the necessary information. External conditions include the presence of someone modelling the target attitude and reinforcing the desirable related actions.

The extent to which a cognitive base is required for attitude change is usually of interest to educators. Gagne (1991) has also addressed this issue, concluding that 'while intellectual skills may be prerequisite to attitude formation in some instances, they are not themselves the attitude, nor do they insure the learning of an attitude' (p143).

Similarly, there is a question as to the relationship between attitudes and behaviour. Do positive attitudes precede positive behaviour? Does behaviour precede attitude change? Is there any relationship at all between the two? The mixed literature on this topic has been previously noted. Nevertheless, the training industry typically expects on-the-job behaviour to be the ultimate evidence of one's attitudes and beliefs. In addition, training designers often strive for attitude changes as a follow-up to cognitively-oriented instruction.

The major STD factors affecting attitude changes after training

Factors with direct influence

Unlike knowledge acquisition and retention, attitude improvement is more difficult to impact in a training programme. Among other reasons, this difficulty stems from the large influence of systemic factors, factors which are not typically addressed in traditional instructional design techniques and procedures. The role of these systemic factors appears to be almost the exact opposite of their part in knowledge acquisition and retention. With respect to knowledge, systemic factors directly account for no more than 40 per cent of the outcome variance; in relation to attitude changes, the *design factors* seem to directly account for no more than 35–40 per cent of the outcomes variance with the remaining variance attributed to systemic factors (see Figures C.3–C.5).

Figure 6.2 presents the most conservative explanation of employee attitude changes after participation in a training programme. *Given the presence of high quality instructional design and delivery*, two things seem to occur:

- the instruction itself accounts for a large part of the outcomes, but it appears to explain only a maximum of 40 per cent of the variation in training outcomes; and
- a person's level of related knowledge exerts some influence on attitudes change, increasing the instructional effects slightly beyond the 40 per cent mark.

The other factors *directly* influencing attitude change parallel the model of knowledge acquisition. They are:

- the trainees' attitudes toward the instructional delivery systems; and
- the employees' expressions of their pre-training attitudes.

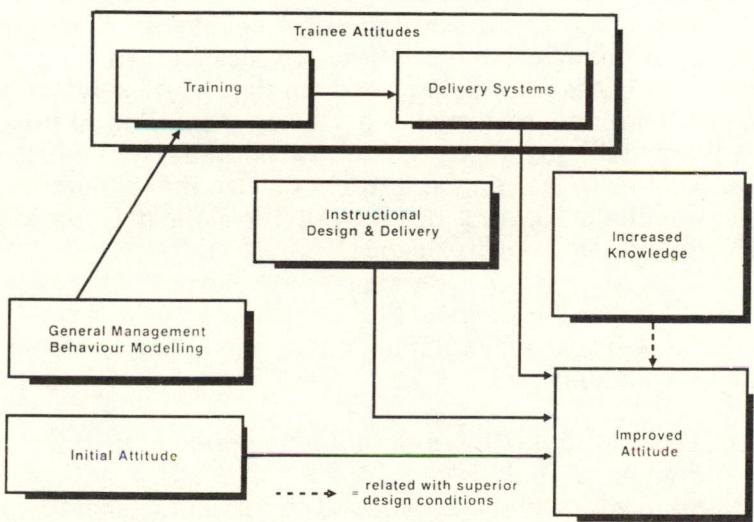

Figure 6.2 *The STD model of replicated factors predicting improved attitudes after training*

The role of trainees' initial attitudes is identical in many respects to the role played in relation to knowledge improvement. This is true with respect to delivery system attitudes where positive attitudes are more likely to lead to ultimate change in attitudes after training; it is also true with respect to the effects of the trainee's established attitudes which are targeted in the training programme. One is more likely to see evidence of some improvement among those employees with the more *negative* pre-training attitudes.

There is also evidence here of another pattern which is also seen in each of the other STD conceptual sub-models. In those learning situations where the instructional design controls a larger portion of the outcome variance, the effects of learner's pre-training capabilities (be they knowledge, skills or attitudes) are somewhat suppressed. Conversely, when design effects appear to be less pronounced, the pre-training capabilities are more predominant in terms of their impact. This latter case is the situation with attitude changes; trainees' initial attitudes repeatedly carry greater weight than the design itself.

This principle is especially clear in relation to knowledge retention. The quality of the instructional design has profound effects on knowledge acquisition. However, while the pre-training knowledge level is still important, it has less impact when the design is better. On the other hand, when the design is less rigorous, or when the training is less intensive, initial knowledge levels again have a more pronounced impact. It seems that the instructional intervention has not counteracted trainee characteristic effects. This same pattern exists with respect to both attitude and behaviour changes after training even though the variations in design effects are less extreme. In this case the data are reminding us of a fundamental purpose of instructional design and formal education: to provide a process which will compensate for those many factors which form inherent barriers to learning and to emphasize those factors which naturally facilitate learning. Moreover, the data help us identify which factors fit into each category.

Factors with indirect influence

Attitude changes also are explained by the somewhat hidden effects of two other factors:

- the trainees' attitudes toward previous training in which they have participated; and
- the extent to which management and supervisors generally model the target attitudes and behaviours.

A major difference between the systemic design of knowledge-oriented learning and the design of instruction directed toward attitude change is the indirect influence of behaviour modelling. While it has no assured effects on knowledge retention, behaviour modelling does have a consistent influence on attitude change. The fact that the STD attitude change sub-model highlights both training attitudes and management behaviour modelling is not surprising; it is perfectly consistent with Gagne's perceptions of the attitude change research. These two factors are examples of reinforcement and human behaviour modelling in the workplace.

Using the STD approach to expand traditional instructional design to promote attitude change

Expanding the internal and external conditions of learning
It is easiest to comprehend the rationale for STD design tactics directed toward attitude change by once again thinking of systemic training design as an extension of Gagne's (1985) explanation of internal and external conditions of learning. Attitudes are, by definition, internal states with evidence of their existence provided in terms of external behaviour. While traditional design methods are useful in ensuring acquisition of the cognitive prerequisites of attitudes, a key value of systemic procedures comes in addressing the full range of external conditions which serve as precursors of the anticipated attitudinal outcome. These procedures are based upon an assumption that a particular attitude toward a given person, object or event is dependent upon attitudes toward other persons, objects and events. The most effective instructional design, then, will address the entire network of attitudes in addition to developing the attitude's cognitive base. As such, one is addressing an expanded set of internal conditions to affect attitude change. It seems sound and predictable that more variables need to be addressed in the designs of instruction directed toward those outcomes which are typically more difficult to achieve.

Building upon knowledge acquisition and retention design procedures
Gagne has suggested that related knowledge is not a universal prerequisite to attitude change. The position reflected in the final STD sub-model is that while knowledge is not absolutely essential, in the best designed programmes it does enhance attitude change. (The dotted line connecting 'increased knowledge' with 'improved attitude' in Figure 6.2 shows the relationship between these two key training outcomes that appears to occur in those instructional programmes which are either more intensive or have the superior design). In situations where a connection does exist, not only is the acquisition of relevant knowledge predictive of attitude change, but attitude change is also then influenced by those same systemic design factors

and those same STD procedures recommended for affecting knowledge outcomes.

However, with the exception of the influence of management behaviour modelling, the final attitude change sub-model has the same components and the same relationships among these components as does the final knowledge retention sub-model (compare Figures 6.1 and 6.2). Attitudes toward previous training and training delivery systems again create a chain-of-attitude effects pattern. These attitudes, combined with the instructional design quality effects, have a critical influence on both knowledge retention and attitude change.

Addressing management behaviour in attitude training

Attitude improvement designs also need to confront issues related to management behaviour and pre-training attitudes, and these two factors may themselves be related.

> Nearly every group to which we belong, from our immediate families to our society as a whole, has an implicit or explicit set of beliefs, attitudes, and behaviors which are considered appropriate for its members . . . groups regulate beliefs, attitudes, and behaviors through the use of social reward and punishment (Bem, 1970, p79).

One task of the designer of attitude-oriented training is to determine exactly which groups influence the behaviour of the particular trainees in their programmes. This research indicates that management and supervisors are the persons who exert the most influence on post-training attitudes and behaviour. In most situations they not only influence social rewards and punishments, but probably control economic rewards and punishments as well. Therefore, it is logical to believe that they also exert influence on pre-training attitudes similar to their sway on post-training attitudes.

The practical question is 'So, what can I do about that?' Training may not be able to change the root problem, but it can compensate for its results if they do not coincide with the goals of the training programme. Jonassen *et al.* (1991) present a framework which can help address this problem in a training programme. They identify and describe instructional strategies and tactics appropriate for contextualizing instruction. Attending to issues such as the lack of management behaviour modelling in the workplace is an example of contextualizing a training programme.

One particular strategy identified by Jonassen *et al.* (1991) is 'Relating the goals of instruction to the learner's needs' (p82). This is one of the 'events of instruction' which is prominent in the work of both Robert Gagne and Leslie Briggs. One could extend their suggested instructional tactic of explaining the purpose or relevance of the content by analysing the applicability of the training content in light of the pressures and expectations in the work environment.

Designers should not treat this phase as a mere introduction to the 'real' training content. Instead, they should construct instructional events which emphasize ways of overcoming those barriers on the job which prevent employees from behaving in the recommended fashion. These instructional events would then also function as part of a reinforced motivation design in the programme.

Alternative delivery techniques may also be required to assure opportunities for trainees to explore their own reactions to working with these barriers on the job. Role playing or video-taped dramatizations followed by debate and discussion sessions may be appropriate. Others may find using simulations or case studies helpful. Designers and company officials should determine whether or not it would be advantageous for management representatives to be included in these sessions. If so, quality circles or focus group strategies might be utilized.

Confronting pre-training attitudes
It may be that by directly dealing with employee perceptions of management behaviour, negative pre-training attitudes will be addressed simultaneously. Again, acknowledging and building upon these attitudes becomes a combined contextualization and motivation design process. The emphasis given to existing attitudes depends primarily upon how negative the typical employee is. The most extreme cases would have very negative staff with a generally low morale; these situations may require intensive intervention related to these issues alone before the core content of the attitude-oriented training is introduced. These interventions may use similar types of instructional events as used in addressing issues related to management behaviour modelling. Creative approaches are often needed, and clearly it is crucial that such instruction be grounded in a valid needs assessment.

CREATING TRAINING PROGRAMMES DIRECTED TOWARD IMPROVING ON-THE-JOB BEHAVIOUR

There are two major training outcome components of the STD conceptual models which concern on-the-job behaviour. One deals with specific behaviour, those workplace performances which directly parallel the training recommendations. The second concerns general behaviour in the workplace, a more universal application of the training principles to a variety of situations. Both of these goals can be viewed as transfer of training phenomena. Their attainment is essential to any successful training programme, but achieving such objectives demands different design procedures than those suggested for knowledge acquisition and retention or attitude improvement.

Transfer of training

Near and far transfer

Viewing on-the-job behaviour as being either specifically or generally related to the training one has just completed is comparable to viewing transfer of training in terms of near and far transfer. Royer (1979) emphasizes these two constructs, but stresses the importance of seeing transfer as a continuum rather than as two separate phenomena. Near transfer is analogous to training-specific behaviour on the job and suggests a similarity between the training task and the task as it is applied. The context is similar and the task is identical.

Far transfer, on the other hand, involves generalizing the task to contexts other than those presented in the training. General on-the-job behaviour outcomes are akin to far transfer. However, some might say that it is not far transfer in its purest form since the application is still confined to one's work context. For example, if an employee were taught principles of caution in terms of walking safely in a manufacturing plant and he or she then followed these rules religiously back on the job, near transfer would be demonstrated. If that same person then applied those principles of caution to other aspects of work behaviour, far transfer would be demonstrated, even though it was still in the same environment. If this trainee now goes home and applies the principles of caution to daily household tasks, this would be far transfer that was even more generalized.

Clark and Voogel (1985) relate the type of transfer to the types of skills transferred. Specifically, procedural knowledge is more likely to lend itself to near transfer than is declarative knowledge,[1] which tends to involve far transfer. Moreover, they assert that in most situations one type of transfer tends to be achieved at the expense of the other. One can speculate on whether this tends to occur in employee training situations. If it does there are important design ramifications.

Transfer prerequisites

Ripple and Drinkwater (1982) assert that the two major requirements of transfer are learning and retention. The dependency between knowledge acquisition and behavioural change is logical and is supported by conventional wisdom. However, the actual nature of this relationship between knowledge and behaviour has not been verified with respect to adults in training situations.

Clark and Voogel (1985) identify many of the common tenets of transfer of training which have emerged from both the behavioural and cognitive orientations to learning. First is the identical elements model of transfer. This model suggests that transfer of training is dependent upon the extent to which the training context is similar to the application context. In the minds of many trainers, this speaks to the practicality of the training programme. The more practical programme is closer to 'the real world' and easier to apply to daily problems. In other words, near transfer (or training-specific on-the-job behaviour) is facilitated. However, the research literature as presented by Clark and Voogel (1985) also points out the propensity for more generalized instruction, which relies less on rule explanation and practice, to provide more support for far transfer.

The effects of particular learner characteristics on transfer are important to the design process. While high general ability is the best overall predictor of transfer of all types, the particular importance of past experience with similar tasks has been shown in relation to near transfer (Clark and Voogel, 1985). It would appear then that specific on-the-job behaviour would be affected by the trainee's work experience. The more general application of knowledge might be related to one's fluid abilities as evidenced by one's flexibility and adaptability to novel learning tasks. This latter aptitude is more characteristic of one's general ability levels.

While it is usually assumed that knowledge acquisition and retention is prerequisite to transfer of training, the question of the role of learner attitudes in this regard is rarely addressed in the literature. The assumption, however, behind most attitude instruction has already been recognized–that there will be a payoff in terms of employee performance. Thus, the world of practitioners operates as if transfer of training were directly dependent upon both knowledge retention and retrieval and positive attitudes. This premise is addressed in STD theory.

The major STD factors affecting near transfer of training

Overview
The theoretical distinctions made in the literature between near and far transfer appear to be substantiated in the training arena. The STD sub-models on transfer clearly show disparate patterns of factors which influence these two types of training outcomes. The near transfer model is more concise and focused. It is shown in Figure 6.3.

There are three principles of effectiveness that should be kept in mind when thinking about near transfer from short-term training programmes to the workplace. Near transfer is dependent upon:

- the quality of the programme's basic instructional design;

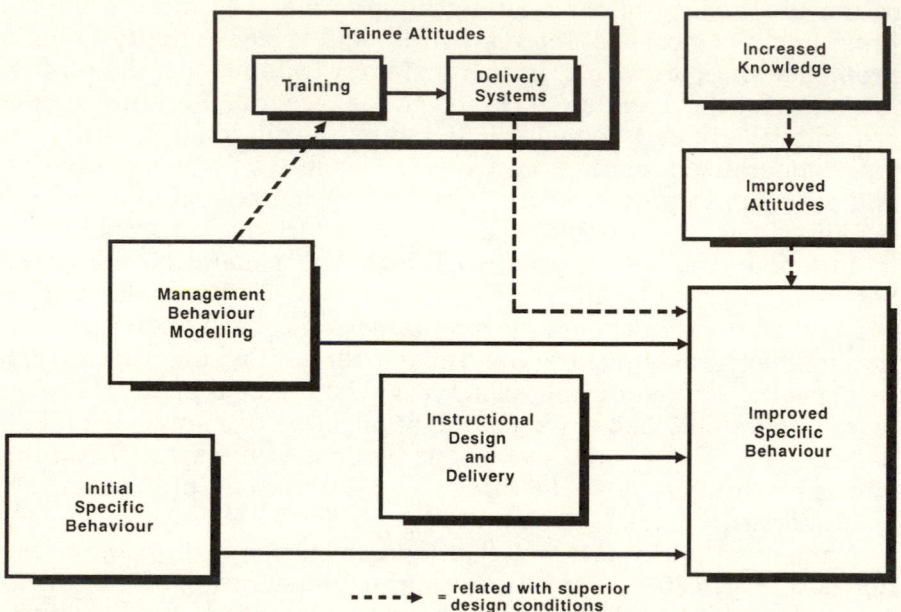

Figure 6.3 *The STD model of replicated factors predicting near transfer of training*

- the extent to which employees are already inclined to those behaviours; and
- the extent to which management supports those behaviours.

The instructional design effects on near transfer

First, let us consider the effects of design quality. While the nature of the instructional design is important in all situations, its impact is magnified with respect to transfer. With quality design one can be assured of trainee gains in both knowledge and attitude improvement. If this foundation has been established, trainee knowledge and attitudes substantially impact on-the-job behaviour. Without the highest quality design, near transfer is overwhelmingly dependent upon the established work habits of the employee and, to a lesser extent, upon the work environment.

Clark and Voogel (1985) would also attribute the large design effects to the nature of the content. Many training programmes concentrate on procedural (or process) knowledge. The content entails step-by-step explanations of those performances which are expected on the job. This instruction is largely dependent upon the given work context. Clark and Voogel also maintain that traditional systematic design models are more influenced by tenets of behavioural learning theory and more applicable to instruction focusing on procedural tasks. Therefore, they would assert that near transfer to that same environment is facilitated by quality instruction using systematic procedures.

If the chained effects of knowledge and attitude improvements are felt on the outcomes of a particular training programme, the sub-model of relevant design factors, in turn, would incorporate the indirect effects of trainee attitudes toward their previous training experiences and the various delivery systems. (Again note those sub-model components in Figure 6.3 connected to the other parts of the diagram with dotted lines. These show the implied impact of trainee attitudes as well as the effects of previous knowledge and attitude changes).

When the quality of the instructional design is not high enough to guarantee the impact of knowledge retention and positive attitudes, near transfer is more difficult to achieve as a natural product of the training programme. In these situations, one can be assured of the heavy influence of pre-training habits and the extent to which management and supervisors demonstrate the target behaviour. In fact, this research has shown that these and other systemic factors may account for up to 80 per cent of the variance in trainee behaviour back on the job when the instructional design and delivery factors do not control the behavioural outcomes of training.

The effects of habit and environment on near transfer
Further discussion of the implications of one's work environment and work habits is warranted. It seems reasonable to expect an employee's pre-training work habits to inhibit near transfer if they do not complement the thrust of the training programme. However, as was the case with both knowledge improvement and attitude change, those who show the most transfer are the employees whose work habits seem to be most lacking. Perhaps the effects of training are most obvious in such situations and less obvious in those situations in which the typical on-the-job behaviour is more acceptable.

However, regardless of the nature of the employee's pre-training work habits, the behaviour of the supervisors is critical as a facilitator of near transfer, even when there is superior training design. Noe and Schmitt's (1986) general concept of 'environmental favourability' is again relevant. Since training effectiveness with respect to near transfer varies so much depending on the design excellence, in those situations in which the design exerts less control a favourable climate can seem to be almost sufficient in itself to facilitate specific behaviour change. However, transfer appears to be based not so much on specific behaviour modelling, but modelling of any type of behaviour, either specifically or generally-related to the training. Such management behaviour shows overall support of the performance targeted in the training programme. This seems adequate as a vehicle for prompting behaviour change provided that the necessary knowledge is available and the trainee is positively oriented toward the topic. The environment serves as a cue to stimulate recall of both the pertinent knowledge and the behaviour, but it does not seem to create a condition in which the performances can be actually learned through imitation alone without some instruction.

Instead of functioning as on-the-job training, routinely supportive management behaviour simply promotes positive rather than negative transfer by facilitating employee application of prior instruction. Non-supportive behaviour, on the other hand, 'teaches' employees lessons which contradict the training and thereby inhibits task performance (Ripple and Drinkwater, 1982). Such lessons, whether they are positive or negative, need not be based only upon replication of training-specific behaviour; generally-related behaviour makes the point as well.

The major STD factors affecting far transfer

Overview
Often trainers are also hopeful that their instruction will result in far transfer of training; they want trainees to use the principles taught in a variety of situations in the workplace. As with near transfer, this is an instance of lateral transfer. Gagne (1974) defines lateral transfer as the application of prior learning to tasks at a similar level of complexity rather than in more complex situations. However, with respect to far transfer, while the training programme may address *representative* situations, the intent is for employee on-the-job behaviour to change in many respects.

When designing training programmes from a systemic orientation, far transfer demands a very different process than is required when designing instruction directed toward near transfer since many more systemic variables are addressed. The far transfer sub-model is shown in Figure 6.4.

Effective far transfer training design is the most complex type of design, building upon all factors involved in the other three major training outcomes. Moreover, the importance of directly addressing this wide range of factors can not be overemphasized, since it appears that approximately 60 per cent of the variance in a given training outcome can be controlled by the systemic factors. This leaves only approximately 40 per cent of the transfer outcome determined by the quality of the training design. This pattern is similar to

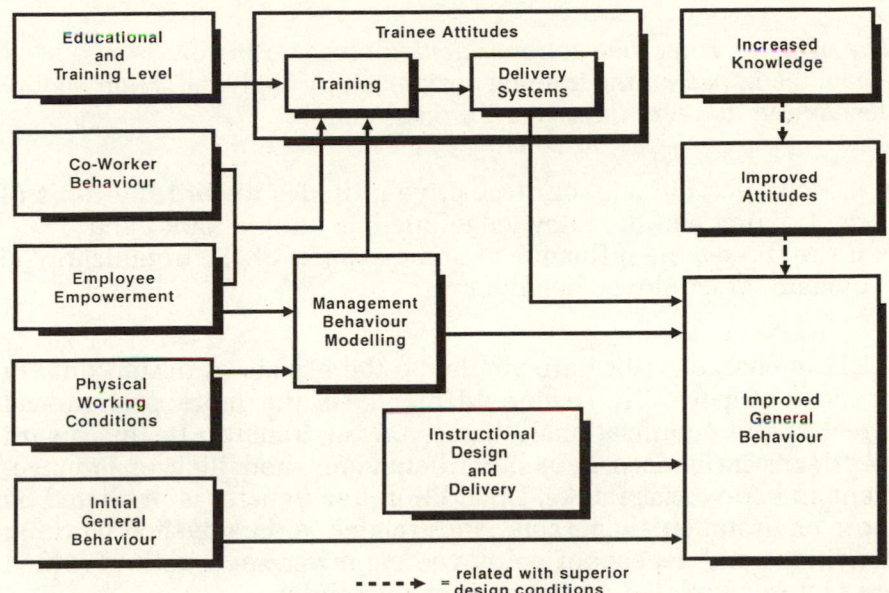

Figure 6.4   *The STD model of replicated factors predicting far transfer of training*

the pattern observed in attitude change situations. The far transfer sub-model reflects a complex network of important elements. Like knowledge retention and attitude change, the outcomes are directly influenced by:

- employee attitudes toward training delivery systems;
- general management behaviour modelling; and
- pre-training work habits.

In those programmes with the highest design quality, far transfer is also influenced directly by:

- those attitudes which have been changed by the training.

However, there are a great many other factors which indirectly influence far transfer in a training situation and they are primarily responsible for the general complexity of the sub-model. They are:

- the trainee's education and training background;
- a variety of organizational climate characteristics; and
- the trainee's knowledge related to the target performances.

What are the implications of these relationships for the training designer?

The effects of the instructional design on far transfer

Again the impact of the training design quality is pivotal. High quality design and delivery does two things:

- it facilitates the impact of positive attitudes toward the topic of the training and the knowledge one has on this topic; and
- it suppresses the influence of some aspects of the organizational climate on employee behaviour.

These characteristics are similar to the effects of design quality on near transfer. The major difference is the more pronounced effect of the organizational climate on far transfer. In this regard transfer is influenced by general behaviour modelling of management and co-workers alike. In addition, far transfer is predicted by those environmental characteristics related to the physical working conditions and aspects of employee empowerment, both of which are factors unrelated on the surface to training.

The effects of context on far transfer

The literature tends to speak to the value of decontextualized instruction if far transfer is the goal. However, the STD model cites the sustained influence of work context on the general application of training principles. How can this be explained?

In non-training instructional settings, far transfer tends to refer to application of knowledge in widely diverse settings. For example, if someone learns to compute the area of various geometric shapes in the abstract, transfer might involve calculating yardage needed for a sewing project or determining the amount of turf necessary for a landscape design. The essential task is the same, even though the stimuli vary. In addition, the contexts vary. In employee training programmes transfer, even far transfer, takes place in the same general work environment in which the training occurs. The essential task is the same, and even though the stimuli which generate performance vary, the general context is still the same. The work environment is an integral part of both the task learned and the transfer task. It is not unexpected then that environmental variables would be more prominent in determining training effectiveness with respect to far transfer.

The effects of trainee differences on far transfer

The literature reviewed by Clark and Voogel (1985) emphasizes the role of fluid intelligence in far transfer and the role of crystallized, more experience-based intelligence in near transfer. While this latter phenomenon was not supported by the STD research, the education and training background of the trainee does play a role in far transfer, and this measure is usually highly correlated with fluid intelligence. In the systemic approach to training design one object of addressing a wider range of variables is to be assured that the design interventions counteract the typical effects of trainee background characteristics. With respect to far transfer, the most complex training outcome, it is not possible to totally offset the effects of these traits, even though their impact is only of an indirect nature.

The greater role of learner characteristics in far transfer is also evident in the consistent influence of trainee attitudes, even with high quality design. This can be contrasted to near transfer which is only influenced by trainee attitudes indirectly through their roles in attitude change and knowledge retention. Trainee attitudes toward the delivery system used and toward past training exert much the same influence on far transfer as they do on knowledge retention and attitude change. When the effects of these learner attitudes are combined with the effects of relevant background characteristics and the profound effects of existing habits, the general impact of learner characteristics can rival that of design and institutional effects on transfer. This may be a learning phenomenon peculiar to adults as a consequence of their having personalities and habits which tend to be set.

Using the STD approach to expand traditional instructional design to promote transfer of training

Current approaches to teaching to transfer
Using the existing research literature base, there is a general consensus as to the design techniques which promote transfer of learning. Gagne *et al.* (1988) summarize those techniques which are most commonly used when teaching for transfer:

- teach foundational intellectual skills in a meaningful context to provide possible cues for use in future retrieval;
- provide practice in retrieving prerequisite information and spaced review of the information and skills which are prerequisite to transfer; and
- provide practice in applying what has been learned in a variety of novel situations.

These tactics are explicitly directed toward transfer of training. Butterfield and Nelson (1989) note that most designers simply take the position that transfer is best served by 'full task-specific instruction on the training task' (p25). However, they differ from those who use a generic approach and consequently advocate using additional methods to promoting transfer of learning. These strategies include:

- emphasizing inferential reasoning and metacognitive instruction (eg, self-interrogation, self-monitoring, self-directing and self-checking); and
- adding feedback to the unaided transfer attempt and, when necessary, providing additional prompts which may be carefully sequenced and structured to make the transfer process more efficient.

Finally, Sternberg and Wagner (1989) have enhanced the views of teaching to transfer through their experiments with adults on the transfer of school learning to job settings. They introduce a particular form of practical knowledge called 'tacit knowledge'. Tacit knowledge is that which is seldom explicitly taught, or even verbalized, but is acquired through job experience and is critical to job success. They propose that tacit knowledge is a fundamental ingredient in transfer in the 'real world', at least with respect to adult learning and use of practical information.

In summary, teaching to transfer in work-related situations involves providing learning activities which focus on multiple contexts, retrieval practice and review, inferential reasoning, feedback and prompts and the use of practical wisdom about effective routines and mores on the job. These measures are derived from current research literature. What else does STD methodology offer?

General systemic transfer procedures

The tactics just discussed primarily fit into the traditional notions of design. They address ways of creating and prescribing instructional actions which result in learning; they are process-oriented. The two atypical topics above–inferential reasoning and tacit knowledge–introduce new content rather than describe techniques of presenting content. In some respects these components are more similar to systemic factors than are the others.

Systemic variables reach beyond the confines of the target training content; they reach beyond activities which manipulate aspects of this content. Systemic variables encompass the entire range of factors which impinge upon learning, including aspects of the training supra-system as well as design tactics. However, this range varies considerably depending upon the type of transfer intended. Near transfer in a training context is simpler to address than is far transfer. Near transfer can be achieved by following those same procedures recommended for changing attitudes. In some respects this supports the position that transfer is best promoted by simply providing full instruction on the task.

Systemic procedures which promote far transfer

Far transfer, on the other hand, depends not only upon the same factors pertinent to near transfer, but additionally relies to a greater extent upon the nature of the work climate and the educational background of the trainee. The additional design implications here pertain to trainee motivation, reinforcement in the workplace, and direct practice on-the-job using the target content to solve problems.

The prescriptive propositions pertaining to organizational climate presented in Chapter 5 are particularly relevant with respect to far transfer. These included discussions of management training, using performance prompts in the workplace, providing substitute (or additional) role models and emphasizing consequences of the recommended behaviour.

To achieve far transfer goals, designers should also be cognizant of the education and training background of the trainees. If the training population is generally lacking in this regard, it has previously been suggested that increased attention be given to design aspects, such as examples, practice exercises and non-traditional test formats. In addition, it may be important to be more flexible in terms of the time allowed for training with more opportunities provided for refresher and review sessions.

Confronting established work habits
Both near and far transfer are dependent upon the effects of the employee's pre-training work habits. Habits become more stable as adults age. There tends to be a general growth cycle from late adolescence into young adulthood which is often slowly reversed into middle age. There are a variety of patterns which occur in older adults. While the extent of change is dependent upon one's personality, change is still possible even for the most resistant (Knox, 1977).

How can a training designer promote transfer in the light of the intensity of established work habits? Kidd (1973) points to the positive effects of small group participation on changing daily routines of training participants. His premise is that small groups foster a sense of ownership not typical in large group presentations, even though both delivery strategies can result in increased knowledge. Relationships and bonds are established among the small-group members, and they assume an obligation to the group and the leader to do something about what they learned.

Knox (1986) also recommends group discussions as an inducement to helping adults apply what they learn. He supports encouraging trainees,

> to discuss their interests in using what they learn (including importance and benefits), to analyze likely facilitators of and barriers to application in the setting where application is to occur, and throughout the program to devote time to exploring and practicing ways to use what they learn under conditions similar to those they are likely to confront (p190).

Knox (1986) also emphasizes the importance of incentives and resources, facilities and people to support application. These factors reflect the relationships between changing habits and critical organizational climate factors such as physical working conditions and management and co-worker support.

Maintaining changed work behaviour
Habits are products of attitudes, knowledge, and environment and have profound effects on transfer of training, near and far. A systemic orientation to design is more likely to address all of the factors which impact changing work habits and, by definition, transfer is impossible without changing work habits. However, the changed habits must be maintained over time.

Harris (cited in Baine, 1986) identifies some specific procedures by which one can address maintenance of changed behaviour. They are based upon prolonged and in-depth training which addresses a variety of tasks, settings and conditions. In addition, the target behaviours need to be compatible with the elements of the environment in which they will be used. Baine also cites other practical research which supports more extended maintenance of the transferred behaviour following conceptual instruction rather than concrete instruction on a specific task.

These suggestions are rooted not only in an understanding of a particular work environment, but in actually building learning activities which address and respond to characteristics of the environment. Creative training design can promote and sustain both near and far transfer by accurately assessing the task, the work environment and the employees.

INCORPORATING THE 'LAYERS OF NECESSITY' APPROACH INTO STD

An overview of the 'Layers of Necessity' approach

A key concern throughout this explanation of the STD approach has been the feasibility of adhering to these procedures within the normal pressures of a corporate training environment. Efforts have been made to merge STD tactics into routine tasks. When synthesizing all STD principles into one generic orientation, the issue of practicality emerges once again. At this point, it is clear that STD is a process which gradually grows in complexity depending upon the nature of the desired training outcomes. It is rooted in direct instruction for knowledge acquisition and retention and, by incorporating a broader scope of systemic design factors, expands to the point where it can address issues of far transfer. This is graphically shown in Figure 6.5 using the sequential waterfall model in which the output of one design stage serves as the input to the next (Maher and Ingram, cited in Tessmer and Wedman, 1990).

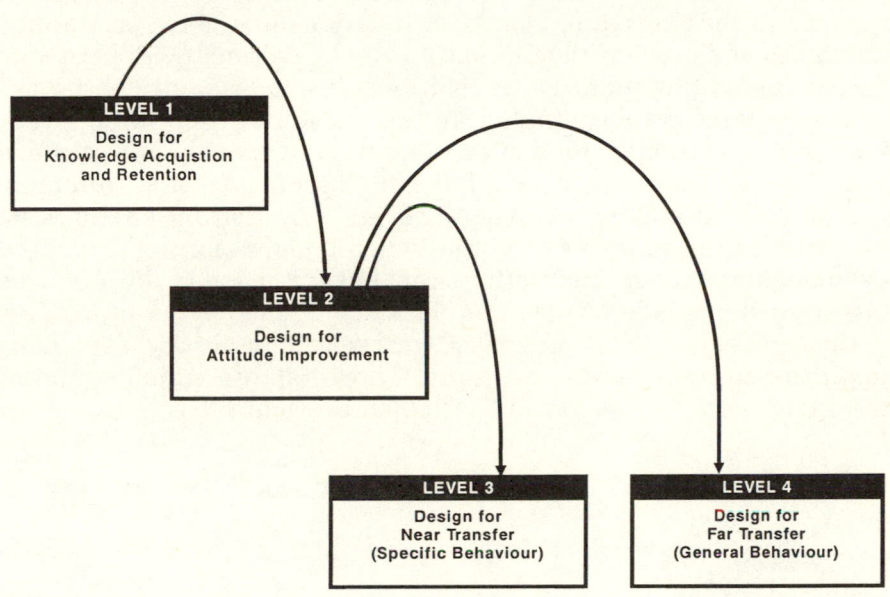

Figure 6.5 *The sequential waterfall view of systemic training design*

Tessmer and Wedman's (1990) use of the waterfall model has been duplicated here because of their expansion of this concept into the Layers of Necessity model of instructional development. They divide the instructional design process into phases of priority activities which can be matched to the necessity of the specific project. For example, in those projects 'with severe time and resource limitations, only the simplest layer may be possible; for situations with more time and resources, a more sophisticated layer may be used' (p79).

It is possible to describe a synthesized STD approach in terms of a modified Layers of Necessity model. The layers, however, can be viewed in two dimensions. The first dimension does not distinguish the layers in terms of time and resource demands but rather the layers are viewed as the four target training outcomes. Is the programme supposed to result in an expanded knowledge base? Or attitude changes? Or modified work behaviour? This is the dimension reflected in Figure 6.5.

The second dimension is, in effect, a layer of necessity. This dimension reflects the extent to which a designer is able to address those variables which are likely to influence a particular training outcome. The final STD model is presented in terms of those factors whose influence is essentially assured. This is the consistently replicated, conservative position presented in this synthesis chapter.

However, the approach is also presented in a more hypothetical manner in the preceding chapters. Relationships between training outcomes and other systemic factors were described which provide further design direction. These relationships have empirical support and were largely substantiated by the literature, even though they were not consistently replicated. The STD approach suggests that attending to the first layer of design factors assures minimum competency attainment. However, it is likely that by attending to the second or third layers of unreplicated factors one could produce even higher quality instruction and ensure mastery by an even larger portion of the trainee population.

Even this first layer, however, varies in complexity depending upon the desired training outcome. Those factors which comprise the first layer of necessity are reflected in Figure 6.6.

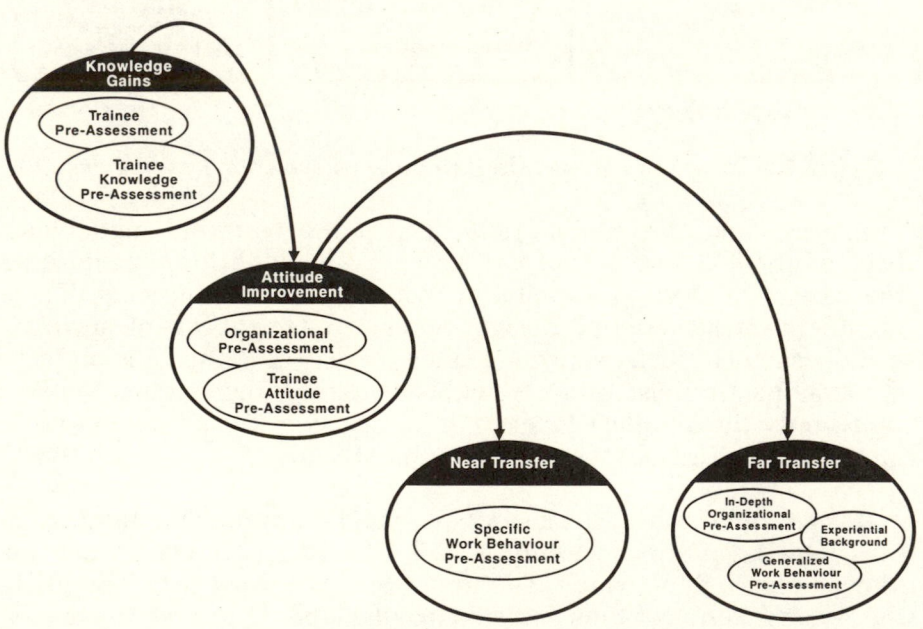

Figure 6.6 *The sequential waterfall view of systemic training design factors in the first layer of necessity*

Even though time may be short and resources scarce, designers should complete a pre-assessment which at least minimally addresses those factors which are apt to influence training outcomes. The time expenditure is initially dependent not so much upon design sophistication, but rather upon the complexity of the desired outcomes expected from the programme. For example, if one is designing a Level 1 training programme (i.e., only knowledge gains are anticipated), only three pieces of information are critical: the attitudes of the typical trainee toward past training in that organization, the delivery system attitudes and the typical employee's pre-training knowledge of the target content. The efficient designer would have representative data on the first two variables on hand; the knowledge level could be determined as part of the training needs assessment.

Multiple layers in STD

If a designer has the time and resources available which permit more detailed work, or if the programme's content is especially critical, he or she may choose to go beyond the first layer of necessity factors. In this situation design variables in layer 2, or perhaps even layer 3, could be addressed. Tessmer and Wedman (1990) have provided one conception of multiple layers which is organized around five major phases of a systematic procedural design model: situational assessment, goal analysis, instructional strategy development, materials development and evaluation and revision. The Tessmer-Wedman Layers of Necessity model then identifies extensions of the primary required phases; these more detailed approaches are the second, third and fourth layers of necessity. For example, if one wanted to move beyond situational assessment, one could conduct a full-blown needs assessment at the second level, or a learner pre-assessment at the third level of necessity.

This paradigm can be directly applied to STD. In the STD approach there is continual interaction between the phase 'Analyse employee and organizational characteristics' and the other stages of the model. Using the Tessmer-Wedman terminology, one could say that the situational assessment phase is not discrete from goal analysis, or evaluation or strategy and materials development. Rather, the results of this phase penetrate into the processes of the other phases.

It is this complex situational assessment emphasis which can best be described using the Layers of Necessity orientation. The 'layered' approach easily allows designers to select the systemic factors which are best to use in their particular situation.

The STD Layers of Necessity model is shown in Figures 6.7a–6.7d. These four diagrams portray those factors which are critical to achieving each training outcome. It is possible to identify three 'layers

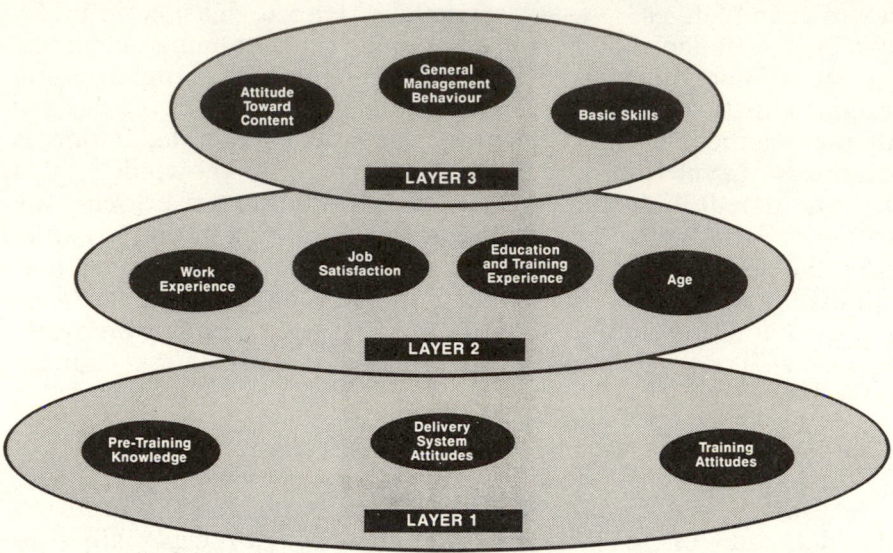

Figure 6.7a   *An application of the Layers of Necessity model to systemic training design for knowledge gains*

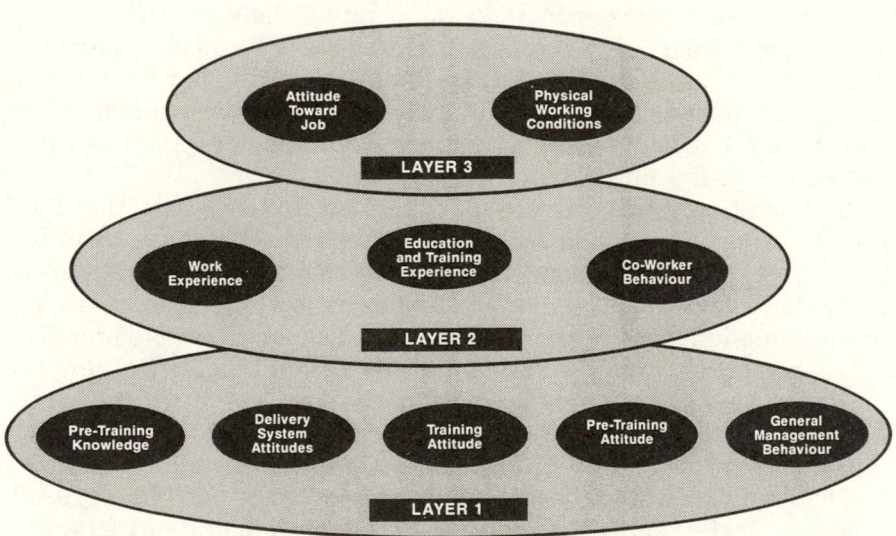

Figure 6.7b   *An application of the Layers of Necessity model to systemic training design for training attitudes*

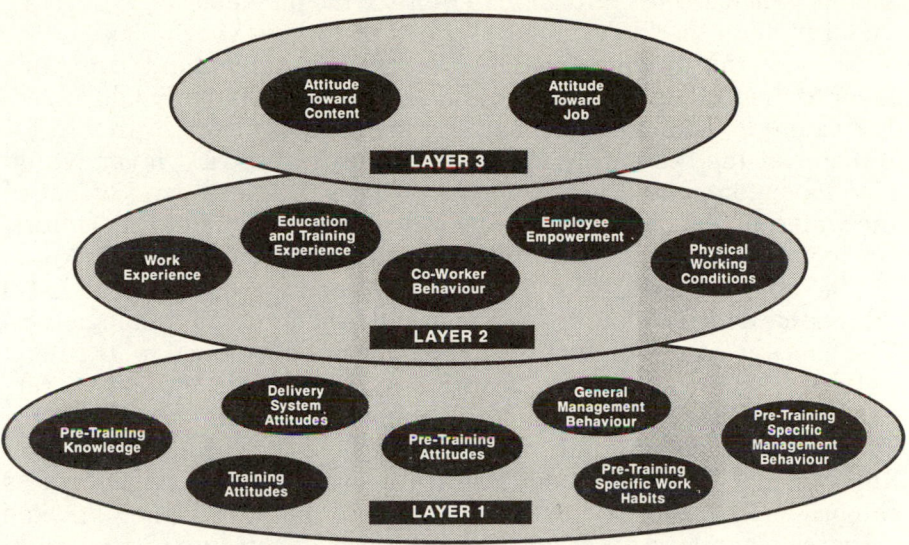

Figure 6.7c *An application of the Layers of Necessity model to systemic training design for near transfer*

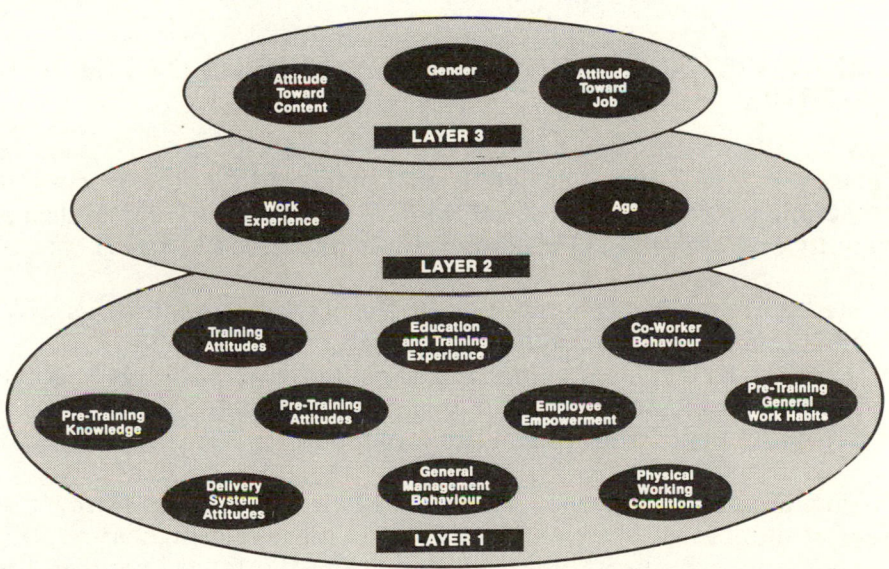

Figure 6.7d *An application of the Layers of Necessity model to systemic training design for far transfer*

of necessity' with each succeeding layer showing those systemic factors which are *less* critical than those in the previous layer. Layers 2 and 3 include the 'nice to have–not need to have' variables.

As with the Tessmer-Wedman model, the movement from one layer to the next implies that all factors are cumulatively addressed. For example, if one were designing instruction directed toward far transfer at the second layer, those factors in the first layer would also be encompassed in the design. This is the 'spill over' effect of the waterfall, and accounts for the large number of first layer factors, for example, in Figure 6.7c relating to near transfer.

The application of the Layers of Necessity concepts to STD addresses some limitations Tessmer and Wedman noted themselves. The concept, as originally presented, was not developed to its fullest extent. By using it in combination with another more concrete design model such as the STD framework, guidelines emerge for determining the appropriate depth of design. In the current description Tessmer and Wedman (1990) use time and resource constraints as the primary basis of layer selection; within the STD framework, the research foundation serves this purpose. Therefore, one would determine the depth of required analysis on an empirical and theoretical basis as well as an understanding of the unique demands of a particular organization. However, by adding the layer-of-necessity dimension to STD, there is an increased need for designers to be creative and have a keen perspective of the training's organizational context.

CREATIVITY, EFFICIENCY AND SYNTHESIS OF THE STD FACTORS

Earlier, the relationship between science and art was discussed in relation to instructional design. It was suggested that the process of integrating the various systemic design propositions demands ingenuity and creativity. This creativity is expressed in terms of:

- incorporating the complexities of the STD approach in as efficient a manner as possible;
- using the STD factors, alone and in combination, as tools to solve training problems unique to a given setting; and
- designing instruction for multiple outcomes.

Efficiency can be attained in at least two ways: 1. by using the fewest number of systemic factors to achieve the highest quality design, and 2. by using the most data from the fewest sources for multiple design purposes. Thus, efficiency not only demands an intimate understanding of the organization and a sensitivity to both its unique constraints and the latitude available, but also a knowledge of instructional design theory and the manner in which adults learn in a training context. Combining these factors in an interesting and imaginative fashion is the essence of creative training design.

Efficient instructional design does not mean constructing the best programme possible; rather it means constructing the programme which best meets the needs of the organization at the lowest cost. A cursory application of this principle within the STD framework might first appear to mean only incorporating those factors at the first layer of necessity for each desired training outcome. However, the best design for a given situation could address either more factors or, in some situations, fewer factors.

In the ideal training situation, there is a work environment in which both management and other employees are fully supportive of, and consistently practise, those principles which are taught. In addition, the physical resources necessary for the targeted behaviours are always available and all employees are involved in decisions relevant to their own jobs.

In the ideal training situation, those persons who participate in the training are well educated and experienced workers. They have all had positive training experiences in the past and are eager to attend other programmes. They are comfortable with a variety of training delivery techniques. In general, they are motivated learners.

The training design for this utopian setting could afford to address only the demands of the new content, ignoring those factors in the large learning and work environment which can affect outcomes. Consequently, even those factors in the first layer of necessity would not all need to be addressed.

In most situations, conditions vary; some aspects of the environment are favourable, others are not. It is not unusual for particular work climates to have one element which needs major attention, requiring factors at the second level of necessity to be incorporated into the design. For example, perhaps many lay-offs have been necessary over the past few years. Consequently, employees tend to be older and morale is not as high as it previously had been. Even training programmes with only confined knowledge goals might want to especially address age, educational and additional training motivation factors, in addition to the first layer attitude variables–attitudes toward training and training delivery systems. All these factors might be essential for effective instruction in this situation.

Finally, creative designers are always stretching to achieve the highest outcome level required by the organization. Instead of developing instruction to promote knowledge retention and simply hoping that transfer or attitude change will occur as natural by-products, the best design will directly attack each desired outcome. The most creative designs, however, will not address each outcome in a serial fashion (ie first, the facts; second, the attitudes). Instead the instruction directed toward various outcomes can often be integrated. Not only is the result likely to be more cohesive and more interesting, but the programme will probably be shorter.

Integration of STD factors is a two-dimensional process. First, the STD procedural model itself suggests using a knowledge of systemic factors throughout each phase of the traditional systems approach. Second, it is now suggested that the systemic factors can serve as a vehicle for constructing learning activities which integrate instruction and direct it toward multiple training outcomes. Thus, instruction is more coordinated and less linear.

Such integration is facilitated by knowing those outcomes which are associated with each factor. Table 6.1 provides a skeleton composite of information designers need to synthesize the STD procedures and integrate designs directed toward multiple outcomes.

Designers need to first determine which factors are most relevant for their situations. Then data sources need to be identified. To a great extent, this stage determines the complexities of using the STD approach. If data banks can be established for a given organization or if several pieces of data can be gathered from the same sources, the time needed for the training needs assessment can be reduced. Finally, the designer can select those systemic factors which must be addressed for a given programme by analysing the intended use and identifying the layer of necessity appropriate for that situation. At this point, skilled design work is enhanced by one's creativity and perceptiveness.

CONCLUSION

A review of the thesis

Overview
This book has been about instructional design, about adults as learners and about the training business. The merger of these three domains is forced by market place conditions, as much as by philosophy or theory. In addition, this discussion has joined the debate on the evolution of instructional design by suggesting an expanded approach to design theory and practice.

The STD theory and its concomitant design procedures stem from a very quantitative research orientation, even though these results were supplemented and substantiated by extensive participant interviews, reflection and analysis. The fact that the conclusions are not only data-based but are based upon replicated observations, provides one type of verification for the tenets of the STD approach, even though it is recognized that over-reliance on and over-simplification of statistical results can produce constricted,

SYSTEMIC TRAINING DESIGN FACTOR	DATA SOURCE	UTILIZATION OF FACTORS	
		Outcome	Necessity Level
TRAINEE BACKGROUND			
AGE	Personnel Files	Knowlege	2
		Far Transfer	2
EDUCATIONAL LEVEL	Personnel Files	Knowledge	2
		Attitude	2
		Near Transfer	2
		Far Transfer	1
TRAINING EXPERIENCE	Personnel Files Training Records	Knowledge	2
		Attitude	2
		Near Transfer	2
		Far Transfer	1
WORK EXPERIENCE	Personnel Files	Knowledge	2
		Attitude	2
		Near Transfer	2
		Far Transfer	2
GENDER	Personnel Files	Far Transfer	3
TRAINEE ATTITUDES			
TRAINING	Post-test from previous training or Needs Assessment survey of represent-ative employees	Knowledge	1
		Attitude	1
		Near Transfer	2
		Far Transfer	1
DELIVERY SYSTEMS	Post-test from previous training or Needs Assessment survey of represent-ative employees	Knowledge	1
		Attitude	1
		Near Transfer	2
		Far Transfer	1
CONTENT	Needs Assessment survey of represent-ative employees	Knowledge	3
		Near Transfer	3
		Far Transfer	3
JOB	Post-test from previous training or Needs Assessment survey of represent-ative employees	Knowledge	2
		Attitude	3
		Near Transfer	3
		Far Transfer	3

Table 6.1 *A Summary of the Uses of STD Factors*

perhaps distorted and often naïve orientations. Nonetheless, there has been an attempt to logically sort through the complexities surrounding human learning and instruction.

This book is based upon a conviction that systematic instructional design has provided extraordinary benefits to education and training; however, changes and growth are necessary and the changes, like the existing procedures, are not simple. Instructional systems design is based, to a great extent, upon construction of learning stimuli and conditions which are dependent upon the type of learning task and the learner's prerequisite capabilities. The macro-approach to design is rooted traditionally in general systems theory; the micro-approach to lesson design is based upon an understanding of human learning, currently relying upon an essentially cognitive orientation.

STD does not deviate from traditional design principles but expands upon them by emphasizing and focusing upon other elements, elements which are certainly not new but perhaps have not been addressed as directly as is suggested here. The unique features of STD include:

- non-linear, iterative design procedures;
- outcomes-oriented procedures which vary for different training goals;
- emphases on an expanded set of learner attitude and background characteristics; and
- emphases on characteristics of the learner's natural environment beyond the immediate learning setting.

STD is adapted to the peculiar characteristics and demands of the adult learner in an employee training setting. Consequently, environmental considerations are seen in terms of the work setting and the instruction is geared to varied groups of adult learners participating in vocationally-oriented programmes, usually in non-voluntary arrangements.

Implications

There has been speculation as to the extent to which the STD principles apply to other adult learning situations as well as to pre-adult learning. Even though these principles were generated from adult training settings, it seems plausible to test the four generalized characteristics of STD in other design endeavours. There is supportive research in other settings substantial enough to warrant such experimentation.

Regardless of the instructional setting in which systemic design principles may be used, the larger questions centre on the feasibility of its use given the fact that it is fundamentally more complex than traditional design orientations. This complexity, even when addressed within a layered framework, can limit widespread application. However, the complexities of STD and other newer approaches to design emphasize the growing importance of computer-based design tools. They can ease the difficulties in managing the large data bases required to make intelligent design decisions. They can ease the decision-making process itself by structuring the alternatives. Moreover, they can expand the range of creative design options leading to more interesting instruction for individual learners.

STD in the genealogy of instructional design

Instructional design as a discipline has a family tree of intellectual growth. The tree has various theoretical roots and application branches, and the need for continued nurturing and growth of the field is always present. Much of the current growth is guided by emphases on:

- psychological foundations, especially among the constructivists;
- philosophical foundations, especially among the post-modernists; and
- technological foundations, especially among those advancing interactivity.

STD also represents new growth, stemming most naturally from the psychological roots of the field. This orientation can be enhanced through use of new technologies, although they are not essential for either design or delivery. STD's emphasis on integrated use of the systemic factors supports many of Merrill *et al*'s (1990a) criticisms of traditional ISD which were cited in Chapter 2. STD's emphasis on variables which reflect one's past experience is also reflective of the constructivist position, and perhaps one could even say that recognizing and building upon complex arrays of variables is evidence of some post-modernist overtones. However, these relationships are not the most significant aspect of STD.

The important point is that STD is part of a growing movement to expand the prevailing approaches to instructional design. Some promote progress with extreme viewpoints, calling for a fairly clean break with past tradition. Other more moderate approaches, like that of STD, are building upon practices and beliefs held by many, but seldom actually applied. For example, few assert that using a systematic design model should be a linear, lock-step sequence, but in reality this is the usual practice.

The more common growth pattern for a discipline is one of gradual evolution rather than abrupt change. At this time, the growth of instructional design may be accelerating because of the concurrent activity in several arenas–philosophical exploration, research in new contexts and the technological development of advanced design and delivery tools.

This period of activity is exciting for the field and can result in new levels of expertise, providing there is still dedication to creating a firm theoretical foundation which is not compromised by the pressures of expediency or the excitement of using new technologies. The fact that events have led the field into working with adults as learners in the employee training context clearly provides opportunities for instructional design expansion. The challenge must be not only for design practice to effectively meet the needs of adult learners and the demands of training situations, but for design theory to precede and dictate the direction of new design practice.

NOTE

[1]The terms 'procedural knowledge' and 'declarative knowledge' are comparable to Howe's (1988) terminology introduced earlier in this chapter. Her term 'process understanding' clearly is analogous to 'procedural knowledge', and 'conceptual knowledge' parallels 'declarative knowledge'. 'Physical knowledge may combine procedural and declarative knowledge in the course of describing, for example, technician and operator skills.

Appendix A
The training programmes

AN OVERVIEW OF THE PROGRAMMES

There were three training programmes involved in the research which serves as a foundation for STD. Each programme was a major corporate-wide effort to promote manufacturing plant safety. These programmes were cooperatively sponsored by the United Automobile Workers and The Ford Motor Company's National Joint Committee on Health and Safety.

Energy control and power lock-out training

The first study involved a programme related to energy control and power lock-out (ECPL) in the plant. Over 50,000 Ford employees (hourly and salaried) participated in this programme. The topic emerged as a result of previous research and an examination of company accident records.

Locking-out is a critical safety procedure in a manufacturing plant. It involves shutting down the assembly line while completing diagnosis and/or repair tasks. Failure to lock-out has resulted in serious injury and even death on occasion. The locking-out process, however, is expensive since it completely stops production.

The ECPL training programme was professionally designed by a firm contracted with by the National Joint Committee. It consisted of seven two-hour sessions spanning two work weeks. There were approximately 25 persons in a class. The classes were conducted in each plant until all participating personnel had attended.

The training was group-oriented lecture and discussion with supporting videotapes. The instructional materials consisted of:

- eight modules;
- a videotape;
- an instructor's manual;
- a participant's workbook; and
- a pocket manual.

The first module in the series was a leadership commitment module for local plants and union management. The remaining seven were aimed at the employees who are expected to follow lock-out procedures on their jobs. They dealt with behaviour change and skill development. The seven participant modules were:

- Believe It
- Check It
- Prep It
- Lock It
- Release It
- Verify It
- Use It

There were pairs of trainers (one hourly and one supervisory employee). They were experienced Ford employees with expertise in the subject matter who were released from their normal job assignments for this particular task. They were not professional trainers. However, each person had received four days of training to prepare themselves to serve as instructors in the ECPL training programme. In a typical training programme the trainers presented the programme content, led the discussion and demonstrated the ECPL procedures.

Powered material handling vehicle operator training

The second safety training programme related to training operators of powered material handling vehicles (PMHV). The content focused on proper techniques for driving and controlling these vehicles in the plants. This programme was offered for approximately 15,000 plant vehicle operators and their supervisors throughout the corporation.

This programme paralleled the ECPL training in many respects. It was also professionally designed and developed by a vendor outside the corporation. The PMHV operator programme was also conducted by trainer teams. Again these teams consisted of one hourly and one salaried Ford employee knowledgeable in the content area. Even though these persons were non-professional trainers, some had also served as trainers in the ECPL programme; thus, the training role was not completely new to them. Again, there was a four-day train-the-trainers programme directed specifically toward the PMHV operator training.

The PMHV operator training programme consisted of four hours of group instruction supported by videotapes. Union leadership and plant management also had a one-hour leadership orientation session. The instructional materials included:

- videotapes segmented to match each portion of the four operator modules;
- a coordinator's guide;
- an operator manual/workbook for each participant; and
- an operator's handbook for each participant.

As with the ECPL training, the entire series was preceded by a leadership commitment session for local plant and union management. The operator training itself consisted of four major modules. They were:

- Skills + commitment = accident prevention;
- Controlling your vehicle and handling the load;
- The responsible operator – mastering the details (including operator certification, lift trucks and stackers, motorized hand and hand/rider trucks, tow tractors and unique vehicles); and
- Skills performance.

Classes with approximately 15 people were conducted at each Ford manufacturing plant. The operator programme was designed to be delivered in four consecutive days. Participants attended those portions of module 3 which pertained to the type of vehicle for which they had been licensed. Finally, completion of the PMHV operator training resulted in operator certification or recertification.

Plant pedestrian safety training

The third programme studied was a one-hour plant pedestrian safety course. This programme was delivered to approximately 125,000 persons, hourly and salaried, who were regular pedestrians in Ford Motor Company plants. Plant vehicle operators all took the pedestrian safety course immediately prior to the vehicle operation training. The same trainer teams were used for both the pedestrian and PMHV operator training.

The pedestrian training programme was a group-oriented seminar with supporting videotapes. The classes varied in size, although the programme was designed for groups of 20 to 25 persons. The programme was professionally produced by the same firm which designed the PMHV operator training programme. The pedestrian instructional materials consisted of:

- a pedestrian safety training videotape with five segments;
- a coordinator's guide; and
- pedestrian booklets for all participants.

The videotape segments organized this programme. The major topics included the human costs of accidents, safe pedestrian skills, personal involvement in accident prevention and recognizing hazards. After each videotape segment there was a planned participant activity.

Appendix B
The research process and the measurement of variables

OVERVIEW OF THE RESEARCH PROCESS

The research design overview

Not only was a common model of research variables used in these separate studies, there were also parallel data collection instruments and research designs. The research was conducted within the context of extensive evaluations of these safety training programmes, and all procedures were approved by the UAW-Ford National Joint Committee on Health and Safety.

The research employed a pre- and post-test survey design with structured follow-up interviews of trainees and trainers to refine and verify the survey data. The post-tests were administered 30–90 days after training to facilitate the collection of knowledge retention data, as well as a more realistic estimation of on-the-job behaviours.

There were two trainee populations for each study: hourly and salaried personnel. The samples were selected on a stratified basis from plants representative of the corporation primarily in terms of plant type and size. Five plants were involved in each study, and the trainees were in randomly selected classes within each plant. (Classes are formed in the plants randomly assuring roughly equal representation from each plant department).

The ECPL trainee sample consisted of 380 employees (307 hourly and 73 salaried). The PMHV operator trainee sample consisted of 317 employees, and the pedestrian trainee sample consisted of 201 employees.

The trainee samples used for the telephone interviews were randomly selected from a list of volunteers from each pre-test population. Approximately 50 trainees were interviewed from each programme. The rate of volunteering for the interviews was comparable from plant to plant in each study. All trainers in each of the programmes were interviewed from each of the target plants.

Path analysis techniques were used to validate and estimate the dimensions of a hypothetical model of adult learning in employee training. The result was a set of causal models of variables which influence training outcomes in the various studies. The measurement details for each variable in the resulting path diagrams follow in this Appendix.

The path analyses were based upon pre-test data for measures of learner background characteristics, learner attitudes and organizational climate variables. The training outcome measures (knowledge, attitude, general behaviour and specific behaviour) were gain scores. Conclusions relating to instructional design and delivery characteristics were based upon interviews with the trainers and an analysis of all programme evaluation data.

THE DATA COLLECTION INSTRUMENTS

Pre-test and post-test surveys

The same instruments were used for both pre- and post-testing in each study. The instruments had two forms, one for hourly employees and one for supervisory employees. The supervisor version of the survey instrument paralleled the one directed toward hourly employees with minor variations in selected items to reflect their job situations.

The surveys consisted of measures in the following areas:

- trainee attitudes;
- demographic information;
- reactions to training delivery methods; and
- a knowledge test of the target safety procedures.

The attitude questions in each instrument related to perceptions of: a. the plant, b. Ford Motor Company, c. communication in the plant, d. health and safety on the job, e. immediate supervision, f. product quality, g. management and union commitment to health and safety, and h. overall job satisfaction. These questions were developed with the assistance of industrial psychologists from the Ford personnel research department to ensure comparability with previous Ford employee attitude surveys.

The attitude questions also included those from the Mayflower Group, a firm which has established a bank of validated questions commonly used in American corporate research. Finally, the instrument included the measures of perceived job risks of Dr Scott Geller of Virginia Polytechnic Institute and State University.

The instruments were peer reviewed and piloted at a Ford manufacturing plant which was not included in the studies. Modifications were made based upon that input, as well as from representatives of the

UAW-Ford National Joint Committee on Health and Safety. This latter group subsequently approved all data collection instruments.

Interview instruments

Trainee interviews.
The trainee telephone interviews lasted 20–30 minutes, providing detailed comments on their reactions to the training and the trainers, including:

- trainer preparation and delivery;
- physical environment of the training;
- the instructional materials;
- the instructional methods; and
- safety performance in the plant.

Trainer interviews.
Each trainer was also interviewed in person using a structured protocol. These instruments covered trainer demographics profiles and their reactions to the following:

- programme organization and methodology;
- trainer preparation;
- student difficulties;
- physical environment of the training; and
- the instructional media.

MEASUREMENT OF VARIABLES

All measures listed below were used in each of the four studies unless otherwise noted. The following key relates those unique variables to the appropriate study:

◆ Energy control and power lock-out safety training
▶ Plant pedestrian safety training
| Truck operator safety training

Only measures included on path diagrams are listed.

Dependent variables

There were four dependent variables in each of the three studies representing the various training outcomes. These were measured in the following manner:

1. *Gains in knowledge retention.* The pre-test/post-test differences (ie, post − pre = difference) between the sums of the correct answers of those objective test items covering training content. (ECPL, 23 items; PMHV operator, 25 items; pedestrian, 14 items)
2. *Gains in attitude toward safety.* The pre-test/post-test differences between the measure 'The safety risks of my job concern me quite a bit'.
3. *Gains in general on-the-job safety behaviour.* The pre-test/post-test differences between the measure 'Before starting a job, how often do you consciously evaluate the consequences of not doing the job safely?'
4. *Gains in specific on-the-job safety behaviour.* The pre-test/post-test differences between the measure 'In the last month, how often did you follow the _____ safety rules?'

Exogenous variables

Trainee profile characteristics

1. Age. In years.
2. Gender. A dummy variable, 1 = male; 2 = female.
3. Education level. 1–5 graduated levels.
4. Rating of self as student. 1–4 above-average student to less than average student (◆).
5. Amount of previous training. 1–5 graduated levels (◆); 1–6 graduated levels (▶ and **l**).

Trainee work experience characteristics

1. Years on present job. 1–5 graduated levels.
2. Years employed by company. 1–5 graduated levels.
3. Accident experience. 1 = yes, 2 = no (◆); 1 = none; 2 = known someone in accident; 3 = minor accident; 4 = major accident (▶ and **l**).

General organizational climate characteristics

Employee perceptions of management actions:

1. Supervisor's rating. 1–5 very good to very poor.

Employee empowerment:

1. Involvement in decision making. 1–5 very satisfied to very dissatisfied.
2. Encouraged to devise new work methods. 1–5 strongly agree to strongly disagree.

Collegial relationships:

1. Co-workers cooperate. 1–5 strongly agree to strongly disagree.

Physical conditions:

1. Physical working conditions. 1–5 strongly agree to strongly disagree.
2. Conditions promote productivity. 1–5 strongly agree to strongly disagree.

Quality of work:

1. Quality of work. 1–5 strongly agree to strongly disagree.

Endogenous variables

Trainee attitudes

1. Job satisfaction. 1–5 strongly agree to strongly disagree.
2. Like the work I do. 1–5 strongly agree to strongly disagree.
3. Safety attitude. 1–5 strongly agree to strongly disagree.

Attitudes toward training:

1. Volunteer for other training. 1–5 strongly agree to strongly disagree (▶ and |); a dummy variable 0 = no 1 = yes (◆).
2. Information from past training useful. 1–5 strongly agree to strongly disagree (▶ and |); a dummy variable 0 = no 1 = yes (◆).
3. Enjoy past training. 1–5 strongly agree to strongly disagree (▶ and |); a dummy variable 0 = no 1 = yes (◆).

Trainee attitudes toward delivery systems:

1. Like learning with instructor/videotape best; a dummy variable 0 = no 1 = yes
2. Enjoy learning with instructor/videotape. 0 = never experienced; 1–5 strongly agree to strongly disagree (▶ and |).
3. Enjoy learning with lecture/discussion. 0 = never experienced; 1–5 strongly agree to strongly disagree (▶ and |).
4. Enjoy learning with self-instructional workbook. 0 = never experienced; 1–5 strongly agree to strongly disagree (▶ and |).
5. Enjoy learning with individualized instruction with computer. 0 = never experienced; 1–5 strongly agree to strongly disagree (▶ and |).

Organizational climate generally related to training

Employee perceptions of management actions:

1. Operation more important than safety. 1–5 strongly agree to strongly disagree, 5 = most desirable (▶ and |).
2. Plant manager aware of safety issues. 1–5 strongly agree to strongly disagree.
3. Union/management support safety. 1–5 strongly agree to strongly disagree.
4. Supervisor corrects safety hazards quickly. 1–5 strongly agree to strongly disagree.
5. Safety top plant priority. 1–5 strongly agree to strongly disagree.

Collegial relationships:

1. Co-workers support safety. 1–5 strongly agree to strongly disagree.

Organizational climate specifically related to training

Employee perceptions of management actions:

1. Union/management support lock-out/truck operator/pedestrian safety rules. 1–5 strongly agree to strongly disagree.
2. Accountable for not following lock-out/truck operator/pedestrian safety rules. 1–5 strongly agree to strongly disagree.
3. Lock-out not a common practice. 1–5 strongly agree to strongly disagree (◆).
4. Supervisor requires one to submit daily log form 3382. 1–5 always to hardly ever (|).

Collegial relationships:

1. Pedestrians/truck operators follow safety rules. 1–5 strongly agree to strongly disagree (▶ and |).

Physical conditions:

1. Shortage of locks. 1–5 strongly agree to strongly disagree (◆).
2. Impossible to lock-out on my job. 1–5 strongly agree to strongly disagree (◆).
3. Equipment provides for easy lock-out. 1–5 strongly agree to strongly disagree (◆).
4. Plant conditions promote safe travel. 1–5 strongly agree to strongly disagree (▶ and |).

Appendix C
The path diagrams and their supporting data

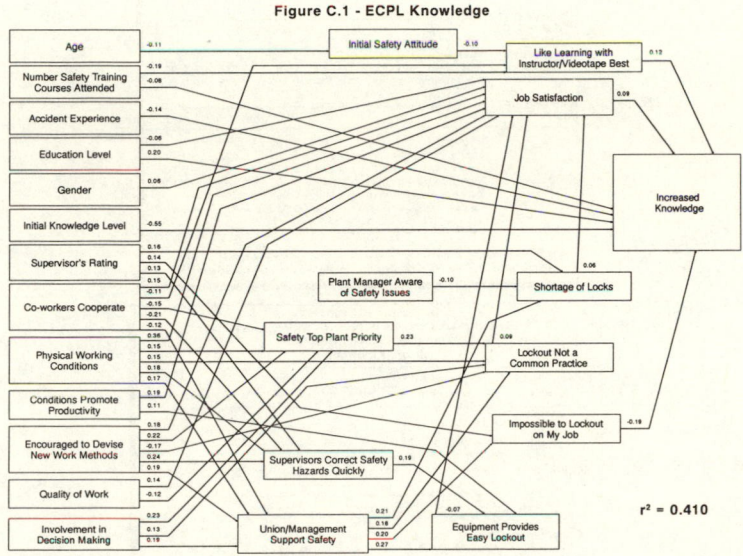

Figure C.1 - ECPL Knowledge

TABLE C.1
Hypothesized Effects of Factors Which Predict Training Knowledge Retention (ECPL Knowledge)

Endogenous Variable	Causal Variable	B	SE B	T	p
Liked Learning with Instructor/ Videotape Best	Constant	0.768	0.067		
	Number of Programs	-0.025	0.007	-3.830	➡0.000+
	Rating of Self	-0.036	0.017	-2.189	➥0.029
	Mutual Safety Attitude	-0.054	0.028	-1.927	0.054
	r^2 = 0.068		N = 388		
Job Satisfaction	Constant	0.052	0.247		
	Physical Conditions	0.310	0.036	8.707	➡0.000+
	Conditions Promote	0.160	0.040	4.017	➡0.000+
	Co-workers Cooperate	0.147	0.040	3.683	➡0.000+
	Encouraged to Devise	0.187	0.040	4.690	➡0.000+
	Quality of Work	0.104	0.033	3.162	➡0.002
Mean = 2.15	Lockout Not Common	0.068	0.029	2.327	➥0.021
S.D. = 1.27	Easy to Lockout	-0.091	0.038	-2.392	➥0.017
	Educational Level	-0.056	0.025	-2.231	➥0.026
	Gender	0.212	0.113	1.876	0.062
	Lockout Shortage	0.036	0.021	1.706	0.086
	Age	-0.064	0.039	-1.644	0.101
	r^2 = 0.657		N = 381		
Initial Safety Attitude	Constant	1.850	0.163		
	Age	-0.110	0.047	-2.149	➥0.032
Mean = 1.51 *S.D. = 0.88*	r^2 = 0.012		N = 381		
Impossible to Lockout on My Job	Constant	1.379	0.212		
	Union/Mgmt Support	0.322	0.081	3.956	➡0.000+
	Supervisor's Rating	0.177	0.065	2.719	➡0.007
Mean = 2.42 *S.D. = 1.76*	r^2 = 0.070		N = 388		
Lockout Not Common Practice	Constant	1.296	0.159		
	Safety Top Priority	0.238	0.059	4.074	➡0.000+
	Union/Mgmt Support	0.212	0.070	3.052	➡0.002
	Physical Conditions	0.149	0.053	2.642	➡0.009
	Encouraged to Devise	-0.162	0.058	-2.787	➡0.006
	Decision Involvement	0.112	0.050	2.270	➥0.024
Mean = 2.52 *S.D. = 1.31*	r^2 = 0.190		N = 388		

➥Significant at 0.05 level or less ➡Significant at 0.01 level or less

TABLE C.1 (Continued)
Hypothesized Effects of Factors Which Predict Training Knowledge Retention (ECPL Knowledge)

Endogenous Variable	Causal Variable	B	SE B	T	p
Lock Shortage	Constant	2.017	0.226		
	Union/Mgmt Support	0.335	0.082	4.071	➡0.000+
	Supervisor's Rating	0.203	0.065	3.103	➡0.002
Mean = 2.94 *S.D. = 1.77*	Plant Manger Aware	-0.120	0.061	-1.970	➥0.050
	r^2 = 0.082		N= 388		
Equipment Provides Easy Lockout	Constant	1.261	0.124		
	Union/Mgmt Support	0.252	0.049	5.113	➡0.000+
	Supervisors Correct	0.172	0.046	3.722	➡0.000+
	Conditions Promote	0.077	0.035	2.228	➥0.026
Mean = 2.21 *S.D. = 1.03*	r^2 = 0.171		N = 388		
Union/ Management Support Safety	Constant	1.145	0.122		
	Decision Involvement	0.133	0.041	3.231	➡0.001
	Encouraged to Devise	0.146	0.051	2.867	➡0.004
	Physical Conditions	0.139	0.048	2.812	➡0.005
	Co-workers Cooperate	-0.099	0.050	-1.985	➥0.048
Mean = 1.96 *S.D. = 1.09*	r^2 = 0.160		N = 388		
Supervisors Correct Hazards Quickly	Constant	1.893	0.133		
	Encouraged to Devise	0.198	0.052	3.787	➡0.000+
	Physical Conditions	0.147	0.051	2.878	➡0.004
	Co-workers Cooperate	-0.194	0.056	-3.454	➡0.000+
	Supervisor's Rating	0.107	0.049	2.194	➥0.029
Mean = 2.56 *S.D. = 1.16*	r^2 = 0.125		N = 388		
Safety Top Plant Priority	Constant	1.500	0.144		
	Decision Involvement	0.187	0.049	3.842	➡0.000+
	Encouraged to Devise	0.199	0.060	3.332	➡0.000+
	Quality of Work	-0.110	0.053	-2.059	➡0.040
	Physical Conditions	0.135	0.056	2.397	➥0.017
Mean = 2.26 *S.D. = 1.27*	Co-workers Cooperate	-0.146	0.062	-2.333	➥0.020
	r^2 = 0.159		N = 388		

➥Significant at 0.05 level or less ➡Significant at 0.01 level or less

TABLE C.1 (Continued) Hypothesized Effects of Factors Which Predict Training Knowledge Retention (ECPL Knowledge)					
Dependent Variable	**Causal Variable**	**B**	**SE B**	**T**	**p**
	Constant	15.199	1.638		
Gain in	Initial Knowledge Level	-1.038	0.088	-11.787	� 0.000+
ECPL	Educational Level	0.489	0.117	4.195	0.000+
Knowledge	Lockout Impossible	-0.392	0.098	-3.977	0.000+
Retained	Accident Experience	-0.528	0.180	-2.925	0.004
	Inst/Videotape Best	0.824	0.340	2.420	0.016
Mean = 2.48	Job Satisfaction	0.261	0.144	1.806	0.072
S.D. = 3.69	Number of Programs	-0.075	0.045	-1.680	0.094
	$r^2 = 0.410$		N = 283		
➥Significant at 0.05 level or less		➤Significant at 0.01 level or less			

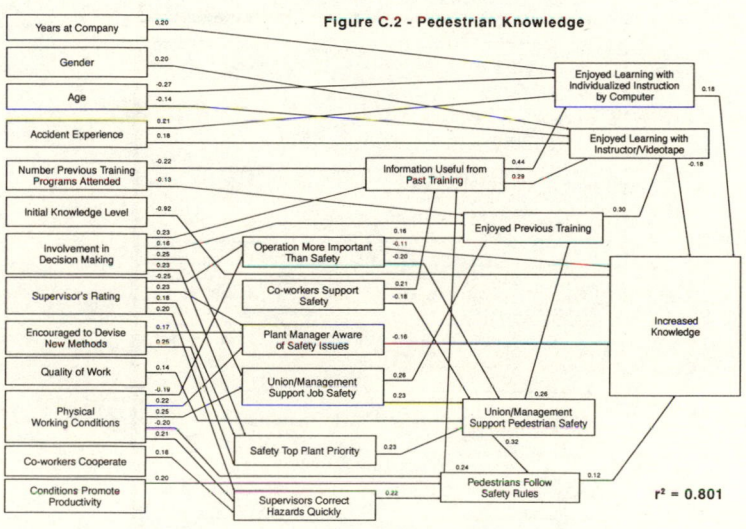

Figure C.2 - Pedestrian Knowledge

$r^2 = 0.801$

TABLE C.2
Hypothesized Effects of Factors Which Predict
Training Knowledge Retention
(Pedestrian Knowledge)

Endogenous Variable	Causal Variable	B	SE B	T	p
Enjoyed Learning with Instructor/ Videotape	Constant	0.269	0.354		
	Past Tng Info Useful	0.352	0.107	3.297	➡0.001
	Enjoyed Past Training	0.366	0.108	3.401	➡0.001
	Accident Experience	0.150	0.060	2.509	➡0.013
	Gender	-0.130	0.065	-2.011	➡0.046
Mean = 2.06	$r^2 = 0.369$		N = 138		
Enjoyed Learning with Individualized Instruction by Computer	Constant	1.304	0.440		
	Past Tng Info Useful	0.689	0.127	5.416	➡0.000+
	Accident Experience	0.229	0.090	2.538	➡0.013
	Age	-0.306	0.120	-2.547	➡0.012
	Years at Company	0.133	0.070	1.886	0.062
Mean = 2.65	$r^2 = 0.295$		N = 112		
Union/Mgmt Support Pedestrian Safety Rules	Constant	1.059	0.259		
	Safety Top Plant Priority	0.160	0.048	3.355	➡0.001
	Union/Mgmt Support	0.192	0.056	3.418	➡0.000+
	Operation Important	-0.153	0.050	-3.053	➡0.003
	Co-workers Support	0.165	0.055	2.974	➡0.003
Mean = 2.12 S.D. = 0.87	Quality of Work	0.126	0.058	2.178	➡0.030
	$r^2 = 0.365$		N = 187		
Safety Top Plant Priority	Constant	0.591	0.247		
	Decision Involvement	0.272	0.089	3.041	➡0.003
	Encouraged to Devise	0.298	0.084	3.543	➡0.001
	Supervisor's Rating	0.207	0.080	2.604	➡0.010
Mean = 2.50 S.D. = 1.26	$r^2 = 0.265$		N = 194		
Supervisors Correct Hazards Quickly	Constant	0.616	0.247		
	Supervisors Rating	0.406	0.071	5.761	➡0.000+
	Physical Conditions	0.249	0.080	3.126	➡0.002
	Co-workers Cooperate	0.223	0.076	2.927	➡0.004
Mean = 2.82 S.D. = 1.21	$r^2 = 0.324$		N = 194		

➡Significant at 0.05 level or less   ➡Significant at 0.01 level or less

TABLE C.2 (Continued)
Hypothesized Effects of Factors Which Predict
Training Knowledge Retention
(Pedestrian Knowledge)

Endogenous Variable	Causal Variable	B	SE B	T	p
Plant Mgr Aware of Safety Issues	Constant	0.785	0.256		
	Supervisor's Rating	0.233	0.075	3.106	➡0.002
	Physical Conditions	0.252	0.081	3.110	➡0.002
	Encouraged to Devise	0.191	0.075	2.527	➡0.012
Mean = 2.46 S.D. = 1.15	$r^2 = 0.205$		N = 190		
Enjoyed Past Training Programs	Constant	1.626	0.230		
	Programs Attended	-0.130	0.030	-4.340	➡0.000+
	Union/Mgmt Support	0.199	0.060	3.290	➡0.001
	Decision Involvement	0.101	0.045	2.239	➡0.026
	Operation Important	0.092	0.044	2.098	➡0.037
Mean = 2.12 S.D. = 0.69	$r^2 = 0.169$		N = 179		
Past Training Information Useful	Constant	1.279	0.190		
	Decision Involvement	0.142	0.044	3.219	➡0.002
	Co-workers Support	0.153	0.051	3.015	➡0.003
	Pedestrians Follow	0.145	0.044	3.298	➡0.001
	Number of Programs	-0.093	0.030	-3.120	➡0.002
Mean = 2.03 S.D. = 0.70	$r^2 = 0.247$		N = 164		
Pedestrians Follow Safety Rules	Constant	1.293	0.247		
	Union/Mgmt Support	0.388	0.082	4.715	➡0.000+
	Supervisors Correct	0.192	0.064	2.993	➡0.003
	Conditions Promote	0.200	0.071	2.792	➡0.006
	Physical Conditions	-0.212	0.077	-2.744	➡0.007
Mean = 2.58 S.D. = 1.06	$r^2 = 0.240$		N = 187		
Operation More Important	Constant	3.522	0.239		
	Supervisor's Rating	-0.258	0.076	-3.413	➡0.001
	Physical Conditions	-0.218	0.083	-2.635	➡0.009
Mean = 2.33 S.D. = 1.16	$r^2 = 0.134$		N = 192		

➡Significant at 0.05 level or less   ➡Significant at 0.01 level or less

TABLE C.2 (Continued) Hypothesized Effects of Factors Which Predict Training Knowledge Retention (Pedestrian Knowledge)					
Dependent Variable	Causal Variable	B	SE B	T	p
Gain in Knowledge Retained Mean = 1.02 S.D. = 2.56	Constant	14.147	0.847		
	Initial Knowlege Level	-1.070	0.058	-18.615	➡0.000+
	Plant Manager Aware	-0.272	0.095	-2.862	➡0.005
	Enjoy Inst/Videotape	-0.446	0.140	-3.185	➡0.002
	Pedestrians Follow	0.252	0.106	2.379	➡0.020
	Operation Important	-0.175	0.086	-2.039	➡0.045
	Enjoy Individualized	0.385	0.116	3.305	➡0.001
	$r^2 = 0.801$		N = 95		
➡Significant at 0.05 level or less			➡Significant at 0.01 level or less		

Figure C.3 - ECPL Attitude

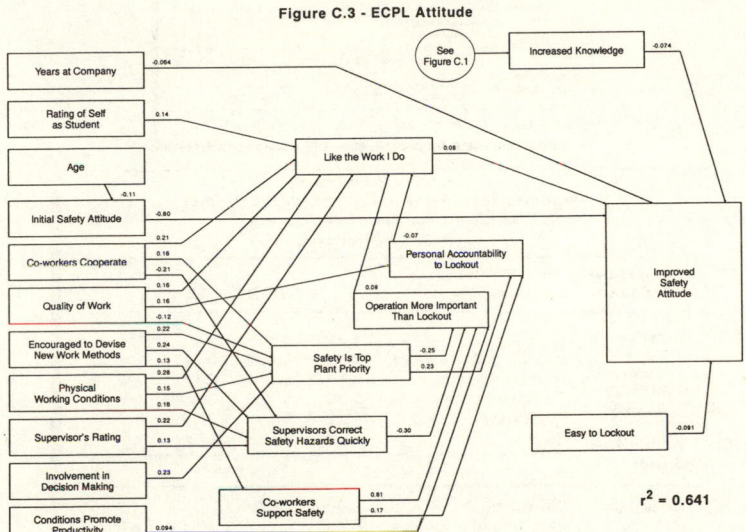

TABLE C.3
Hypothesized Effects of Factors Which Predict
Attitude Changes After Training
(ECPL Attitude)

Endogenous Variable	Causal Variable	B	SE B	T	p
Knowledge Gain	See Table C.1 for Knowledge Gain Data.				
Mean = 2.38 S.D. = 3.59	r^2 = 0.410 N = 283				
I Like the Work I Do	Constant	-0.750	0.183		
	Co-workers Cooperate	0.218	0.048	4.576	⇒0.000+
	Working Conditions	0.269	0.041	6.605	⇒0.000+
	Supervisor's Rating	0.213	0.042	5.119	⇒0.000+
	Student Rating	0.120	0.032	3.778	⇒0.000+
	Quality of Work	0.153	0.043	3.592	⇒0.000+
	Operation Before ECPL	0.083	0.033	2.530	⇒0.012
	ECPL Accountability	0.089	0.045	1.979	⇒0.049
Mean = 1.93 S.D. = 1.33	r^2 = 0.545 N = 388				
Personal Accountability to Lockout	Constant	1.044	0.152		
	Safety Top Priority	0.193	0.041	4.731	⇒0.000+
	Co-workers Support	0.181	0.051	3.560	⇒0.000+
	Quality of Work	0.115	0.036	3.147	⇒0.002
Mean = 2.12 S.D. = 1.06	r^2 = 0.132 N = 388				
Operation More Important Than Safety	Constant	3.897	0.220		
	Supervisor Corrects	-0.379	0.066	-5.787	⇒0.000+
	Safety Top Priority	-0.288	0.061	-4.750	⇒0.000+
	Conditions Promote	0.096	0.048	-4.991	⇒0.047
	Co-workers Support	0.116	0.067	1.716	0.087
Mean = 2.77 S.D. = 1.45	r^2 = 0.202 N = 388				
Safety Is Top Plant Priority	Constant	1.500	0.144		
	Decision Involvement	0.187	0.049	3.842	⇒0.000+
	Encouraged to Devise	0.199	0.060	3.332	⇒0.000+
	Quality of Work	-0.110	0.053	-2.059	⇒0.040
	Working Conditions	0.135	0.056	2.397	⇒0.017
	Co-workers Cooperate	-0.146	0.062	-2.333	⇒0.020
Mean = 2.26 S.D. = 1.27	r^2 = 0.159 N = 388				

⇒Significant at 0.05 level or less   ⇒Significant at 0.01 level or less

---

TABLE C.3 (Continued)
Hypothesized Effects of Factors Which Predict
Attitude Changes After Training
(ECPL Attitude)

Endogenous Variable	Causal Variable	B	SE B	T	p
Supervisor's Correct Safety Hazards Quickly	Constant	1.893	0.133		
	Encouraged to Devise	0.198	0.052	3.787	⇒0.000+
	Working Conditions	0.147	0.051	2.878	⇒0.004
	Co-workers Cooperate	-0.194	0.056	-3.454	⇒0.000+
	Supervisor's Rating	0.107	0.049	2.194	⇒0.029
Mean = 2.56 S.D. = 1.16	r^2 = 0.125 N = 388				
Co-workers Support	Constant	1.999	0.101		
	Encouraged to Devise	0.093	0.037	2.514	⇒0.012
Mean = 2.22 S.D. = 1.02	r^2 = 0.016 N = 388				

Dependent Variable	Causal Variable	B	SE B	T	p
Improved Safety Attitude	Constant	1.766	0.175		
	Initial Attitude	-1.022	0.048	-21.297	⇒0.000+
	Easy to Lockout	-0.092	0.037	-2.466	⇒0.014
	Knowledge Gain	-0.022	0.011	-2.046	⇒0.042
	Years at Ford	-0.056	0.032	-1.740	0.083
	Like Work I Do	0.065	0.030	2.129	⇒0.034
Mean = -0.102 S.D. = 1.05	r^2 = 0.641 N = 273				

⇒Significant at 0.05 level or less   ⇒Significant at 0.01 level or less

Figure C.4 - Operator Attitude

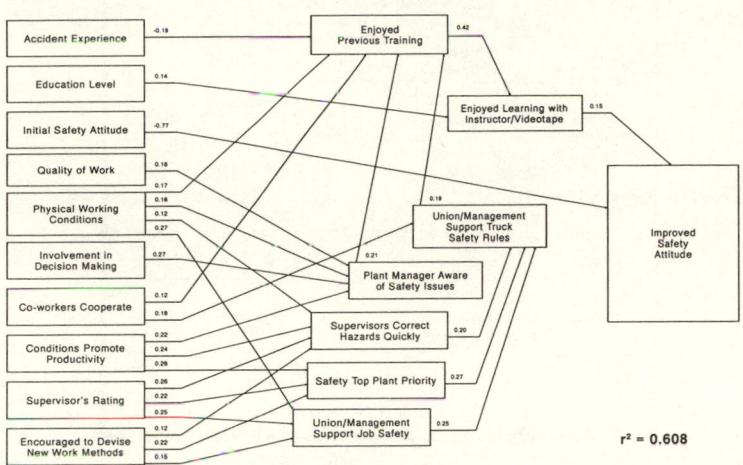

$r^2 = 0.608$

TABLE C.4
Hypothesized Effects Factors Which Predict
Attitude Changes After Training
(Operator Attitude)

Endogenous Variable	Causal Variable	B	SE B	T	p
Enjoyed Learning with Instructor/ Videotape	Constant	0.667	0.201		
	Enjoyed Past Training	0.471	0.064	7.329	➡0.000+
	Educational Level	0.148	0.061	2.416	0.016
Mean = 1.99	$r^2 = 0.194$		N = 252		
Enjoyed Past Training Programs	Constant	1.250	0.141		
	Plant Manager Aware	0.132	0.040	3.296	➡0.001
	Union/Mgmt Support	0.161	0.049	3.266	➡0.001
	Accident Experience	-0.148	0.042	-3.529	➡0.000+
	Physical Conditions	0.120	0.043	2.761	➡0.006
Mean = 2.07 S.D. = 0.72	Co-workers Cooperate	0.093	0.045	2.052	➡0.041
	$r^2 = 0.230$		N = 281		
Union/ Management Support Truck Safety Rules	Constant	0.362	0.130		
	Supervisor Corrects	0.147	0.046	3.219	➡0.001
	Safety Top Priority	0.170	0.046	3.721	➡0.000+
	Union/Mgmt Support	0.159	0.051	3.112	➡0.002
	Operators Follow	0.131	0.041	3.164	➡0.002
Mean = 1.93 S.D. = 0.89	Co-workers Cooperate	0.096	0.043	2.204	➡0.028
	$r^2 = 0.401$		N = 296		
Safety Top Plant Priority	Constant	0.489	0.160		
	Conditions Promote	0.275	0.057	4.846	➡0.000+
	Supervisor's Rating	0.272	0.064	4.266	➡0.000+
	Encouraged to Devise	0.218	0.059	3.705	➡0.000+
Mean = 2.21 S.D. = 1.11	$r^2 = 0.302$		N = 307		
Supervisors Correct Hazards Quickly	Constant	0.606	0.175		
	Conditions Promote	0.239	0.062	3.844	➡0.000+
	Supervisor's Rating	0.337	0.068	4.940	➡0.000+
	Physical Conditions	0.132	0.064	2.081	➡0.038
	Encouraged to Devise	0.124	0.061	2.030	➡0.043
Mean = 2.46 S.D. = 1.13	$r^2 = 0.297$		N = 306		
➡Significant at 0.05 level or less		➡Significant at 0.01 level or less			

TABLE C.4 (Continued) Hypothesized Effects of Factors Which Predict Attitude Changes After Training (Operator Attitude)					
Endogenous Variable	**Causal Variable**	**B**	**SE B**	**T**	**p**
Plant	Constant	0.488	0.178		
Manager	Physical Conditions	0.201	0.067	3.015	�0.003
Aware of	Conditions Promote	0.220	0.057	3.884	➤0.000+
Safety	Quality of Work	0.236	0.072	3.280	➤0.001
Issues	Decision Involvement	0.172	0.058	2.966	➤0.003
Mean = 2.38					
S.D. = 1.12	$r^2 = 0.300$		N = 301		
Dependent Variable	**Causal Variable**	**B**	**SE B**	**T**	**p**
Gains in	Constant	1.188	0.145		
Safety	Initial Safety Attitude	-1.059	0.062	-17.216	➤0.000+
Attitude	Enjoy Inst/Videotape	0.180	0.054	3.353	➤0.001
Mean = 0.00+					
S.D. = 1.08	$r^2 = 0.608$		N = 199		
➤Significant at 0.05 level or less			➤Significant at 0.01 level or less		

Figure C.5 - Pedestrian Attitude

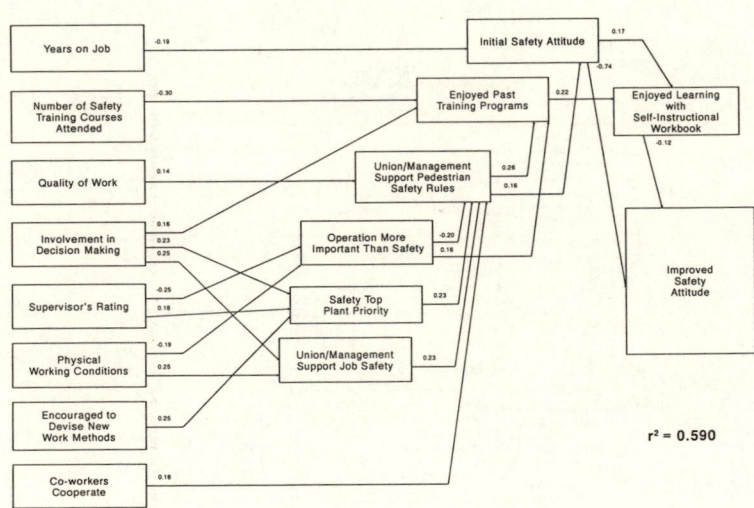

TABLE C.5
Hypothesized Effects of Factors Which Predict
Attitude Changes After Training
(Pedestrian Attitude)

Endogenous Variable	Causal Variable	B	SE B	T	p
Enjoyed Learning with Self-Inst Workbook	Constant	1.738	0.259		
	Enjoyed Past Training	0.296	0.110	2.701	➟0.008
	Initial Safety Attitude	0.146	0.070	2.080	➟0.039
Mean = 2.57	$r^2 = 0.078$		N = 145		
Enjoyed Past Training Programs	Constant	1.626	0.230		
	Number of Programs	-0.130	0.030	-4.340	➟0.000+
	Union/Mgmt Support	0.199	0.060	3.290	➟0.001
	Decision Involvement	0.101	0.045	2.239	➟0.026
	Operation Important	0.092	0.044	2.098	➟0.037
Mean = 2.12 S.D. = 0.693	$r^2 = 0.169$		N = 179		
Initial Safety Attitude	Constant	1.545	0.207		
	Years on Job	-0.124	0.045	-2.731	➟0.007
	Union/Mgmt Support	0.177	0.079	2.248	➟0.026
Mean = 1.67 S.D. = 0.98	$r^2 = 0.066$		N = 191		
Union/ Management Support Pedestrian Safety Rules	Constant	1.059	0.259		
	Safety Top Priority	0.160	0.048	3.355	➟0.001
	Union/Mgmt Support	0.192	0.056	3.418	➟0.000+
	Operation Important	-.0153	0.050	-3.053	➟0.003
	Co-workers Support	0.165	0.055	2.974	➟0.003
	Quality of Work	0.126	0.058	2.178	➟0.031
Mean = 2.12 S.D. = 0.87	$r^2 = 0.365$		N = 187		
Union/Mgmt Support Safety	Constant	0.867	0.210		
	Physical Conditions	0.261	0.074	3.514	➟0.000+
	Decision Involvement	0.239	0.070	3.433	➟0.000+
Mean = 2.14 S.D. = 1.03	$r^2 = 0.177$		N = 194		
Safety Top Plant Priority	Constant	0.591	0.247		
	Decision Involvement	0.272	0.089	3.041	➟0.003
	Encouraged to Devise	0.298	0.084	3.543	➟0.000+
	Supervisor's Rating	0.207	0.080	2.604	➟0.010
Mean = 2.50 S.D. = 1.16	$r^2 = 0.265$		N = 194		

➟Significant at 0.05 level or less   ➟Significant at 0.01 level or less

TABLE C.5 (Continued)
Hypothesized Effects of Factors Which Predict
Attitude Changes After Training
(Pedestrian Attitude)

Endogenous Variable	Causal Variable	B	SE B	T	p
Operation More Important Than Safety	Constant	3.522	0.239		
	Supervisor's Rating	-0.258	0.076	-3.413	➟0.000+
	Physical Conditions	-0.218	0.083	-2.635	➟0.009
Mean = 2.33 S.D. = 1.16	$r^2 = 0.134$		N = 192		

Dependent Variable	Causal Variable	B	SE B	T	p
Gain in Safety Attitude	Constant	2.152	0.238		
	Initial Safety Attitude	-1.024	0.077	-13.260	
	Enjoy Self-Inst Wkbook	-0.165	0.080	-2.068	➟0.041
Mean = 0.00+ S.D. = 1.27	$r^2 = 0.590$		N = 135		

➟Significant at 0.05 level or less   ➟Significant at 0.01 level or less

Figure C.6 – ECPL Specific Behavior

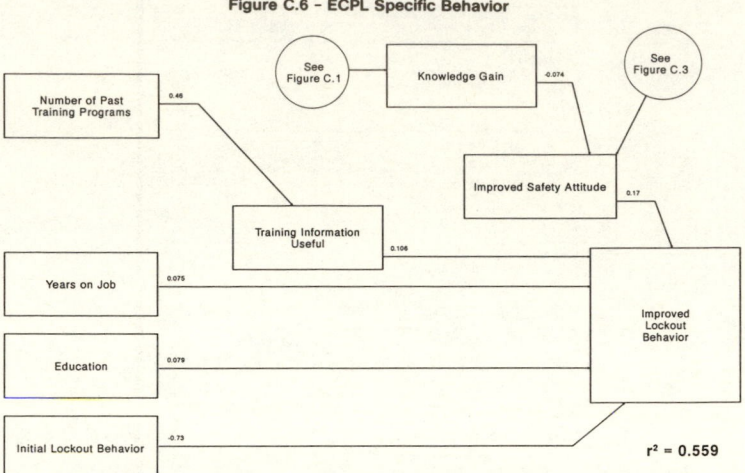

r² = 0.559

	TABLE C.6				
	Hypothesized Effects of Factors Which Predict **Specific Behavior Changes After Training** **(ECPL Specific Behavior)**				
Endogenous **Variable**	**Causal** **Variable**	**B**	**SE B**	**T**	**p**
Improved *Safety* *Attitude*	*See Table C.3 for Attitude Change Data*				
Mean = -0.102 *S.D. = 1.05*	r² = 0.641		N = 273		
Training *Info Useful*	Constant No. of Trng Courses	3.133 0.477	0.276 0.276	11.344	0.000+
Mean = 5.20 *S.D. = 4.00*	r² = 0.209		N = 381		
Knowledge *Gain*	*See Table C.1 for Knowledge Gain Data*				
Mean = 2.38 *S.D. = 3.59*	r² = 0.410		N = 283		
Dependent **Variable**	**Causal** **Variable**	**B**	**SE B**	**T**	**p**
Improved *Lockout* *Behavior*	Constant Initial Behavior Improved Attitude Training Info Useful Education Level Years on Job	1.689 -1.001 0.373 0.062 0.129 0.105	0.310 0.055 0.089 0.024 0.066 0.057	-18.106 4.173 2.591 1.962 1.848	⇒0.000+ ⇒0.000+ ⇒0.010 0.051 0.066
Mean = -0.676 *S.D. = 2.34*	r² = 0.559		N = 283		
⇒Significant at 0.05 level or less			⇒Significant at 0.01 level or less		

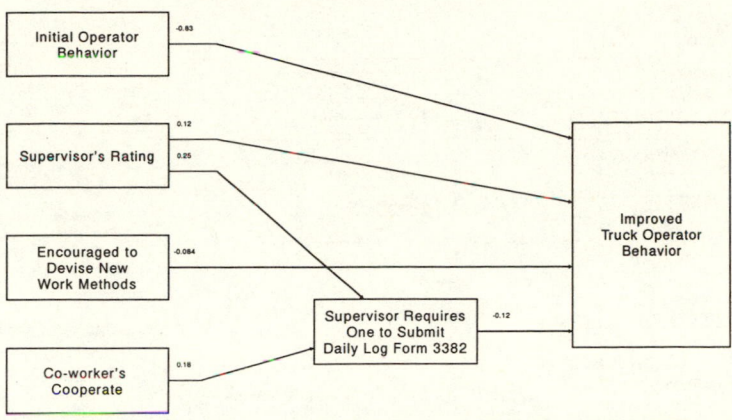

Figure C.7 - Operator Specific Behavior

Initial Operator Behavior	-0.83			
Supervisor's Rating	0.12 / 0.25		Improved Truck Operator Behavior	
Encouraged to Devise New Work Methods	-0.084			
Co-worker's Cooperate	0.18	Supervisor Requires One to Submit Daily Log Form 3382	-0.12	

$r^2 = 0.695$

TABLE C.7
Hypothesized Effects of Factors Which Predict
Specific Behavior Changes After Training
(Operator Specific Behavior)

Endogenous Variable	Causal Variable	B	SE B	T	p
Supervisors Remind Employees of Form 3382	Constant	1.674	0.347		
	Supervisor's Rating	0.339	0.131	2.579	➡0.011
	Co-workers Cooperate	0.326	0.116	2.814	➡0.005
	Operators Follow	0.269	0.097	2.769	➡0.006
Mean = 3.16 S.D. = 1.55		$r^2 = 0.139$		N = 234	

Dependent Variable	Causal Variable	B	SE B	T	p
Gain in Frequency of Following Truck Safety Rules	Constant	1.885	0.223		
	Initial Behavior	-1.024	0.061	-16.772	➡0.000+
	Supervisor Reminds	-0.108	0.044	-2.453	➡0.015
	Supervisor's Rating	0.184	0.079	2.332	➡0.021
	Encouraged to Devise	-0.111	0.062	-1.804	0.073
Mean = -0.22 S.D. = 1.31		$r^2 = 0.695$		N = 153	

➡Significant at 0.05 level or less	➡Significant at 0.01 level or less

Figure C.8 - Pedestrian Specific Behavior

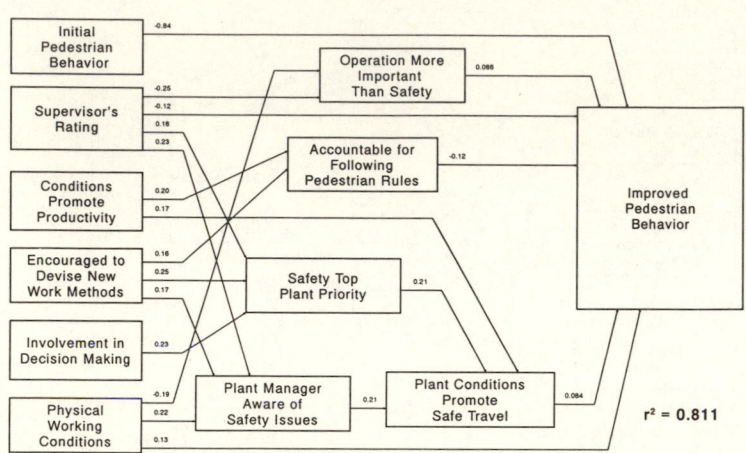

TABLE C.8						
Hypothesized Effects of Systemic Entry Variables						
on Specific Behavior After Training						
(Pedestrian Specific Behavior)						

Endogenous Variable	Causal Variable	B	SE B	T	p
Operation More Important Than Safety	Constant	3.522	0.239		
	Supervisor's Rating	-0.258	0.076	-3.413	➡0.001+
	Physical Conditions	-0.218	0.083	-2.635	➡0.009
Mean = 2.33 S.D. = 1.16	r^2 = 0.134		N = 192		
Accountable for Following Ped. Rules	Constant	1.632	0.175		
	Conditions Promote	0.161	0.062	2.594	➡0.010
	Encouraged to Devise	0.133	0.064	2.086	➡0.038
Mean = 2.32 S.D. = 1.16	r^2 = 0.093		N = 192		
Plant Conditions Promote Safe Travel	Constant	1.491	0.216		
	Safety Top Priority	0.173	0.064	2.711	➡0.007
	Plant Manager Aware	0.193	0.067	2.874	➡0.005
	Conditions Promote	0.165	0.068	2.414	➡0.017
Mean = 2.81 S.D. = 1.07	r^2 = 0.191		N = 187		
Safety Top Plant Priority	Constant	0.591	0.247		
	Decision Involvement	0.272	0.089	3.041	➡0.003
	Encouraged to Devise	0.298	0.084	3.543	➡0.001
	Supervisor's Rating	0.207	0.080	2.604	➡0.010
Mean = 2.50 S.D. = 1.16	r^2 = 0.265		N = 194		
Plant Mgr. Aware of Safety Issues	Constant	0.785	0.256		
	Supervisor's Rating	0.233	0.075	3.106	➡0.002
	Physical Conditions	0.252	0.081	3.110	➡0.002
	Encouraged to Devise	0.191	0.075	2.527	➡0.012
Mean = 2.46 S.D. = 1.15	r^2 = 0205		N = 190		
➡Significant at 0.05 level or less			➡Significant at 0.01 level or less		

TABLE C.8 (Continued) Hypothesized Effects of Systemic Entry Variables on Specific Behavior After Training (Pedestrian Specific Behavior)					
Dependent Variable	Causal Variable	B	SEB	T	p
	Constant	1.628	0.329		
	Initial Behavior	-1.009	0.050	-20.063	➡0.000+
Improved	Operation Important	0.103	0.053	1.955	0.053
Pedestrian	Physical Conditions	0.194	0.065	3.006	➡0.003
Behavior	Accountable for Rules	-0.194	0.068	-2.865	➡0.005
Mean = - 0.164	Supervisors Rating	-0.156	0.059	-2.647	➡0.009
S.D. = 1.353	Conditions Promote	0.116	0.056	2.046	➡0.043

$r^2 = 0.811$ N = 126

➡Significant at 0.05 level or less   ➡Significant at 0.01 level or less

Figure C.9 - ECPL General Behavior

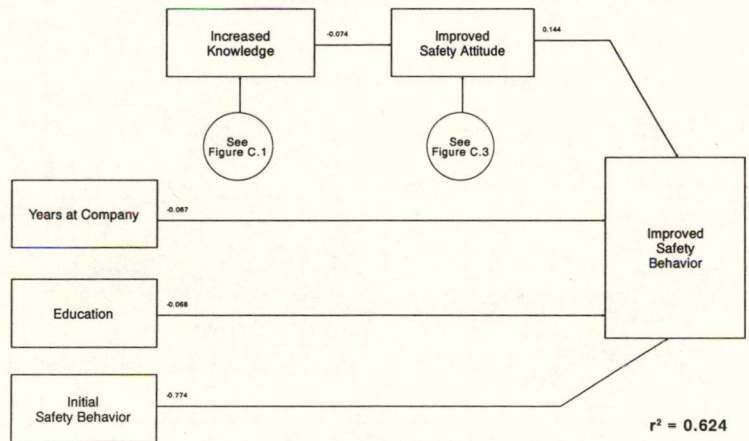

$r^2 = 0.624$

TABLE C.9
Hypothesized Effects of Factors Which Predict
General Behavior Changes After Training
(ECPL General Behavior)

Endogenous Variable	Causal Variable	B	SE B	T	p
Improved Safety Attitude	See Table C.3 for Attitude Change Data				
Mean = -0.102 S.D. = 1.05	$r^2 = 0.641$ N = 273				
Knowledge Gain	See Table C.1 for Knowledge Gain Data				
Mean = 2.38 S.D. = 3.59	$r^2 = 0.410$ N = 283				

Dependent Variable	Causal Variable	B	SE B	T	p
Improved Safety Behavior	Constant	2.355	0.297		
	Initial Behavior	-0.967	0.047	-20.404	➡0.000+
	Improved Attitude	0.231	0.060	3.877	➡0.000+
	Education Level	-0.080	0.044	-1.828	0.069
Mean = -0.356 S.D. = 1.70	Years at Ford	-0.096	0.053	-1.805	0.072
	$r^2 = 0.624$ N = 283				

➡Significant at 0.05 level or less   ➡Significant at 0.01 level or less

Figure C.10 - Operator General Behavior

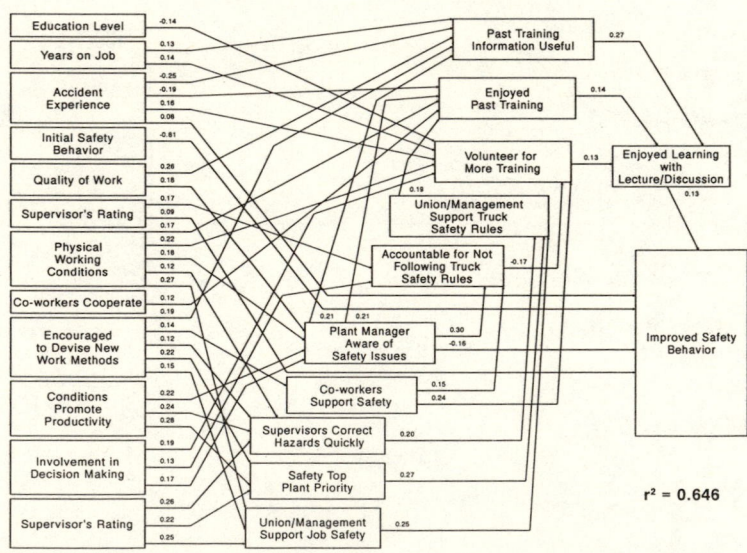

$r^2 = 0.646$

Table C.10

Hypothesized Effects of Factors Which Predict General Behavior Changes After Training (Operator General Behavior)

Endogenous Variable	Causal Variable	B	SE B	T	p
Enjoyed Learning with Lecture/ Discussion Mean = 1.91	Constant	0.845	0.141		
	Past Tng Info Useful	0.290	0.080	3.596	➡0.000+
	Volunteer for Training	0.102	0.052	1.960	0.051
	Enjoyed Past Training	0.140	0.076	1.846	0.066
	$r^2 = 0.205$		N = 255		
Volunteer for Other Training Mean = 2.09 S.D. = 0.93	Constant	1.582	0.270		
	Physical Conditions	0.203	0.064	3.189	➡0.002
	Co-workers Support	0.228	0.062	3.700	➡0.000+
	Educational Level	-0.173	0.078	-2.218	➡0.028
	Decision Involvement	0.164	0.058	2.802	➡0.006
	Accountable for Rules	-0.159	0.065	-2.461	➡0.015
	Accident Experience	-0.159	0.066	-2.388	➡0.018
	Years on Job	0.082	0.037	2.166	➡0.031
	$r^2 = 0.199$		N = 214		
Past Training Information Useful Mean = 2.04 S.D. = 0.71	Constant	1.217	0.162		
	Quality of Work	0.217	0.054	4.028	➡0.000+
	Plant Manager Aware	0.132	0.042	3.123	➡0.002
	Accident Experience	-0.202	0.049	-4.089	➡0.000+
	Encouraged to Devise	0.124	0.042	2.946	➡0.004
	Years on Job	0.059	0.028	2.121	➡0.035
	$r^2 = 0.260$		N = 212		
Enjoyed Past Training Programs Mean = 2.07 S.D. = 0.72	Constant	1.250	0.141		
	Plant Manager Aware	0.132	0.040	3.296	➡0.001
	Union/Mgmt Support	0.161	0.049	3.266	➡0.001
	Accident Experience	-0.148	0.042	-3.529	➡0.000+
	Physical Conditions	0.120	0.043	2.761	➡0.006
	Co-workers Cooperate	0.093	0.045	2.052	➡0.041
	$r^2 = 0.230$		N = 281		
Co-workers Support Safety Mean = 1.83 S.D. = 1.00	Constant	0.544	0.129		
	Encouraged to Devise	0.132	0.053	2.507	➡0.013
	$r^2 = 0.020$		N = 305		

➡Significant at 0.05 level or less   ➡Significant at 0.01 level or less

Table C.10 (Continued)

Hypothesized Effects of Factors Which Predict General Behavior Changes After Training (Operator General Behavior)

Endogenous Variable	Causal Variable	B	SE B	T	p
Accountable For Not Following Truck Safety Rules Mean = 1.95 S.D. = 0.954	Constant	0.148	0.171		
	Union/Mgmt Support	0.239	0.065	3.658	➡0.000+
	Plant Manager Aware	0.164	0.052	3.168	➡0.002
	Supervisor's Rating	0.115	0.059	1.953	0.052
	Co-workers Support	0.121	0.048	2.496	➡0.013
	Operators Follow Rules	0.110	0.051	2.159	➡0.031
	Decision Involvement	0.010	0.048	2.082	➡0.038
	$r^2 = 0.321$		N = 291		
Union/ Management Support Truck Safety Rules Mean = 1.93 S.D. = 0.89	Constant	0.362	0.130		
	Supervisor Corrects	0.147	0.046	3.219	➡0.001
	Safety Top Priority	0.170	0.046	3.721	➡0.000+
	Union/Mgmt Support	0.159	0.051	3.112	➡0.002
	Operators Follow	0.131	0.041	3.164	➡0.002
	Co-workers Cooperate	0.096	0.043	2.204	➡0.028
	$r^2 = 0.401$		N = 296		
Plant Manager Aware of Safety Issues Mean = 2.38 S.D. = 1.12	Constant	0.488	0.178		
	Physical Conditions	0.201	0.067	3.015	➡0.003
	Conditions Promote	0.220	0.057	3.884	➡0.000+
	Quality of Work	0.236	0.072	3.280	➡0.001
	Decision Involvement	0.172	0.058	2.966	➡0.003
	$r^2 = 0.300$		N = 301		

Dependent Variable	Causal Variable	B	SE B	T	p
Gain in General Safety Behavior Mean = -0.15 S.D. = 0.93	Constant	1.324	0.175		
	Initial Safety Behavior	-1.017	0.064	-15.955	➡0.000+
	Enjoy Lecture/Discussion	0.166	0.058	2.841	➡0.005
	Plant Manager Aware	-0.132	0.041	-3.250	➡0.001
	Accident Experience	0.083	0.047	1.759	0.080
	Supervisor's Rating	0.097	0.055	1.776	0.078
	$r^2 = 0.646$		N = 184		

➡Significant at 0.05 level or less   ➡Significant at 0.01 level or less

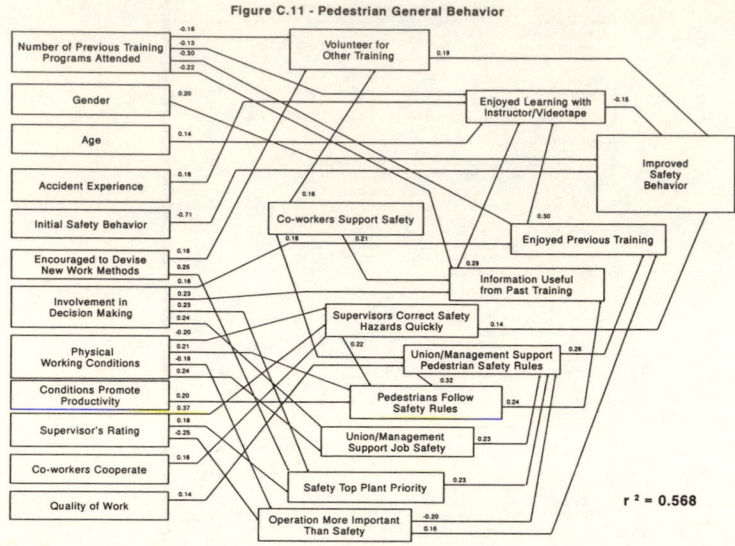

Figure C.11 - Pedestrian General Behavior

$r^2 = 0.568$

TABLE C.11
Hypothesized Effects of Factors Which Predict
General Behavior Changes After Training
(Pedestrian General Behavior)

Endogenous Variable	Causal Variable	B	SE B	T	p
Enjoyed Learning with Instructor/ Videotape	Constant	0.269	0.354		
	Past Tng Info Useful	0.352	0.107	3.297	➡0.001
	Enjoyed Past Training	0.366	0.108	3.401	➡0.001
	Accident Experience	0.150	0.060	2.509	➡0.013
	Gender	-0.130	0.065	-2.011	➡0.046
Mean = 2.06					
	$r^2 = 0.369$		N = 138		
Enjoyed Past Training Programs	Constant	1.626	0.230		
	Programs Attended	-0.130	0.030	-4.340	➡0.000+
	Union/Mgmt Support	0.199	0.060	3.290	➡0.001
	Decision Involvement	0.101	0.045	2.239	➡0.026
	Operation Important	0.092	0.044	2.098	➡0.037
Mean = 2.12 S.D. = 0.69					
	$r^2 = 0.169$		N = 179		
Past Training Information Useful	Constant	1.279	0.190		
	Decision Involvement	0.142	0.044	3.219	➡0.002
	Co-Workers Support	0.153	0.051	3.015	➡0.003
	Pedestrians Follow	0.145	0.044	3.298	➡0.001
	Number of Programs	-0.093	0.030	-3.120	➡0.002
Mean = 2.03 S.D. = 0.70					
	$r^2 = 0.247$		N = 164		
Volunteer for Other Training	Constant	1.882	0.238		
	Co-workers Support	0.166	0.067	2.475	➡0.014
	Number of Programs	-0.089	0.040	-2.207	➡0.029
	Encouraged to Devise	0.129	0.059	2.268	➡0.032
Mean = 2.22 S.D. = 0.89					
	$r^2 = 0.089$		N = 183		
Pedestrians Follow Safety Rules	Constant	1.293	0.247		
	Union/Mgmt Support	0.388	0.082	4.715	➡0.000+
	Supervisors Correct	0.192	0.064	2.993	➡0.003
	Conditions Promote	0.200	0.071	2.792	➡0.006
	Physical Conditions	-0.212	0.077	-2.744	➡0.007
Mean = 2.58 S.D. = 1.06					
	$r^2 = 0.240$		N = 187		
➡Significant at 0.05 level or less		➡Significant at 0.01 level or less			

TABLE C.11 (Continued)
Hypothesized Effects of Factors Which Predict
General Behavior Changes After Training
(Pedestrian General Behavior)

Endogenous Variable	Causal Variable	B	SE B	T	p
Union/Mgmt Support Pedestrian Safety Rules	Constant	1.059	0.259		
	Safety Top Plant Priority	0.160	0.048	3.355	0.001
	Union/Mgmt Support	0.192	0.056	3.418	0.000+
	Operation Important	-0.153	0.050	-3.053	0.003
	Co-workers Support	0.165	0.055	2.974	0.003
Mean = 2.12 S.D. = 0.87	Quality of Work	0.126	0.058	2.178	0.030

r² = 0.365   N = 187

Endogenous Variable	Causal Variable	B	SE B	T	p
Operation More Important	Constant	3.522	0.239		
	Supervisor's Rating	-0.258	0.076	-3.413	0.001
Mean = 2.33 S.D. = 1.16	Physical Conditions	-0.218	0.083	-2.635	0.009

r² = 0.134   N = 192

Endogenous Variable	Causal Variable	B	SE B	T	p
Safety Top Plant Priority	Constant	0.591	0.247		
	Decision Involvement	0.272	0.089	3.041	0.003
	Encouraged to Devise	0.298	0.084	3.543	0.001
Mean = 2.50 S.D. = 1.26	Supervisor's Rating	0.207	0.080	2.604	0.010

r² = 0.265   N = 194

Endogenous Variable	Causal Variable	B	SE B	T	p
Supervisors Correct Hazards Quickly	Constant	0.616	0.247		
	Supervisor's Rating	0.406	0.071	5.761	0.000+
	Physical Conditions	0.249	0.080	3.126	0.002
Mean = 2.82 S.D. = 1.21	Co-workers Cooperate	0.223	0.076	2.927	0.004

r² = 0.324   N = 194

Dependent Variable	Causal Variable	B	SE B	T	p
Gain in General Safety Behavior	Constant	1.430	0.362		
	Initial Safety Behavior	-0.963	0.079	-12.237	0.000+
	Volunteer for Programs	0.309	0.097	3.185	0.002
	Enjoy Inst/Videotape	-0.265	0.105	-2.515	0.013
Mean = 0.18 S.D. = 1.38	Supervisors Correct	0.164	0.068	2.405	0.018

r² = 0.568   N = 134

Significant at 0.05 level or less	Significant at 0.01 level or less

References

Ajzen, I. and Fishbein, M. (1980) *Understanding Attitudes and Predicting Social Behavior*. Englewood Cliffs, NJ: Prentice Hall.

Anderson, C. S. (1982) 'The search for school climate: A review of the research', *Review of educational research, 52*, 368–420.

Andrews, D. H. and Goodson, L. A. (1991) 'A comparative analysis of models of instructional design', in G. J. Anglin (ed.) *Instructional Technology: Past, Present, and Future* (pp. 133–55). Englewood, CO: Libraries Unlimited, Inc.

Aslanian, C. B. and Brickell, H. N. (1980) *Americans in Transition: Life Changes as Reasons for Learning*. New York: College Entrance Examination Board.

Baine, D. (1986) *Memory and Instruction*. Englewood Cliffs, NJ: Educational Technology Publications.

Baltes, P. B., Kliegl, R. and Dittmann-Kohli, F. (1988) 'On the locus of training gains in research on the plasticity of fluid intelligence in old age', *Journal of Educational Psychology, 80*, 392–400.

Banathy, B. H. (1968) *Instructional Systems*. Palo Alto, CA: Fearon Publishers.

Barrett, J. B., Gradous, D. B., Lydell, M. K., Sengbusch, S., Swanson, B. E., Swanson, R. A., Theobald, J. D. and Warner, D. K. (1991), 'Lessons for managers: England's human resource dilemmas', *Performance Improvement Quarterly, 4*(2), 59–68.

Beauchamp, M. (1990) 'The validation of an integrative model of learner affect variables and instructional system design', Doctoral dissertation, Wayne State University, Detroit, MI.

Becker, M. H. and Maiman, L. A. (1975) 'Sociobehavioral determinants of compliance with health and medical care recommendations', *Medical care, 13*, 10–24.

Beckwith, D. (1988) 'The future of educational technology', *Canadian Journal of Educational Communications, 17*(1), 3–20.

Bem, D. J. (1970) *Beliefs, Attitudes, and Human Affairs*. Belmont, CA: Brooks/Cole Publishing Company.

Bloom, B. S. (1976) *Human Characteristics and School Learning*. New York: McGraw-Hill Book Company.

Bonner, J. (1988) 'Implications of cognitive theory for instructional design: revisited', *Educational Communication and Technology Journal, 36*, 3–14.

Boshier, R. (1989) 'Participant motivation', in C. J. Titmus (ed.) *Lifelong Education for Adults: An International Handbook* (pp 147–51). Oxford: Pergamon Press.

Bowers, D. G. (1977) *Systems of Organization: Management of the Human Resource.* Ann Arbor, MI: The University of Michigan Press.

Bowsher, J. E. (1989) *Educating America: Lessons Learned in the Nation's Corporations*. New York: John Wiley & Sons, Inc.

Branson, R. K. (1991) 'Major issues in large ISD projects', in L. J. Briggs, K. L. Gustafson and M. H. Tillman (eds) *Instructional Design: Principles and Applications* (2nd edn, pp 345–73). Englewood Cliffs, NJ: Educational Technology Publications.

Brookfield, S. D. (1986) *Understanding and Facilitating Adult Learning*. San Francisco: Jossey-Bass Publishers.

Brown, J. S., Collins, A. and Duguid, P. (1989) 'Situated cognition and the culture of learning', *Educational Researcher, 18*(1), 32–42.

Bruner, J. (1982) *The Process of Education*. New York: Vintage Books.

Butterfield, E. C. and Nelson, G. D. (1989) 'Theory and practice of teaching for transfer', *Educational Technology Research and Development, 37*(3), 5–38.

Caffarella, R. S. and O'Donnell, J. M. (1987) 'Self-directed adult learning: A critical paradigm revisited', *Adult Education Quarterly, 37*, 199–211.

Carey, L. M. and Dick, W. (1991) 'Summative evaluation', in L. J. Briggs, K. L. Gustafson and M. H. Tillman (eds) *Instructional Design: Principles and Applications* (2nd edn, pp 269–311). Englewood Cliffs, NJ: Educational Technology Publications.

Carnevale, A. P. (1988) 'Management training: today and tomorrow', *Training and Development Journal, 42*(12), 18–29.

Carnevale, A. P. and Schulz, E. R. (1988) 'Technical training in America: how much and who', *Training and Development Journal, 42*(11), 18–32.

Carroll, J. B. (1963) 'A model of school learning', *Teachers College Record, 64*, 723–33.

Carroll, J. B. (1989) 'The Carroll model: a 25-year retrospective and prospective view', *Educational Researcher, 18*(1), 26–31.

Cattell, R. B. (1963) 'Theory of fluid and crystallized intelligence: a critical experiment', *Journal of Educational Psychology, 54*, 445–59.

Cennamo, K. S., Savenye, W. C. and Smith, P. L. (1991) 'Mental effort and video-based learning: The relationship of preconceptions and the effects of interactive and covert practice', *Educational Technology Research and Development, 39*(1), 5–16.

Clark, R. E. and Salomon, G. (1986) 'Media in teaching', in M. C. Wittrock (ed.) *Handbook of Research on Teaching* (pp 464–78). New York: Macmillan Publishing Company.

Clark, R. E. and Voogel, A. (1985) 'Transfer of training principles for instructional design', *Educational Communications and Technology Journal, 33*(2), 113–23.

Cookson, P. S. (1986) 'A framework for theory and research on adult education participation', *Adult Education Quarterly, 36*, 130–41.

Cross, K. P. (1981) *Adults as Learners: Increasing Participation and Facilitating Learning*. San Francisco: Jossey-Bass Publishers.

Darkenwald, G. G. and Merriam, S. B. (1982) *Adult Education: Foundations of Practice*. New York: Harper and Row, Publishers.

Darkenwald, G. G. and Valentine, T. (1985) 'Factor structure of deterrents to public participation in adult education', *Adult Education Quarterly. 35*, 177–93.

Davies, I. (1984) 'Instructional development: themata, archetypes, paradigms and models', in R. K. Bass and C. R. Dills (eds) *Instructional Development: The State of the Art, II* (pp 8–17). Dubuque, IA: Kendall/Hunt Publishing.

Davies, I. K. (1991) 'Instructional development as an art: one of the three faces of ID', in D. Hlynka and J. C. Belland (eds) *Paradigms Regained: The Uses of Illuminative, Semiotic and Post-modern Criticism as Modes of Inquiry in Educational Technology* (pp 93–106). Englewood Cliffs, NJ: Educational Technology Publications.

Dick, W. and Carey, L. (1990) *The Systematic Design of Instruction* (3rd edn). Glenview, IL: Scott, Foresman and Company.

Dijkstra, S. (1991) 'Instructional design models and the representation of knowledge and skills', *Educational Technology, 31*(6), 19–26.

DiVesta, F. J. and Rieber, L. P. (1987) 'Characteristics of cognitive engineering: the next generation of instructional systems', *Educational Communications and Technology Journal, 35*, 213–30.

Dixon, R. A. and Baltes, P. B. (1986) 'Toward life-span research on the functions and pragmatics of intelligence', in R. J. Sternberg and R. K. Wagner (eds) *Practical Intelligence: Nature and Origins of Competence in the Everyday World* (pp 203–35). Cambridge: Cambridge University Press.

Dixon, R. A., Kramer, D. A. and Baltes, P. B. (1985) 'Intelligence: A life-span developmental perspective', in B. B. Wolman (ed.) *Handbook of Intelligence: Theories, Measurements, and Applications* (pp 301–50). New York: John Wiley & Sons.

Duffy, T. M. and Jonassen, D. H. (1991) 'Constructivism: new implications for instructional technology?', *Educational Technology, 31*(5), 7–12.

Ellington, H. and Harris, D. (1986) *Dictionary of Instructional Technology*. London/New York: Kogan Page/Nichols Publishing Company.

Erickson, E. H. (1963) *Childhood and Society* (2nd edn). New York: W. W. Norton and Company, Inc.

Feuer, D. and Geber, B. (1988) 'Uh-oh . . . second thoughts about adult learning theory', *Training*, pp 31–9.

Fisher, J. C. (1986) 'Participation in educational activities by active older adults', *Adult Education Quarterly, 36*, 202–10.

Flynn, M. L. (1988–9) 'The potential of older adults for response to computer-assisted instruction', *Journal of Educational Technology Systems, 17*, 231–41.

Ford, J. M. and Roth, W. T. (1980) 'Do cognitive abilities decline with age?', in D. Rogers (ed.) *Issues in Life-span Human Development* (pp 67–71). Monterey, CA: Brooks/Cole Publishing Company.

Gage, N. L. (1979) 'The generality of dimensions of teaching', in P. L. Peterson and H. J. Walberg (eds) *Research on Teaching: Concepts, Findings, and Implications* (pp 264–88). Berkeley, CA: McCutchan Publishing Corporation.

Gagne, R. M. (1965) *The Conditions of Learning* (1st edn). New York: Holt, Rinehart and Winston.

Gagne, R. M. (1974) *Essentials of Learning for Instruction*. Hinsdale, IL: Dryden Press.

Gagne, R. M. (1985) *The Conditions of Learning and Theory of Instruction* (4th edn). New York: Holt, Rinehart and Winston.

Gagne, R. M. (1991) 'Analysis of objectives', in L. J. Briggs, K. L. Gustafson and M. H. Tillman (eds) *Instructional Design: Principles and Applications* (2nd edn, pp 123–50). Englewood Cliffs, NJ: Educational Technology Publications.

Gagne, R. M., Briggs, L. J. and Wager, W. W. (1988) *Principles of Instructional Design* (3rd edn). New York: Holt, Rinehart and Winston, Inc.

Gardner, H. (1983) *Frames of Mind*. New York: Basic Books.

Gardner, H. and Hatch, T. (1989) 'Multiple intelligences go to school: educational implications of the theory of multiple intelligences', *Educational Researcher, 18*(8), 4–10.

Guskey, T. R. (1986) 'Staff development and the process of teacher change', *Educational Researcher, 15*(5), 5–11.

Gustafson, K. L. and Reeves, T. C. (1990) 'IDioM: a platform for a course development expert system', *Educational Technology, 30*(3), 19–25.

Hall, A. D. and Fagen, R. E. (1975) 'Definition of a system', in B. D. Ruben and J. Y. Kim (eds) *General Systems Theory and Human Communication* (pp 52–65). Rochelle Park, NJ: Hayden Book Company, Inc.

Hannafin, M. J. and Rieber, L. P. (1989a) 'Psychological foundations of instructional design for emerging computer-based instructional technologies: Part I', *Educational Technology Research and Development, 37*(2), 91–101.

Hannafin, M. J. and Rieber, L. P. (1989b) 'Psychological foundations of instructional design for emerging computer-based instructional technologies: Part II', *Educational Technology Research and Development, 37*(2), 102–14.

Havighurst, R. J. (1972) *Developmental Tasks and Education*. New York: David McKay.

Hiemstra, R. and Sisco, B. (1990) *Individualizing Instruction: Making Learning Personal, Empowering, and Successful.* San Francisco: Jossey-Bass Publishers.

Hlynka, D. (1991) 'Post-modern excursions into educational technology', *Educational technology, 31*(6), 27–30.

Hlynka, D. and Belland, J. C. (1991) 'Critical study of educational technology', in D. Hlynka and J. C. Belland (eds) *Paradigms Regained: The Uses of Illuminative, Semiotic and Post-modern Criticism as Modes of Inquiry in Educational Technology* (pp 5–20). Englewood Cliffs, NJ: Educational Technology Publications.

Hlynka, D. and Nelson, B. (1991) 'Educational technology as metaphor', in D. Hlynka and J. C. Belland (eds) *Paradigms Regained: The Uses of Illuminative, Semiotic and Post-modern Criticism as Modes of Inquiry in Educational Technology* (pp 107–19). Englewood Cliffs, NJ: Educational Technology Publications.

Howe, A. (1988) 'Training technology', in D. Unwin and R. McAleese (eds) *The Encyclopaedia of Educational Media Communications and Technology* (2nd edn, pp 528–36). New York: Greenwood Press.

Hultsch, D. F. and Dixon, R. A. (1990) 'Learning and memory in aging', in J. E. Birren and K. W. Schaie (eds) *Handbook of the Psychology of Aging* (3rd edn, pp 258–74). San Diego: Academic Press, Inc.

Industry Report, 1990 (1990) *Training*, October, pp 31–76.

Institute of Training and Development (1991) *Reports of 'Training in Britain' surveys.* Marlow, Buckinghamshire.

Jarvis, P. (1987) *Adult Learning in the Social Context.* Beckenham, Kent: Croom Helm.

Jennings, M. K. and Markus, G. B. (1984) 'Partisanship over the long haul: results from the three wave political socialization panel study', *American Political Science Review, 78*, 1000–1018.

Jonassen, D. H., Grabinger, R. S. and Harris, N. D. C. (1991) 'Analyzing and selecting instructional strategies and tactics', *Performance Improvement Quarterly, 4*(2), 77–97.

Kaufman, R. and English, F. W. (1979) *Needs Assessment: Concept and Application.* Englewood Cliffs, NJ: Educational Technology Publications.

Kaufman, R. and Thiagarajan, S. (1987) 'Identifying and specifying requirements for instruction', in R. M. Gagne (ed.) *Instructional Technology: Foundations* (pp 113–40). Hillsdale, NJ: Lawrence Erlbaum Associates, Publishers.

Keller, J. M. (1979) 'Motivation and instructional design: a theoretical perspective', *Journal of Instructional Development, 2*(4), 26–34.

Keller, J. M. (1983) 'Motivational design of instruction', in C. M. Reigeluth (ed.) *Instructional-design Theories and Models: An Overview of Their Current Status* (pp 383–434). Hillsdale, NJ: Lawrence Erlbaum Associates, Publishers.

Keller, J. M. (1987a) 'Strategies for stimulating the motivation to learn', *Performance and Instruction, 26*(9), 1–7.

Keller, J. M. (1987b) 'The systematic process of motivational design', *Performance and Instruction, 26*(10), 1–8.

Kemp. J. E. (1985) *The Instructional Design Process.* New York: Harper & Row, Publishers.

Kidd, J. R. (1973) *How Adults Learn.* Chicago: Association Press.

Kirkpatrick, D. L. (1976) *Evaluating Training Programs.* New York: McGraw-Hill Book Company.

Knirk, F. G. and Gustafson, K. L. (1986) *Instructional Technology: A Systematic Approach to Education.* New York: Holt, Rinehart and Winston.

Knowles, M. S. (1980) *The Modern Practice of Adult Education.* Chicago: Association Press, Follett Publishing Company.

Knox, A. B. (1977) *Adult Development and Learning.* San Francisco: Jossey-Bass Publishers.

Knox, A. B. (1986) *Helping Adults Learn: A Guide to Planning, Implementing, and Conducting Programs.* San Francisco: Jossey-Bass Publishers.

Kogan, N. (1990) 'Personality and aging', in J. E. Birren and K. W. Schaie (eds) *Handbook of the Psychology of Aging* (3rd edn, pp 330–46). San Diego: Academic Press, Inc.

Kozma, R. B. (1991) 'Learning with media', *Review of Educational Research, 61*(2), 179–211.

Levinson, D. J. (1978) *The Seasons of a Man's Life.* New York: Random House.

Lick, H. B. (1989) 'The effects of organizational and environmental climate factors on a joint union-management safety training program at a U.S. automaker', Doctoral dissertation, Wayne State University, Detroit, MI.

Lloyd, B. H. and Gressard, C. (1984) 'The effects of sex, age, and computer experience on computer attitudes', *AEDS Journal, 8*(2) 67–77.

McFarland, T. D. and Parker, R. (1990) *Expert Systems in Education and Training*. Englewood Cliffs, NJ: Educational Technology Publications.

McGuire, W. J. (1985) 'Attitudes and attitude change', in G. Lindzey and E. Aronson (eds) *Handbook of Social Psychology* (3rd edn, pp 233–346). New York: Random House.

Mahmood, M. A. and Medewitz, J. N. (1989) 'Assessing the effect of computer literacy on subjects' attitudes, values, and opinions toward information technology: an exploratory longitudinal investigation using the linear structural relations (LISREL) model', *Journal of Computer-based Instruction, 16*(1), 20–28.

Martin, B. L. and Briggs, L. J. (1986) *The Affective and Cognitive Domains: Integration for Instruction and Research*. Englewood Cliffs, NJ: Educational Technology Publications.

Merriam, S. B. (1987) 'Adult learning and theory building: a review', *Adult Education Quarterly, 37*, 187–98.

Merriam, S. B. and Caffarella, R. S. (1991) *Learning in Adulthood: A Comprehensive Guide*. San Francisco: Jossey-Bass Publishers.

Merriam, S. and Mullins, L. (1981) 'Havighurst's adult developmental tasks: a study of their importance relative to income, age, and sex', *Adult Education, 31*(3), 123–41.

Merrill, M. D. (1983) 'The component display theory', in C. M. Reigeluth (ed.) *Instructional-design Theories and Models: An Overview of Their Current Status* (pp 279–333). Hillsdale, NJ: Lawrence Erlbaum Associates, Publishers.

Merrill, M. D. (1991) 'Constructivism and instructional design', *Educational Technology, 31*(5), 45–53.

Merrill, M. D., Li, Z. and Jones, M. K. (1990a) 'Limitations of first generation instructional design', *Educational Technology, 30*(1), 7–11.

Merrill, M. D., Li, Z. and Jones, M. K. (1990b) 'The second generation instructional design research program', *Educational Technology, 30*(3), 26–31.

Miller, J. G. (1978) *Living Systems*. New York: McGraw Hill Book Company.

Morgan, R. M. (1987) 'Planning for instructional systems', in R. M. Gagne (ed.) *Instructional Technology: Foundations* (pp 379–96). Hillsdale, NJ: Lawrence Erlbaum Associates, Publishers.

Morris, D. C. (1988–9) 'A survey of age and attitudes toward computers', *Journal of Educational Technology Systems, 17*, 73–8.

Morse, S. W. (1984) *Employee Educational Programs: Implications for Industry and Higher Education*. ASHE-ERIC Higher Education Research Report No. 7, Washington, DC: Association for the Study of Higher Education.

Murphy, S. R. (1989) 'Effects of attitudes on behavior after participation in an industrial safety training program', Doctoral dissertation, Wayne State University, Detroit, MI.

Murray, F. B. and Mosberg, L. (1982) 'Cognition and memory', in H. E. Mitzel (ed.) *Encyclopedia of Educational Research* (5th edn, pp 279–85). New York: The Free Press.

Nadler, L. and Nadler, Z. (1989) *Developing Human Resources* (3rd edn). San Francisco: Jossey-Bass Publishers.

Noe, R. A. (1986) 'Trainees' attributes and attitudes: neglected influences on training effectiveness', *Academy of Management Review, 11*, 736–49.

Noe, R. A. and Schmitt, N. (1986) 'The influence of trainee attitudes on training effectiveness: test of a model', *Personnel Psychology, 39*, 497–523.

Perkins, D. N. and Salomon, G. (1989) 'Are cognitive skills context-bound?', *Educational Researcher, 18*(1), 16–25.

Peters, L. H., O'Connor, E. J. and Rudolf, C. J. (1980) 'The behavioral and affective consequences of performance-relevant situational variables', *Organizational Behavior and Human Performance, 25*, 79–96.

Pfeffer, J. (1985) 'Organizations and organization theory', in G. Lindzey and E. Aronson (eds) *Handbook of Social Psychology, Volume 1–Theory and Method* (3rd edn, pp 379–440). New York: Random House.

Prescott, J. E. (1986) 'Environments as moderators of the relationship between strategy and performance', *Academy of Management Journal, 29*, 329–46.

Rachal, J. R. (1989) 'The social context of adult and continuing education', in S. B. Merriam and P. M. Cunningham (eds) *Handbook of Adult and Continuing Education* (pp 3–14). San Francisco: Jossey-Bass Publishers.

Reiser, R. A. and Gagne, R. M. (1983) *Selecting Media for Instruction*. Englewood Cliffs, NJ: Educational Technology Publications.

Resnick, L. B. (1987) 'Learning in school and out', *Educational Researcher, 16*(9), 13–20.

Richey, R. C. (1986) *The Theoretical and Conceptual Bases of Instructional Design*. London/New York: Kogan Page/Nichols Publishing Company.

Richey, R. C. (1991) 'Adult attitudes toward alternative delivery systems and industrial training outcomes', in M. R. Simonson (ed.) *Proceedings of Selected Research Paper Presentations at the 1991 Annual Convention of the Association for Educational Communications and Technology* (pp 635–80). Ames, IA: University of Iowa.

Ripple, R. E. and Drinkwater, D. J. (1982) 'Transfer of learning', in H. E. Mitzel (ed.) *Encyclopedia of Educational Research* (5th edn, pp 1947–55). New York: The Free Press.

Romiszowski, A. J. (1981) *Designing Instructional Systems: Decision Making in Course Planning and Curriculum Design*. London/New York: Kogan Page/Nichols Publishing Company.

Romiszowski, A. J. (1988) *The Selection and Use of Instructional Media*. (2nd edn) London/New York: Kogan Page/Nichols Publishing Company.

Rossett, A. (1987) *Training Needs Assessment*. Englewood Cliffs, NJ: Educational Technology Publications.

Royer, J. M. (1979) 'Theories of the transfer of learning', *Educational Psychologist, 14*(1), 53–69.

Rybash, J. M., Hoyer, W. J. and Roodin, P. A. (1986) *Adult Cognition and Aging: Developmental Changes in Processing, Knowing and Thinking*. New York: Pergamon Press.

Salomon, G. (1983) 'The differential investment of mental effort in learning from different sources', *Educational Psychologist, 18*, 42–50.

Schaie, K. W. (1990) 'Intellectual development in adulthood', in J. E. Birren and K. W. Schaie (eds) *Handbook of the Psychology of Aging* (3rd edn, pp 291–309). San Diego: Academic Press, Inc.

Schaie, K. W. and Willis, S. L. (1982) 'Life-span development', in H. E.

Mitzel (ed.) *Encyclopedia of Educational Research* (5th edn., pp 1093–1101). New York: The Free Press

Schmid, R. F. and Gerlack, V. S. (1986) 'An analysis of algorithmic processes and instructional design', *Educational Communication and Technology Journal, 34*, 163–74.

Schubert, W. H. (1980) 'Recalibrating educational research: toward a focus on practice', *Educational Researcher, 9*(1), 17–24.

Schwab, D. P. and Cummings, L. L. (1975) 'Theories of performance and satisfaction: a review', in R. M. Steers and L. W. Porter (eds) *Motivation and Work Behaviour* (pp 223–41) New York: McGraw-Hill Book Company.

Seels, B. (1989) 'The instructional design movement in educational technology', *Educational Technology, 29*(5), 11–15.

Seels, B. and Glasgow, Z. (1990) *Exercises in Instructional Design*. Columbus, OH: Merrill Publishing Company.

Shavelson, R. J. and Bolus, R. (1982) 'Self-concept: the interplay of theory and methods', *Journal of Educational Psychology*, 74, 3–17.

Shaver, J. P. (1979) 'The productivity of educational research and the applied-basic research distinction', *Educational Researcher, 8*(1), 3–9.

Shipp, T. and McKenzie, L. R. (1981) 'Adult learners and non-learners: demographic characteristics as an indicator of psychographic characteristics', *Adult Education, 31*, 187–98.

Snow, R. E. (1977) 'Individual differences and instructional theory', *Educational Researcher, 6*(10), 11–15.

Snow, R. E. (1989) 'Aptitude-treatment interaction as a framework for research on individual differences in learning', in P. L. Ackerman, R. J. Sternberg and R. Glaser (eds) *Learning and Individual Differences: Advances in Theory and Research* (pp 13–60). New York: W. H. Freeman and Company.

Steers, R. M. and Porter, L. W. (1975) 'The role of motivation in organizations', in R. M. Steers and L. W. Porter (eds) *Motivation and Work Behavior* (pp 3–30) New York: McGraw-Hill Book Company.

Sternberg, R. J. and Wagner, R. K. (1989) 'Individual differences in practical knowledge and its acquisition', in P. L. Ackerman, R. J. Sternberg and R. Glaser (eds) *Learning and Individual Differences: Advances in Theory and Research* (pp 255–78). New York: W. H. Freeman and Company.

Streibel, M. J. (1991) 'Instructional plans and situated learning: the challenge of Suchman's theory of situated action for instructional designers and instructional systems', in G. J. Anglin (ed.) *Instructional Technology: Past, Present, and Future* (pp 117–32). Englewood, CO: Libraries Unlimited, Inc.

Strike, K. A. (1979) 'An epistemology of practical research', *Educational Researcher, 8*(1), 10–16.

Suchman, L. (1987) *Plans and Situated Actions*. New York: Cambridge University Press.

Swisher, J. D., Vicary, J. R. and Nadenishek, P. E. (1983) 'Humanistic education: a review of the research', *Journal of humanistic Education and Development, 22*(1), 8–15.

Tennyson, R. D. and Rasch, M. (1988) 'Linking cognitive learning theory to instructional prescriptions', *Instructional Science, 17*, 369–85.

Tessmer, M. (1990) 'Environment analysis: a neglected stage of instructional design', *Educational Technology Research and Development, 38*(1), 55–64.

Tessmer, M. and Harris, D. (1990) 'Beyond instructional effectiveness: key environmental decisions for instructional designers as change agents', *Educational Technology, 30*(7), 16–20.

Tessmer, M. and Wedman, J. F. (1990) 'A layers of necessity instructional development model', *Educational Technology Research and Development, 38*(2), 77–85.

Triandis, H. C. (1971) *Attitude and Attitude Change.* New York: John Wiley & Sons, Inc.

Troll, L. (1982) *Continuations: Adult Development and Aging.* Monterey, CA: Brooks/Cole.

US Department of Commerce, Bureau of Census (1990) *Statistical Abstract of the United States.* Washington, DC: US Government Printing Office.

Wagner, R. K. and Sternberg, R. J. (1986) 'Tacit knowledge and intelligence in the everyday world', in R. J. Sternberg and R. K. Wagner (eds) *Practical Intelligence: Nature and Origins of Competence in the Everyday World* (pp 51–83). Cambridge: Cambridge University Press.

Wallace, W. A. (1979) *From a Realist Point of View: Essays on the Philosophy of Science.* Washington, DC: University Press of America.

Watkins, K. E. (1989) 'Business and industry', in S. B. Merriam and P. M. Cunningham (eds) *Handbook of Adult and Continuing Education* (pp 422–35). San Francisco: Jossey-Bass Publishers.

Williams, M. D. (1990) *Self-guided Learning: What the Literature Says to Designers* (Young Professors Program). Washington, DC: National Society for Performance and Instruction.

Winn, W. (1989a) 'Toward a rationale and theoretical basis for educational technology', *Educational Technology Research and Development, 37*(1), 35–46.

Winn, W. (1989b) 'Rethinking cognitive approaches to instructional design'. Paper presented at the Annual Meeting of the American Educational Research Association, San Francisco, CA.

Wlodkowski, R. J. (1985) *Enhancing Adult Motivation to Learn.* San Francisco: Jossey-Bass Publishers.

Index

SUBJECT INDEX